VERSATILE GUARDIAN

RESEARCH IN NAVAL HISTORY

U.S.S. *Constitution*

VERSATILE
GUARDIAN
RESEARCH IN NAVAL HISTORY

EDITED BY

RICHARD A. VON DOENHOFF

HOWARD UNIVERSITY PRESS

WASHINGTON, D.C.

1979

This Special Edition
Published by Howard University Press for the
National Archives Trust Fund Board
National Archives and Records Service
General Services Administration
Washington, D.C.

Printed in the United States of America.

Endleaves: U.S. Coast Survey's first published nautical chart of Annapolis Harbor, 1846. (Records of the Coast and Geodetic Survey, Cartographic Archives Branch, National Archives.)

LIBRARY OF CONGRESS CATALOGING IN PUBLICATION DATA
Conference on Naval History, Washington, D.C., 1974.
    Versatile guardian.

    (National Archives conferences; v. 14)
    Bibliography: p.
    Includes index.
    1. United States—History, Naval—Congresses. 2. United States—History, Naval—Sources—Congresses. I. von Doenhoff, Richard A., 1940- II. Title. III Series: United States. National Archives and Records Service. National Archives conferences; v. 14.
E182.C725   1974   359'.00973   79-15678
ISBN 0-88258-078-7

NATIONAL ARCHIVES CONFERENCES/VOLUME 14

Papers and proceedings of the National Archives Conference on Naval History

Sponsored by the National Archives and Records Service
May 29-31, 1974
The National Archives Building
Washington, D.C.

Preface

This volume contains the papers and commentaries prepared for and presented at the Conference on Naval History held on May 30 and 31, 1974, at the National Archives. This was the fourteenth in a series of National Archives conferences on a variety of timely and significant subjects for the exchange of ideas and information among archivists, researchers, and other members of the scholarly community. The conferences are designed to inform scholars about the wealth of useful and pertinent research materials available in the National Archives and Records Service, as well as to provide a forum for archivists and researchers to suggest new avenues of approach to the subject of each conference.

The National Archives and Records Service, a part of the General Services Administration, administers the permanently valuable, noncurrent records of the federal government. These archival holdings date from the days of the Continental Congress to the present. The nearly one million cubic feet of records comprising the National Archives of the United States consist of textual records, photographs, motion pictures, sound recordings, and maps which are preserved because of their continuing practical utility for the orderly processes of government and as a record of our national heritage.

One goal of the National Archives staff is to explore and make more widely known these historical records. These conferences are a positive step in that direction. The papers of each conference are published in the belief that this fruitful exchange of ideas and information should be preserved and made available in printed form.

The Conference on Research on the Second World War, which was held in 1971, largely neglected the naval contributions to the war effort. The Conference on Naval History undertook to fill in this gap and further provided an opportunity for many of the nation's leading scholars in the field of naval history to suggest new avenues of approach and research in other time periods.

The director of this conference and editor of this volume was Richard A. von Doenhoff, who joined the National Archives staff in 1972 after nine years as a historian with the U.S. Naval History Division.

JAMES B. RHOADS
Archivist of the United States

Contents

III

TECHNOLOGY AND THE NAVY

IV

THE NAVY IN EARLIER WARS:
SOURCES AND RESEARCH POTENTIALS

V

SOME NAVAL ASPECTS OF THE SECOND WORLD WAR

List of Illustrations

Introduction

In the years since Rear Adm. Samuel Eliot Morison, U.S.N. (ret.), published his notable fifteen-volume work on U.S. naval operations in World War II, there has seemed to be a waning of productivity in the field of naval history. Morison clearly stood above his contemporaries and in many respects dominated the field.

Naval history has held the attention and fascination of such noted scholars as Alfred T. Mahan, Charles O. Paullin, and Samuel Eliot Morison, to name a few. President Theodore Roosevelt wrote a naval history of the War of 1812, and Franklin D. Roosevelt was an avid collector of naval prints, manuscripts, and memorabilia. While we honor and learn from these men, we must also look toward the future. Generally, one envisions naval history in terms of great sea battles, such as the *Constitution* and *Guerriere*, the *Monitor* and *Virginia*, Dewey at Manila Bay, or the momentous struggles at Coral Sea, Midway, Okinawa, and Savo Island. These are, indeed, the hallmarks of the U.S. Navy. Victories such as these, however, are merely the highlights of the history of the naval establishment. Within the scope of its far-reaching responsibilities, the navy exercised important influence in the development of American foreign policy, unique shipwright techniques, naval aviation, and nuclear propulsion.

In the first decade of its creation, the navy established its traditional bureau system. Within this structure, the navy categorized functions and activities and efficiently administered the naval establishment through a vast array of technological and military changes, which remained essentially unchanged until 1967. In that time period, steam replaced sail, aircraft carriers supplanted frigates, task forces assumed the duties of squadrons, and our first line of deterrent defense in 1967 extended over millions of square miles of ocean.

The purpose of the National Archives Conference on Naval History was to stimulate ideas for additional research and writing. The speakers were asked to consider the facets within their respective specializations which, to them, exemplified the potential for further study. Prof. W. T. Mallison, for example, combined two disciplines—history and international law—to present a new approach.

The conference incorporated the view that naval history could be used to supplement other specializations in American history. While the navy conducted some notable diplomatic efforts in the nineteenth century, a history of American foreign policy should also consider the influence and impact of worldwide naval presence on negotiations and international relations. Those historians studying the history of technology should not ignore the navy's significant contributions in such areas as radar, aeronautics, metallurgy, oceanography, and weapons systems. And it almost goes without saying that any study of warfare and theories of strategy should incorporate the thinking of American naval planners and leaders.

The success of this conference must be attributed to the spirited cooperation of a great number of people. The conference logistics were ably handled by Elsie F. Freivogel of the Office of Educational Programs. During the first morning of the conference, a broken water main extinguished the lights in the entire National Archives Building. Freivogel immediately undertook to locate the afternoon sessions in the Hotel Washington, thereby preserving the continuity of the program and allowing the conference to proceed. To Vice Adm. Edwin B. Hooper, U.S.N. (ret.), then director of the Naval History Division, who delivered the opening address, I owe a debt of gratitude. I wish to express my appreciation to the session chairmen who graciously introduced each session and maintained a tight schedule: Richard W. Leopold, Thomas P. Hughes, James E. O'Neill, and Philip A. Crowl.

To Mabel E. Deutrich, now assistant archivist for the Office of the National Archives, and her staff in the Military Archives Division—Garry D. Ryan, Robert W. Krauskopf, and Robert Wolfe—who accelerated schedules to produce several inventories and microfilm publications in connection with the conference, I wish to express my appreciation. Frank G. Burke and the Office of Educational Programs carried forward with an exhibit of naval records and artifacts, drawing upon resources not only located in the National Archives Building but from the Franklin D. Roosevelt Library and the Harry S. Truman Library as well, which added significantly to the conference.

The papers and commentaries presented during the conference are contained in this volume. Some of these presentations have been updated by the authors to reflect additional research or events in the years between the conference and the publication of this volume. I owe a tremendous debt of gratitude to David I. Eggenberger for his unflagging support and especially to Angela S. Wilkes for editing the manuscript and seeing the volume through the publication process.

Finally, I want to extend special thanks to Archivist of the United States

James B. Rhoads and to Deputy Archivist of the United States James E. O'Neill for selecting me to direct the conference and for their guidance through the many months of preparation.

RICHARD A. VON DOENHOFF
Conference Director

VERSATILE GUARDIAN

RESEARCH IN NAVAL HISTORY

EDWIN B. HOOPER

The Spectrum of Naval History

Archivist James B. Rhoads, by holding conferences in the National Archives on important areas in history, performs an especially valuable service. Perhaps the most important aspect is the bringing together of writers and teachers of history, other users of historical source materials, and archivists who maintain and service these materials. The focusing of each agenda upon an important area of history stimulates scholarly activity and promotes a fuller and more efficient utilization of the records of our national government.

The theme of naval history, selected for this fourteenth conference in the series, is most appropriate at this time considering the recent courses of events on the world scene and in this country.

One of the more ominous aspects of the more recent past is the extent to which the balance of seapower has been changing. Challenges will be faced that bear some resemblance to those of earlier years. As we evaluate how best we can meet these challenges, we should also weigh the cumulative effects of the many changes within this country and those of our allies that have so profoundly affected naval power and its application in recent years—changes in the means of warfare; changes in the organization, command, and support of United States military forces; and other changes influencing the elements which make a nation powerful upon the sea.

The light of history may be crucial in determining whether the courses on which we are now embarked are the correct ones and also in helping to chart new courses into the future. Human progress over the centuries has been made possible largely through benefiting from the accumulated wisdom of historical experiences. When the experiences and the lessons of the past have been neglected the result has often been retrogressive rather than progressive.

Insofar as navies and seapower are concerned, the historical input into the decision-making process has proven to be especially critical during periods of instability and major changes on the world scene, or when advancing technology has had its greatest impact. A notable example in United States history was during the last two decades of the nineteenth century. This was the time, after the deemphasis of the navy following the Civil War, that the decision was reached to initiate the final breakaway from the age of sail. This was a time of intensified intellectual activity within the corps of naval officers, a time of innovative thinking and exploration of new concepts, particularly by some in the more junior ranks.

Fortunately, when the potentials of the "new navy" were explored, the past was reevaluated. It was more than coincidental that the Naval War College was established in 1884. Alfred Thayer Mahan gave a series of lectures on history at the college, and these lectures formed the basis for his famous work, *The Influence of Sea Power upon History, 1660-1783,* published in 1890.

It will be recalled that Mahan set forth his interpretation of history in that book with some misgivings, noting that steam navies had as yet no history considered as decisive in its teaching. He observed "the great changes that have been brought about in naval weapons by the scientific advances of the past half century, and by the introduction of steam as the motive power," and warned that "theories about the naval warfare of the future are almost thoroughly presumptive." Nevertheless, he was convinced that, "while many of the conditions of war vary from age to age, there are certain teachings in the school of history which remain constant."[1]

Mahan's book had a profound impact upon naval policies throughout the world. In the case of the United States, it led to a freeing of naval strategic concepts from the limiting objectives of coastal defense and commerce destruction of a quarter century. In the years that followed, adjustments in naval forces and tactics were dictated by spectacular advances in submarine performance and by the development of aircraft. Yet, concepts derived from the study of history in Mahan's seminal work, when interpreted in the light of such adjustments, proved enduring for half a century and more.

That Mahan's work had lasting significance is evidenced by the recent series of articles, "Navies in War and in Peace," by Admiral of the Fleet of the Soviet Union S. G. Gorshkov, published in this country by the U.S. Naval Institute Press. The admiral's approach to his subject is, in a number of respects, reminiscent of that of Mahan, whom Gorshkov acknowledges as the creator of the "theory of Sea Power."[2]

Since World War II we have been going through another transitional phase of great significance with regard to United States naval power, a phase of uncertainty highlighted by an unending series of changes, in organization for the common defense and its growing superstructure, in national strategy, in the composition of military forces and their weapon systems, in the control and support of these forces, and in policies affecting their balance and readiness. Many influences helped set the stage for these profound and extensive changes. By far the most significant were those stemming from accelerated advances in military technology and, in particular, the advent of the atomic bomb.

In Mahan's great work, he had cautioned that in tracing resemblances from an early era of history to later eras "there is a tendency not only to overlook differences, but to exaggerate points of likeness, — to be fanciful."[3] In the months following V-J Day, the tendency was often the reverse. "Modern science," it was said, "has utterly changed the nature of war."[4] In placing emphasis on "revising concepts inherited from the past," many in the civilian intellectual community, and even in military circles, insisted that lessons of history were no longer valid. At times, they responded with ridicule to attempts to throw the light of history on proposed actions. This was reflected in the accusation of one prominent leader that the Navy Department "frequently seemed to retire from the realm of logic into a dim religious world in which Neptune was God, Mahan his prophet, and the United States Navy the only true church."[5] One respected writer on strategy concluded: "Obviously the relative importance of the army and navy in wartime would be considerably diminished if not eliminated by a device which was capable of producing havoc great enough to effect a decision by itself."[6]

The question was raised as to whether the purpose of an American navy to fight other navies was obsolete, and doubts were expressed as to the continuing significance of seapower. Yet the geography of the land and sea areas of the world had not changed. The physics of the sea had not been altered. The most economical, and only practical means of transportation for the vast bulk of fuel, materials, goods, and military supplies between the land areas of the globe would still be by sea, and quantities so transported would increase. The demand for more and more of the resources of the seas and seabeds would also increase. Competition for the use of the sea and its resources could lead to armed conflict. And the relative opaqueness of water to electro-magnetic radiations would continue to provide an ideal medium for expanding roles of submarines in an age of nuclear power and missiles.

In the aftermath of World War II, major expenditures were required to develop nuclear warfare capabilities. Increasing demands were accommodated within a declining budget. During a period of unchallenged United States naval supremacy, the blessings of control of the sea tended to be taken for granted. The navy and other conventional forces were cut to the point that by 1950 capabilities no longer matched commitments. Lessons of history had to be relearned through harsh experience in the Korean War.

Once that major, though limited, war was over, the process of change resumed. For a time, there was a tendency to be lured by what the British historian Roskill, in referring to an earlier era, described as "the fallacy of the dominant weapon"[7] — in this case the nuclear weapon. Integrated strategy was emphasized, at times to the point of neglect of specialized forms of warfare, such as that upon the sea. Radical departures were made from earlier principles of defense organization and responsibilities. Some effects of the far-reaching changes became evident in the Vietnam War, but their full implications have yet to be tested.

We are now entering a new period, or a new phase, in which it is of extraordinary importance that we draw fully on the experiences, teachings, and indeed the inspiration of history. This is a time for reevaluation. Faced with a changing balance of seapower in the world, crucial decisions will be required at many levels. The United States and her allies of the so-called Free World are confronted by a powerful, modern, and expanding Soviet navy of submarines and surface ships, a navy supplemented by oceanographic research vessels, a vast fishing fleet, and a growing merchant marine. Evidence of the increased influence of Soviet seapower is today apparent in the Middle East, the Indian Ocean, and other areas of the globe.

Because of the subtlety and pervasive nature of much of their influence, in peace and war, naval power and the other elements of seapower have always been difficult subjects for the historian to interpret. The diversification of naval tasks and added roles, such as nuclear deterrence, have made the interpretation far more complex than ever before. Yet never has the need for understanding been greater. Insofar as the navy is concerned, the dimensions of the problems go beyond those relating to ships, aircraft, and weapon systems and the strategies and tactics of their use. There are fundamental problems concerning that key ingredient of all forms of military power, that is, personnel — the motivation of these personnel and their preparations for combat. The problems are, in part, the result of shifting attitudes and turbulence in the nation as a whole. For this reason, personnel policies and their consequences are one segment of the wide spectrum of naval history that is especially critical today and in the future. If adaptations to changed conditions are required, it is even more important that we understand the sources of incentive, of teamwork, of discipline, of professionalism, and of inspirational leadership as practiced by great naval officers of the past.

Having touched briefly on the earlier importance of naval history and on some of the current needs, I should now like to express some broad views as to ways in which we can reap the benefits of history. Within the Naval Historical Center of the Navy Department one of our highest priorities is the providing of support to staff actions and official studies. We are convinced that the fullest practicable use of relevant background contained in past records and secondary sources will facilitate these actions and studies, lead to sounder conclusions, and improve justification of the decisions proposed.

In addition to making available source materials in our own holdings, we lead the researchers to important materials held elsewhere. In this regard, I congratulate Dr. Rhoads and the Archives staff for the accessioning of the "flag files" of important naval commands, previously remotely stored in Mechanicsburg, Pennsylvania. Hopefully, this action will result in increased use of these important materials by researchers.

The use of historical sources in staff actions and in studies is not sufficient within itself. Leaders within the navy and elsewhere in the government need an understanding of naval history and of its impact upon general history, as background for day-to-day decisions related to naval power. Within the navy, there are a few encouraging signs. One is the renewed emphasis on history at the Naval War College in recent years. Another is the establishment of a history major at the U.S. Naval Academy. Also, I am pleased to note that an officer recently selected for flag rank is about to receive a doctoral degree in history from Yale.

As for the contributions of historians toward a better understanding of naval history, we in the Naval Historical Center can fulfill but a very small percentage of the needs. The bulk of the secondary works must be those produced by outside scholars. Their value will be enhanced by the degree to which the writings facilitate extrapolation of historical lessons into the present and the future. In what might be considered an extension of Mahan's thoughts, Sir Julian Corbett stated that "the value of history in the art of war is not only to elucidate the resemblance of past and present but also their essential differences."[8] This observation is even more valid today, providing the historian comprehends the uncertainties involved in comparing the past with the untested present and the future.

In any case, we cannot expect the historian to accomplish the entire task. What is important is that historians' interpretations reflect an awareness of principles and factors that will likely be enduring, along with a perception of those that probably will be subject to change. And regardless of the depth of interpretation, sound writing of history will help readers, in uniform and out, to draw their own conclusions—conclusions based upon their own experiences and perceptions of the problems to be faced.

Most of my shore assignments prior to becoming director of Naval History at the Naval Historical Center were in research and development. During those tours I was deeply impressed with the importance of unfettered research as a complement to programmed research in areas officially recognized as important. From the vantage point of my present assignment, I have seen many parallels between the research and development situation and the historical process. The spectrum of important naval history is so wide that great value should be placed upon research and writings in areas that seem important to individual historians. Such efforts are bound to provide significant insights into history far beyond those that would be produced by programmed activity.

Although the focus of this paper has been on naval history, there has been no intent to place this important element of history out of perspective with other areas with which naval events are associated. I should like, in particular, to stress the importance of histories of all the military services, histories that are important to the readiness of those services and to the effectiveness of the nation's military efforts as a whole. Moreover, only by recording and interpreting such histories, and those of other specialized areas of a country's endeavors, can the building blocks of meaningful general history be provided.

NOTES

1. A. T. Mahan, *The Influence of Sea Power upon History* (Boston: Little, Brown, 1890), p. 2.
2. Sergei G. Gorshkov, *Red Star at Sea* (Annapolis: Naval Institute Press, 1974), p. 30.
3. Mahan, *Influence of Sea Power*, p. 5.
4. Vannevar Bush, "Scientific Weapons and a Future War," *Life Magazine* (14 November 1949), p. 113.
5. Henry L. Stimson and McGeorge Bundy, *On Active Service in Peace and War* (New York: Harper & Brothers, 1947), p. 506.
6. Bernard Brodie, *The Atomic Bomb and American Security* (New Haven: Yale Institute of International Studies, 1945), p. 81.
7. S. W. Roskill, "History: Dust Heap or Cornerstone?", *U.S. Naval Institute Proceedings* 92, no. 1 (January 1966): 70.
8. Quoted in ibid, p. 67.

I

NAVAL HISTORY SOURCES: PLANS, PROGRAMS, AND PROBLEMS

MABEL E. DEUTRICH

"Cognizance"
over Navy Department Records

The Navy Department, created in 1798, has been in existence for 181 years. During 124 of those years it operated under a bureau system. On the whole, the system worked quite satisfactorily; its major defect was the problem of coordination of activities of the entire department. Each bureau chief jealously guarded his little empire and tried to make certain no one impinged upon his—to use the navy's term—"cognizant" area. In describing this phenomenon one naval historian said:

> "Cognizance," a word of mystic significance in naval circles, is the keynote of the Navy Department's century-old bureau system. It implies responsibility and jurisdiction for a specific field of activity, together with a vigorous "Hands off!" toward any outsider threatening to poach in those preserves.[1]

Because one can scarcely find an order enunciating responsibility that does not use the term "cognizance" at least once, it seemed appropriate, in fact almost essential, that the title of this paper be "Cognizance over Navy Department Records."

ADMINISTRATIVE BACKGROUND

There is another reason for mentioning the bureaus at the outset of this paper. In administering its holdings, the National Archives, like all major archival institutions, follows the principle of provenance. Simply stated, this principle requires tracing the origin of each document and filing it with all other documents having the same origin. Records created or accumulated by an organizational element must be kept together and, generally, in their original filing arrangement. It is axiomatic, therefore, that if the navy operated under a bureau system most of the time and that if the National Archives follows the principle of provenance, it has organized the records of each bureau into a separate record group and placed the records of the secretary's office—including records of general import to the entire department—in a record group called "General Records of the Department of the Navy." It follows that records of other organizational elements, such as the Offices of the Judge Advocate General and the Chief of Naval Operations, are in separate record groups.

A very simplified recitation of the administrative structure of the Navy Department may help to bring the picture into focus. Until 1815, naval affairs were managed entirely by the secretary of the navy, with some clerical help. The War of 1812, however, revealed the need of the civilian secretary for professional assistance. Accordingly, in 1815, a three-man Board of Naval Commissioners was created to fill this void. Unfortunately, however, none of the commissioners was responsible for the material functions of naval administration. And so, in 1842 a step was taken in the opposite direction; five bureaus were established, each headed by a chief who was specifically charged with responsibility in a specialized area.[2] During the Civil War three more bureaus were added. In 1915, to force some coordination and direction among the bureaus and offices, an Office of Chief of Naval Operations was created.

Over the years, there were a number of realignments of responsibilities among the bureaus, some designed to effect greater efficiency and some, such as the creation of the Bureau of Aeronautics in 1921, to keep pace with technological developments. The bureau system continued, however, until May 1, 1966, when the four material bureaus then in existence were replaced by six "systems commands."[3] The two bureaus not connected with naval material support—the Bureaus of Naval Personnel and Medicine and Surgery—were continued.[4]

Other organizational elements that created records and whose records are arranged in separate record groups are the naval districts and shore establishments, the naval operating forces, and the Marine Corps.

There is one other very important record group that must be mentioned—the Naval Records Collection of the Office of Naval Records and Library. As indicated by its title, the records in this group are not records created by the Office of Naval Records and Library; they are records relating to naval operations *collected* by that office from official and unofficial sources.[5] They consist primarily of very significant records culled from the Office of the Secretary of the Navy and the various navy bureaus and offices.[6] Included, however, are semiofficial and private records (correspondence, journals, logs, and similar items) of naval officers and, in some instances, copies of records in other archival institutions and in private hands.

The collection of these records by the Office of Naval Records and Library has its strengths and weaknesses. On the credit side is the fact that the hundreds of volumes of records obtained from naval officers and unofficial sources would not have been centralized; some, no doubt, would have found their way to archival institutions, but many would simply have been lost to the scholarly community. As far as the bound volumes of records taken from the Office of the Secretary of the Navy and the bureaus are concerned, such as copies of letters sent and letters received, they can be used just as easily in this record group as in the one to which they belong. If retained in their bound form, the indexes are intact; cross references can easily be inserted in the inventories or other finding aids to the record groups to which they belong. On the other hand, the removal of unbound documents from files without benefit of precise, consistent cross references, and the occasional dismantling of bound volumes, as was done to create the large geographical "area" and "subject" files as well as some other series, is quite another matter.[7] Sometimes the source of the documents in these artificially created files is indicated. Often, however, there is no means of ascertaining the official or private origin of a document or learning about any related documents. Furthermore, the indexes to the series from which the documents were culled have been impaired. We can only tell researchers that if indexes or registers to records of the Office of the Secretary of the Navy or to bureaus—especially the Bureau of Personnel (Navigation)— are missing, maybe they are in the area, subject, or other files set up by the Office of Naval Records and Library.

THE NATIONAL ARCHIVES
AND NAVY DEPARTMENT RECORDS

The first job faced by the National Archives after it was established was to organize and inaugurate a survey of the records of the federal government in the Washington, D.C. area, including the records of the Department of the Navy. This initial survey was begun in May 1935, and by the close of 1936 it had, for all practical purposes, completed the part relating to navy records.

A second step was the accessioning of records. The first navy records accessioned by the National Archives consisted of a series of log books containing engineering data recorded on steam vessels from 1861 to 1924 and the correspondence and other records of the Bureaus of Equipment and of Steam Engineering from 1885 to 1910. These records, consisting of 2,200 cubic feet, were received during the fiscal year ending June 30, 1936.[8] During the following year records were received from six bureaus or offices in the Department of the Navy.[9] This pattern of steady accessioning continued for the next dozen years, except that they were unusually heavy during 1941 and 1942, when the Navy Department, like the War Department, was under great pressure for office space because of its expanded World War II activities. By mid-1943, the National Archives had almost sixty thousand cubic feet of Navy Department records.[10]

A third step was the systematic analysis, arrangement, and description of all of the National Archives holdings. For this purpose the National Archives decided, in the spring of 1941, that it must prescribe the boundaries of the record groups into which its holdings were to be organized, and that when this had been done all series of records within each group must be described in inventories or checklists. Because of the increased accessions and other emergency activities connected with the war effort, the boundaries for all record groups for materials then in custody were not prescribed until the close of fiscal year 1944. Little progress, therefore, had been made in the preparation of inventories or checklists. For several years thereafter, however, excellent progress was made. In 1945 checklists were produced describing the records in the following record groups: Naval Records Collection of the Office of Naval Records and Library, General Records of the Department of the Navy, and Office of the Judge Advocate General. The following year checklists were produced for the records of the Naval Observatory, the U.S. Marine Corps, and the Bureau of Supplies and Accounts. In 1948 preliminary inventories were issued for the records of the Bureaus of Medicine and Surgery and Yards and Docks. Preliminary inventories for the Bureaus of Aeronautics and Ordnance were issued in 1951 and, in the following year, one was produced for the records of the Hydrographic Office.

Being very conscious from the beginning of the need to protect the integrity of the records, the National Archives planned to maintain and administer the records of each executive department and major independent establishment, as well as the records of the legislative and judicial branches, by a distinct and separate division of the National Archives.[11] Thus, the seeds of the record group concept, formally adopted in 1941, had already been sown.

Initially, when the National Archives had only small scatterings of records from many departments and agencies, all accessioned records were placed in one of two divisions, called the "Division of Department Archives, No. 1" or "No. 2." Navy Department records were placed in Division No. 1.[12] As accessions increased, however, separate departmental divisions were established. The Division of Navy Department Archives was created on January 3, 1938.[13]

There were a number of changes in the organizational structure of the National Archives in the years that followed. One trend that continued until 1962, was the centralization of more and more of the total responsibility for administering records in the custodial divisions. Thus, most of the functional divisions, such as accessions, classification, and research, which had been established simultaneously with the departmental divisions, were gradually abolished, and these responsibilities were given to the custodial units.

The name of the custodial unit that administered the navy records changed from time to time. Because the number of division heads reporting to the archivist was too great for effective control, certain divisions were consolidated. This led to a merger of the Divisions of Navy Department Archives and the War Department Archives into a War Records Office on July 1, 1944.[14] At the close of 1947, major operating units previously called "offices" were redesignated "divisions" and the units within them became "branches."[15] Hence, we had a Navy Branch in the War Records Division. But regardless of its name, from 1938 to 1962 Navy Department records were administered by a separate and distinct organizational unit.

The story of the accessioning and administering of navy records by the National Archives, that has been told thus far, extends primarily to the beginning of the 1950s. In a nutshell, it is a story of steady accessions and considerable progress in the preparation of finding aids and the publication of selected series of records on microfilm.[16] To get the full picture, however, it is necessary to return momentarily to the period of World War II. As early as 1940, the National Archives became concerned with the rate of creation of records and the need for the establishment of retention and disposal schedules. It was already evident that the various governmental agencies were retaining all sorts of records not of enduring value. It was soon equally obvious that these agencies needed places to store and process records not needed in day-to-day activities but that could not be either immediately destroyed or sent to the National Archives. Some of the agencies, the military in particular, also needed depositories where they could centralize their highly active personnel records.

This is not the place to tell the story of the development of the records management concept—the scheduling of records for disposal as authorized initially by the Federal Records Disposal Act of 1943 and the establishment of intermediate depositories, first by the various agencies and, beginning in 1950, as the result of recommendations of the first Hoover Commission, the merger of most of them into centers operated by the General Services Administration. Nor is it the place to dwell upon the shortage of storage space with which the National Archives was faced in just a few years after the close of World War II. But all of these factors, especially the establishment of records centers and the lack of space in the National Archives, had a direct bearing upon the activities of the National Archives from the 1950s and the situation which prevails today.

The Navy Department was one of the leaders in the development of a comprehensive records management program. It selected a member of the National Archives to serve as director of records coordination, a position that was created in October 1941.[17] It proceeded to schedule its records at a rapid rate, and it established a series of records centers throughout the country. The first of these centers, established in 1942 in Washington, D.C., was merely a resting place for records that were not sufficiently active to retain in valuable office space and for records that either were awaiting transfer to the National Archives or disposal authorization. This same situation prevailed for many of its centers but one of them had a second purpose—the centralization and servicing of personnel files of civilian and naval personnel separated from the service before World War II.[18]

The establishment of the depository to house permanently valuable records of separated civilian and military personnel was of significance to the National Archives for three reasons. The first was that the National Archives had accessioned about twelve thousand cubic feet of files on civilian and naval personnel separated from the service from about 1885 to 1941. These files were relatively dormant until the attack on Pearl Harbor, when thousands of men who had served as officers and enlisted men sought the opportunity to serve again. The records of their prior service were, therefore, needed and calls for them—about one hundred thousand requests a year in 1942 and 1943—poured into the National Archives. The records had become too active to remain in the National Archives; the requests could be filled only with the assistance of navy personnel and funds.[19] The second reason why the establishment of this center was of significance was that it marked the first large withdrawal of navy records from the National Archives Building. The third reason was that it was an economically sound move—one of the forerunners to the establishment of a specialized federal records center in Saint Louis for separated civilian personnel records of all federal agencies and the personnel records of men and women discharged from the nation's armed services.[20]

In retrospect, the decade of 1951 to 1961 was one of doldrums in comparison with the preceding and succeeding periods. This, perhaps, is not an entirely fair characterization of activities. There was some shifting of navy records to the records centers and, in some instances, the return of portions of them back to the National Archives Building. The rapid accessioning of records prior to this period, and especially during the war years, coupled with the lack of space, equipment, and personnel had prevented the National Archives from arranging its holdings in logical order as they were brought into the building. By 1953 it had become imperative from a standpoint of safety, efficiency, and economy to rearrange them. Thus, for the next three years all available resources were expended on a massive shifting of records, including of course, the records of the Navy Department.[21] Furthermore, by the close of this decade most World War II military records had been accessioned.[22] On the other hand, the only navy inventories produced until the close of the decade were ones describing the cartographic records of the U.S. Marine Corps and the Office of the Chief of Naval Operations, produced in 1954 and 1955, respectively. Finally, in 1960, an inventory was issued for the records of the

Bureau of Naval Personnel and the following year one for the records of the
Bureau of Ships.

The lag in the production of finding aids, as well as the lack of space in the
National Archives Building and in the records centers, were the key factors
which lead to the establishment, in 1962, of a functional organization within
the National Archives. Under this functional organization, two projects divisions
and an appraisal division were established. The projects divisions were to
concentrate on the production of finding aids and microfilm publications;
the appraisal division was to prepare retention plans for federal agencies,
which would reduce to a small core the volume of records considered to be
of enduring value. [23]

Although the functional organization resulted in the demise of the Navy
Branch, navy records did not receive short shrift. Some records were transferred to records centers and a few were destroyed. Inventories were prepared
for all navy record groups where none existed, i.e., the records of Naval
Operating Forces, Naval Districts and Shore Establishments, and the Office
of the Chief of Naval Operations. [24] Most of the inventories prepared earlier
were obsolete, largely because many records were accessioned after they had
been prepared. Supplements, therefore, were issued during this period for all
except two of them. Furthermore, a number of series were reproduced as
microfilm publications; the most significant produced during this period
probably was Microcopy 625, Area File of the Naval Records Collection,
1775-1910.

By 1966, it was apparent that the National Archives must have additional
space. It was obtained by transferring, during the following year, about one-
third of its holdings to the newly constructed Washington National Records
Center building in Suitland, Maryland. The records were housed in space
especially built and equipped for permanently valuable records. [25]

Among the records moved to Suitland were over thirty thousand cubic
feet of Navy Department records. For the most part, they were World War I
and II records of the bureaus and other records used least frequently. Two
record groups—the records of the Bureau of Supplies and Accounts and the
records of Naval Districts and Shore Establishments—were transferred in their
entirety.

About the same time, the functional organization was dropped except for
accessioning and appraisal work, which continued to be carried out by a
separate division. The navy records that were retained in the National Archives
Building were placed organizationally with all other military records. Those
dated prior to World War I were administered by the Old Military Archives
Division; those of World War I and later were administered by the Modern
Military Archives Division. [26]

Once again, navy records were by no means neglected. New revised inventories were produced for the records of the U.S. Marine Corps and the records of the Hydrographic Office. The records of the Naval Academy were segregated and placed in a separate record group after which an inventory was prepared. In addition, two series of records from this new record group have been reproduced as microfilm publications: Microcopy 945, Letters Sent by the Superintendent of the U.S. Naval Academy, 1845-65, and Microcopy 949, Letters Received by the Superintendent of the U.S. Naval Academy, 1845-87.

Filming for four other microfilm publications has also been completed and the accompanying pamphlets are now available. Microcopy 971, Annual Reports of Fleets and Task Forces of the United States Navy, 1920-41, reproduces reports submitted by the commanding officers of the Atlantic, Pacific, United States, and Asiatic Fleets; Special Service Squadron; Naval Forces Europe; and Squadron 40-T. Correspondence and reports pertaining to fleet problems are reproduced on Microcopy 964, Records Relating to United States Fleet Problems I to XXII, 1923-41. A small series of naval attache reports has been reproduced as Microcopy 975, Selected Naval Attache Reports Relating to the World Crisis, 1937-43. The reports reproduced in this microfilm publication were selected by the Navy Department in 1943 in response to a request by President Roosevelt for information on "estimates of potential military strength" and the "probability of an outbreak of war." Microcopy 984, Navy Department General Orders, 1863-1948, includes circulars ("directives") for that period.

Only a few series of navy records have been accessioned and brought into the National Archives Building in recent years — because of a lack of space. For example, approximately 18,000 cubic feet of navy operational records, the so-called flag files, became available for accessioning. Because of the shortage of space, only about 1,700 cubic feet, those dated approximately 1917 to 1940, could be brought into the National Archives Building; the remaining 16,300 cubic feet had to be sent to Suitland, Maryland. The only other significant series brought into the National Archives is approximately 340 cubic feet of naval attache reports, 1900 to 1939. This series was reviewed by the Navy Department and our Declassification Division so that security classifications could be removed from as many documents as possible.

THE NEED FOR CENTRALIZATION OF NAVY RECORDS

At the present time the National Archives has 104,000 cubic feet of Navy Department records in its custody,[27] 57,000 cubic feet of which are in the National Archives Building[28] and 47,000 cubic feet of which are in archives space at Suitland, Maryland. But there are also almost 590,000 cubic feet of Navy Department records in the various records centers. Over half of these are records of Naval Districts and Shore Establishments, and probably should not be centralized. [29] If those records are excluded, and if it is assumed that 10 percent of the remaining records will be found to be permanently valuable, another 26,000 cubic feet of records should be accessioned. In addition, there are approximately 6,500 cubic feet of records in the Naval Historical Center, [30] some of which are vital to its operations and should not be accessioned at this time.

The National Archives hopes that a new building will be constructed just across the street as part of the master plan of the Pennsylvania Avenue Development Corporation. But this building will not be available for several years, and space is needed now. To fill this void, the National Archives is searching for adequate space that can be leased.

When leased space is acquired, a lot of careful planning will be needed so that, if at all possible, we will not end up with an additional dispersal of navy records. It would be most undesirable to have the pre-World War I bureau records in the National Archives Building, the World Wars I and II bureau records in Suitland, Maryland, and post-World War II records in still another location, and, at the same time, the records of the Offices of the Secretary of the Navy and the Chief of Naval Operations scattered in the National Archives Building, the Naval Historical Center, and leased space.

To a certain extent the National Archives will be faced with this same problem for records of most agencies, and it will be neither possible nor economical to shift all records when leased space is acquired. We have a unique situation, however, with the navy records—a situation that warrants special consideration. All of the bureau records, with the exception of two—Personnel and Medicine and Surgery—are closed record groups. [31] The General Records of the Department of the Navy, 1798–1947, is also closed.

Closed record groups are record groups to which no records are being added as a result of current record-creating activities and to which no records will be added in the future. They are highly desirable for a number of reasons: archivists can perfect the arrangement of the records and prepare definitive finding aids to them; they can weed out once and for all the records that are not permanently valuable; they no longer need to constantly shuffle records because of additions that need interfiling; and finding aids no longer become obsolete almost as soon as they are produced because additional records are accessioned.

Sometimes, to prevent a record group from becoming so large that we have problems in the arrangement and description of the records and so that we can reap the benefits of closed record groups, we close a record group when a major reorganization has taken place. Thus, the record groups containing the records of the Offices of the Secretary of War and Navy and the Army

Air Forces were closed at 1947 when the National Defense Establishment was created.

The National Archives staff engaged in accessioning and disposal work should concentrate on holdings in closed record groups. All of the permanently valuable records in these groups should be accessioned and, along with the navy records already among our holdings, should be centralized as soon as possible. If it is not feasible to do this when we acquire leased space, it certainly should be done when we get a new building. In addition, a navy branch or division should be reestablished to service and administer these records. The reestablishment of this branch or division would permit the archivists to concentrate on these holdings — to arrange, organize, and describe them. Then, and only then, will the archivists become subject matter experts in this area — archivists truly steeped in naval history. Then, and only then, will we truly have cognizance over the navy records.

NOTES

1. Robert G. Albion, "The Administration of the Navy, 1798-1945," *Public Administration Review* 5, no. 4 (Autumn 1945): 293.
2. The initial five bureaus were Medicine and Surgery; Yards and Docks; Provisions and Clothing; Ordnance and Hydrography; and Construction, Equipment, and Repairs.
3. Abolished were the Bureaus of Weapons, Ships, Yards and Docks, and Supplies and Accounts. They were replaced by six systems commands — Air, Ship, Ordnance, Electronics, Supply, and Facilities Engineering. These systems were placed organizationally under the chief of naval material, a position created in 1963.
4. For a brief administrative history of the Navy Department from 1798 to 1945, see Albion, "Administration of the Navy;" for a concise statement of organizational changes from 1947-66, see R. P. Smyth, "The Navy Department: The Fulcrum and the Balance," *U.S. Naval Institute Proceedings* 93, no. 5 (May 1967): 70-78.
5. The Naval Records Collection was begun in 1882 by the Office of Library and Naval War Records. Its collecting activities were directed first to Civil War records and later to all old records. In 1915 its name was changed to the Office of Naval Records and Library. In 1918, a Historical Section was organized in the Office of the Chief of Naval Operations for the purpose of soliciting and arranging records relating to United States naval participation in World War I and preparing monographs for publication. The following year both units were placed under the same officer and thus the two were merged.
6. The Office of Naval Records and Library was not intended to be a repository for all old records of enduring value. Records not directly related to naval operations, e.g., most records of the Bureaus of Construction and Repair, Supplies and Accounts, and Medicine and Surgery, were not collected.
7. The system utilized for filing loose documents (primarily into geographical area and

subject files) was developed by the Historical Section for the World War I records. It was not until 1923, when the Historical Section and the Office of Naval Records and Library were physically merged, that the system was imposed upon the older documents.

8. U.S., National Archives, *Second Annual Report of the Archivist of the United States for the Fiscal Year Ending June 30, 1936* (Washington, D.C.:Government Printing Office, 1937), p. 13. (Hereafter annual reports of the National Archives are cited as NA, *Annual Report.*)

9. Ibid., 1937 (Washington, D.C.: Government Printing Office, 1938), p. 35.

10. Ibid., 1942 (Washington, D.C.: Government Printing Office, 1943), pp. 2, 13; and ibid., 1943 (Washington, D.C.: Government Printing Office, 1944), p. 17.

11. Ibid., 1935 (Washington, D.C.: Government Printing Office, 1936), pp. 17–18.

12. Ibid., 1936 (Washington, D.C.: Government Printing Office, 1937), pp. 50 51.

13. Ibid., 1938 (Washington, D.C.: Government Printing Office, 1939), pp. 2-3.

14. Ibid., 1944 (Washington, D.C.: Government Printing Office, 1945), p. 54.

15. Ibid., 1948 (Washington, D.C.: Government Printing Office, 1949), p. 39.

16. The National Archives began publishing significant series of records on microfilm in 1940. Initially, it was a small-scale operation; during World War II most of the filming was for security purposes. After the war, however, the production of microfilm publications became one of the most significant programs of the National Archives. The most important microfilm publications of navy records that had been produced by 1950 were M-75, Records Relating to the United States Exploring Expedition under the Command of Lt. Charles Wilkes, 1836–42; M-88, Records Relating to the United States Exploring Expedition to the North Pacific, 1854–56; M-124, Letters Received by the Secretary of the Navy, Miscellaneous Letters, 1807-15; and M-125, Letters Received by the Secretary of the Navy: Captains' Letters, 1807–61, 1866–85.

17. NA, *Annual Report,* 1942 (Washington, D.C.: Government Printing Office, 1943), p. 5.

18. Naval Depository No. 2 was established in Philadelphia on December 1, 1943. The rapid disestablishing of activities on the east coast after VE day, however, overtaxed the facilities of this center. To remedy this, three annexes were established — at New York City; at the Naval Supply Depot, Mechanicsburg, Pa.; and at the Naval Station, New Orleans, La. The center in Philadelphia was disestablished on June 30, 1947, and the remaining holdings were distributed among the annexes.

19. NA, *Annual Report,* 1942 (Washington, D.C.: Government Printing Office, 1943), p. 29; and ibid., 1943 (Washington, D.C.: Government Printing Office, 1944), pp. 34–35.

20. In the fall of 1951, a records center was established for records of separated civilian employees from all agencies of the federal government. In July 1960, the Department of Defense turned over its Military Personnel Records Center in Saint Louis to the General Services Administration. Although housed in separate buildings and at separate locations in Saint Louis, this complex constitutes a single specialized records center.

21. U.S., General Services Administration, *Annual Report on the National Archives and Records Service, from the Annual Report of the Administrator of General Services for the Year Ending June 30, 1956* (Washington, D.C.: Government Printing Office, 1957), p. 7.

22. Idem, *Tenth Annual Report of the Administrator of General Services, June 30, 1959* (Washington, D.C.: Government Printing Office, 1960), p. 28.

23. There was an Office of Military Archives and an Office of Civil Archives. Within each of these there was a reference division and a projects division. The projects divisions were charged with the production of finding aids and microfilm publications. In addition, there was an Office of Records Appraisal (later redesignated a division), which was responsible for the accessioning and disposal of records. In particular, it was charged with the preparation of retention plans for federal agencies. It was hoped that the identification of the relatively small core of records of enduring value that must be retained to document the functions, responsibilities, and activities of an agency would facilitate the disposal of those records of ephemeral value.

24. An inventory was also prepared for the Records of Joint Army and Navy Boards and Committees, Record Group 225.

25. U.S., General Services Administration, *Administrator's Annual Report, Fiscal Year 1968* (Washington, D.C.: Government Printing Office, 1968), p. 3.

26. All reference service on navy records in the National Archives Building is performed by the Navy and Old Army Branch; projects work is handled by the Military Projects Branch.

27. This figure pertains to Navy Department records per se. Excluded from it are records of related agencies such as the Coast Guard, Maritime Commission, U.S. Shipping Board, Bureau of Marine Inspection and Navigation, and Joint Army and Navy Boards and Committees.

28. Thirteen hundred cubic feet of these records are cartographic records and 5,700 cubic feet are audiovisual records.

29. The permanently valuable records in this record group should be accessioned, but they probably should be housed in our regional archives branches, which were established in 1968.

30. U.S., Department of the Navy, Office of the Chief of Naval Operations, Naval History Division, *U.S. Naval History Sources in the Washington Area and Suggested Research Subjects* (Washington, D.C.: Government Printing Office, 1970), pp. 3-6.

31. In 1966, when most of the bureaus were replaced by systems commands, the record groups for these bureaus were closed and new record groups were established for each of the six systems commands.

DEAN C. ALLARD

The Naval Historical Center
and the Resources of Naval History

The value of research in naval history and the Naval Historical Center's philosophy regarding official and scholarly historical projects are discussed in the paper "The Spectrum of Naval History," and an excellent overview of the programs and outlook of the National Archives is provided in "Cognizance' over Navy Department Records." This paper will cover the evolution and nature of the Naval Historical Center's collections and conclude with remarks on materials held by additional repositories.

By far the oldest component of the Naval Historical Center is the Navy Department Library, which traces its origin to an 1800 letter from President John Adams to Secretary of the Navy Benjamin Stoddert. In this communication, Adams directed the preparation of a catalog of books on naval subjects and requested that arrangements be made to purchase appropriate volumes. Adams's long interest in naval affairs was reflected in the specific advice he gave to Stoddert. According to the president, the collection:

> ought to consist of all the best writings in Dutch, Spanish, French, and especially in English, upon the theory and practice of naval architecture, navigation, gunnery, hydraulics, hydrostatics, and all branches of mathematics subservient to the profession of the sea [, and] the lives of all the admirals, English, French, Dutch, or any other nation, who have distinguished themselves by the boldness and success of their navigation, or their gallantry and skill in naval combats.[1]

In 1882, Congress instructed the Navy Department Library to consolidate other book collections that had been developed throughout the century by Washington naval offices.[2] The expanded organization then came under the direction of James R. Soley, a member of the navy's corps of commissioned professors, author of one of the early histories of naval operations in the Civil War, and for several years after 1890 the assistant secretary of the navy. Organizationally, the library was associated with the newly established Office of Naval Intelligence, indicating the close integration of historical resources with other official naval programs.[3]

Between 1882 and the present, the library shifted from its location in the State-War-Navy building at Seventeenth Street and Pennsylvania Avenue to the Main Navy building and several other locations before moving during 1970 to its current site in the Washington Navy Yard. But throughout its existence, the library has continued to serve as a focal point of the variously named organizations that have served as the navy's central historical office.

Today, the Navy Department Library's holdings include approximately one hundred twenty-five thousand volumes. It has good general coverage of technical subjects of naval interest and of American history. As President Adams had originally suggested, foreign naval history also is well represented. However, the main collection obviously relates to the U.S. Navy. Such resources include superb groups of official naval publications, long runs of the principal periodicals, extensive collections of secondary sources on U.S. naval history, and blocks of naval biographical and autobiographical materials. The holdings are supplemented by microfilm copies of many of the basic archival resources of the nineteenth century, dissertations and theses, and other unpublished manuscripts. In the latter category, the approximately three hundred volumes of administrative histories from major World War II commands deserve particular notice.[4] The concentration of these rich resources in an open-shelf library, and the service provided by a thoroughly experienced and knowledgeable staff, makes the Navy Department Library a research facility of central importance for all naval historians.

Another longstanding naval historical program—the collecting, editing, and publication of the navy's records—started in 1881 when the navy's Bureau of Navigation turned its attention to the printing of Civil War documents. In 1884 this function was transferred to Professor Soley, who headed a combined organization known as the Office of Library and Naval War Records. Starting in 1894 and continuing through 1922, thirty large volumes of the well-known *Official Records of the Union and Confederate Navies in the War of the Rebellion* were produced.[5]

In undertaking such an ambitious project, during an era prior to the existence of the National Archives, it became necessary for the navy's historians to seek out and centralize records that were scattered throughout the Navy Department. During part of this period, the Office of Library and Naval War Records also employed agents to collect privately held papers dealing with the Union and Confederate navies. In the absence of another central repository, the office's collecting efforts further extended to additional early records of the navy. In 1904 and 1906, this enlarged program was recognized by congressional acts directing the Navy Department and other executive departments to transfer older naval records for preservation. On the eve of World War I, as a result of all these efforts, the navy's historical agency (then known as the Office of Naval Records and Library) had become the principal archival repository for naval documentation dating into the 1880s.

With America's entry into the Great War, plans were made by the navy for the centralization and eventual publication of the records of World War I. As it developed, an almost complete absence of printing funds from 1922 to 1934 prevented such a publication project. However, for the first time the Office of Naval Records and Library did start to collect current records. Further, under the influence of British archival procedures—particularly as developed by Julian S. Corbett of the Royal Navy's historical section and adapted by Commodore Dudley Knox, who headed the Office of Naval Records and Library from 1921 to 1946—most of the World War I records and older historical sources were organized in accordance with a subject system that ignored the archival provenance of the material. Although the result was a usable collection, Knox's approach was contrary to today's accepted archival principles. Knox's system was not applied to the post-World War I holdings of the Office of Naval Records and Library.

In 1934, when the availability of funds allowed the Office of Naval Records and Library to resume documentary publications, it turned its attention to much smaller conflicts than World War I. The first of these was the Quasi War with France, for which seven documentary volumes were published between 1935 and 1938. Then, starting in 1939 and continuing through 1944, Commodore Knox's organization issued a six-volume documentary series on the Barbary Wars.[6]

As these volumes appeared, the long-planned U.S. National Archives came into existence. The availability of a central repository for the nation's records, and the need to direct the office's attention to the operational records of World War II, led the Office of Naval Records and Library to deposit in the National Archives in 1942 its records dating from the American Revolution through the early 1920s. Today, these transferred resources are known as Record Group 45 and represent a principal source for all students of early naval history.

Turning to the modern holdings of the Naval Historical Center, the navy's historical office, since the transfer of its early records, has initiated a fourth major documentary publication series comprising the naval and maritime documents of the American Revolution. In connection with this program, the Naval Historical Center has brought together an important group of microfilmed naval and maritime documents, which are readily available for scholarly use.

The collections of the Naval Historical Center also include a special file containing an intermixture of original manuscripts and correspondence or reports representing the results of the navy's historical research regarding the careers of approximately thirty-five thousand naval personnel, as well as some other subjects of particular interest. This so-called Z file continues to be augmented as we add the results of some of our current research and introduce individual manuscripts received from private sources. The group is particularly rich for students of nineteenth-century naval history.

Another useful research file consists of the source folders maintained in the Ships History Branch of the Naval Historical Center concerning ships of the U.S. Navy, particularly those of the twentieth century. Like the Z file, this is something of a hybrid collection insofar as it includes some contemporary documents (notably the annual histories submitted by ships) together with the histories, reports, and correspondence prepared by the Naval Historical Center's staff.

Reference also should be made to the center's nondocumentary resources, including a photographic collection comprised of approximately two hundred thousand views. This is a select group in comparison with the navy's central photographic files accumulated by the Naval Photographic Center and largely deposited in the U.S. National Archives. However, the Historical Center's coverage is unique for certain periods and subjects (including the pre-1940 era and some aspects of post-World War II naval history). The usability of this collection is enhanced by an excellent index. Further, the curators of this collection have developed an excellent cross-reference system to significant pictorial materials in other repositories.

Since 1930, the head of the navy's central historical office also has been designated curator for the Navy Department. In that capacity, the director of Naval History is responsible for a large collection of objects and other relics of the navy's past, many of which have been obtained through the scrapping of naval ships. Some of these materials are on display in the Navy's Memorial Museum at the Washington Navy Yard. Additional items are on loan to other museums or are in storage. As we are often reminded by museum-based scholars, these physical remains of history have value for research as well as for display.[7] In the case of the Naval Historical Center's collection, research is enhanced by a computerized indexing system that is being developed to control each item.

To return to more conventional source material, since 1942 the major archival effort of the Naval Historical Center has been devoted to current records that are accessioned not only for their official utility to the navy but also for their long-run value to historical scholars.[8] The modern record program originated in the early months of World War II when Commodore Knox established a Manuscript Section to centralize, arrange, and index the basic records relating to the navy's operational experience in that conflict. At one point, in explaining the basic purpose of this collection, the commodore quoted Marshal Foch's dictum that history becomes in peacetime "the true method of learning war and of determining the invariable principles of the art of war."[9] Knox's emphasis upon the official uses of these sources also was reflected in the high standards that he established for their control. As he explained in one article:

> It is far from enough to make a mass collection. Equally important and even more difficult and time consuming is the problem of arrangement. The great reservoir of information must be so organized and administered that almost any cross section of data, great or small, that may be called for in the future may be found readily within a reasonable time. Otherwise the information is virtually locked up, with the key lost so far as utility is concerned.[10]

To achieve these goals, Commodore Knox had to overcome formidable problems. The first was to assure that the basic historical documents were actually prepared by the navy, despite the reluctance of some officials to require additional paperwork in time of war. He also had to satisfy other naval officials that his Manuscript Section was a secure repository for documents that originally carried a very high security classification. Finally, Knox needed to recruit a qualified staff to operate the section.

Knox was highly successful in meeting all of these challenges. World War II may be one of the most thoroughly documented conflicts in which any navy has participated. In addition to approximately one hundred thousand action reports, there are massive collections of operational plans and orders, as well as war diaries that cover the noncombat experience of significant commands ashore and afloat. Each of these documents is individually indexed and cross-indexed, allowing rapid and precise retrieval in most instances. Thousands of unit histories, ranging from those of major headquarters components in Washington, D.C., to fleet headquarters and numerous operational commands, also are available.[11] The central classified records of the Navy Department relating to the war are unusually full, as is indicated by their index that occupies hundreds of library index drawers. Knox even initiated one of the early oral history projects. As a result, there are some four hundred interviews giving a personal view of the war by officer and enlisted participants.

In terms of staffing, Knox recruited a number of highly qualified individuals. Under the direction of Capt. P. T. Wright, such reserve officers and scholars as Walter Whitehill, Richard Leopold, John Kemble, Marion V. Brewington, David Tyler, and Charles Summersell worked in that office. One former officer, reporting at the end of World War II — Barbara A. Gilmore — continues to serve in an important capacity in today's Naval Historical Center.

Parenthetically, it is interesting to note that the war diary dutifully maintained by these and other staff members of the Manuscript Section offers interesting insight into wartime Washington and the reactions of fresh-caught reserve officers, who until recently had toiled in academic groves. One of the more interesting passages in the diary recounts how the new officers in the Office of Naval Records and Library were exposed to a series of thirty orientation lectures, including one on naval correspondence by a veteran warrant officer "which consisted chiefly of the reading, with proper gestures and asides, of Articles 75½ and 76 and Chapter 52 of Navy Regulations."[12]

In 1946, upon the departure of the military staff of World War II—but presumably not of the veteran warrant officer—the Office of Naval Records and Library was merged with the Office of Naval History that had been created in 1944 to oversee the volumes of World War II operational history being written by Prof. Samuel E. Morison and an administrative history project under the direction of Prof. Robert G. Albion. This combined organization eventually became known as the Naval Historical Center, while the Manuscript Section became the Operational Archives.

During the first postwar decade, while Rear Adm. John B. Heffernan served as director of Naval History and Loretta I. MacCrindle headed the archives, the primary archival task was to complete the collection, arrangement, and indexing of the operational records of World War II. To make space available for this task, other major transfers of records (including the Navy Department's central files for 1926–39) were made to the National Archives. At the same time, a project was initiated to screen the files of senior fleet commands (the so-called flag files), primarily to obtain copies of action reports, war diaries, and planning documents that had not been received during the war. The basic administrative correspondence in the flag files remains, however, and continues to have great value in documenting the activities of the originating commands.

Also in this period, the Operational Archives received the records of certain key components of the Navy Department, including those of the War Plans Division and the immediate offices of Fleet Admiral King. As a result of arrangements made by Commodore Knox prior to his retirement, the navy's historians further accessioned a collection amounting to almost four thousand reels of microfilmed German naval records and additional associated materials. In recent years, these films have been transferred to the Modern Military Branch of the National Archives.

With the outbreak of the Korean War in 1950, the Operational Archives departed to some extent from its concentration on World War II to collect and organize the basic reports, diaries, and plans of the Korean conflict. At the same time, at the request of the Navy General Board that was disestablished in 1951, the branch took custody of that organization's extremely valuable files. Although the board's records dated back to 1900, their archival arrangement prevented the separation of early materials from the more sensitive records of recent date.

In 1956, Rear Adm. Ernest M. Eller became the director of Naval History. Under his administration and that of his successors—Rear Admiral F. Kent Loomis, Vice Admiral Edwin B. Hooper, and Rear Admiral John D. H. Kane, Jr.—the primary effort of the Operational Archives has been to collect sources on postwar naval operations, strategy, and policy, while continuing to service its rich holdings for the World War II years. Wherever possible, within limited space and the self-imposed constraints of subject specialization, these World War II holdings are augmented.

The materials on the postwar navy have many similarities with the records of 1941–45. Operational reports and operational plans or orders continue to be basic documents. However, especially in the post-Korean War years, many of these were transmitted in message form instead of as letters. As a result, our message files for the last decade are much more extensive and important than for World War II. Unit histories from individual ships and aviation commands are available during most of the postwar period, and starting in 1959 the preparation of accounts of major fleet and shore organizations also was resumed. Due to decentralized filing practices in the postwar years, the central records of the Navy Department, since 1949, are much less valuable than they were for earlier periods. However, selected series from certain divisions within the Office of the Chief of Naval Operations and from senior fleet commands, relating to naval operations, strategy, and policy, serve as space-saving substitutes. The files that we collect from certain senior flag officers also are compact and concentrated data sources in the subject areas that we seek to document.

Closely related to these records are the extensive and valuable series of oral histories by senior naval officers (now numbering about a hundred) that were undertaken in the 1960s by Dr. John T. Mason under the auspices of Columbia University's oral history office and since 1969 through Dr. Mason's association with the U.S. Naval Institute.[13] The director of Naval History has continued an earlier arrangement with Columbia under which the Naval Historical Center purchases copies of each of these oral histories, hence providing a degree of subsidy to this important program.

As was true in World War II, all of these sources are collected initially because of their value for the navy, including the continuous evaluation programs that are such a prominent part of the modern management cycle and the constant need for administrative reference. They also are used in the Naval Historical Center's own programs, including the publications that are described in our current list of books in print.

Yet, the Naval Historical Center continues to welcome and encourage the use of these materials by researchers preparing unofficial works. Fortunately, such research has been greatly simplified in the last few years due to the declassification of most of the records in the Operational Archives dating prior to 1950. Specific lists of these downgraded materials are available to researchers on request. In addition, under the provisions of a presidential executive order, scholars may apply for access to certain naval records that have not yet been declassified.

In addition to the resources held in the Naval Historical Center and the National Archives, researchers will find a number of other collections that might be useful. Among the most elusive and least cared for materials are the massive holdings of twentieth-century naval records deposited by hundreds of naval commands and offices in the various federal records centers located throughout the United States. Many of these files are of marginal value. However, in some instances the National Archives and the U.S. Navy are discovering materials with research significance. In such cases, assuming space permits, steps are being taken by the National Archives to accession the records. Examples include the flag files mentioned by Admiral Hooper, a key collection of naval attaché reports of the 1900–39 period, and the files of the navy's World War II coordinator of Research and Development. As a result of the surveys made by the navy's declassification team and the Operational Archives, the Naval Historical Center has data available on some of the other collections in the records centers. The center will supply this information to researchers interested in particular programs or commands.

Other valuable record holdings are in the custody of specialized naval repositories located outside the Washington area. Of particular interest to many historians is the Naval Historical Collection at the Naval War College in Newport, Rhode Island. That agency's resources include the records of the War College, which are of much use for students of naval strategy and policy, as well as the personal papers of a number of officers associated with the college. The archives of the U.S. Naval Academy holds that institution's official records since the 1920s, while groups of important private manuscripts are in the academy's museum and library. Of further note is the U.S. Naval Construction Battalion Center, Port Hueneme, California, that has the central collection of records relating to the Seabees and extensive historical sources on the Civil Engineering Corps and overseas bases. The Submarine Library and Museum at New London, Connecticut, and the more recent Aviation Museum at Pensacola, Florida, are developing special holdings on these arms of the navy.

Regarding collections of personal papers, the Manuscript Division of the Library of Congress has extensive materials deposited by the Naval Historical

Foundation[14] as well as valuable naval groups that have been collected independently by the library. A number of other important repositories in the national capital region, including the Marine History Division with its excellent groups of personal papers and large oral history collections, are discussed in general terms in the Naval Historical Center's 1970 publication *U.S. Naval History Sources in the Washington Area.* [15]

Many other collections of valuable sources are located throughout the United States in a somewhat amazing variety of presidential libraries, state and local historical agencies, college and university archives, and public or private libraries. Over the last several years, the Naval Historical Center has compiled considerable data on these materials. The card file prepared to date identifies no less than one hundred ninety nonfederal repositories outside the Washington area, holding approximately one thousand separate collections. The center continues to collect references to such materials for inclusion in the next revision of its sources guide. In the meantime, the information presently in the Naval Historical Center's card index is available to researchers.

It is obvious that the very rich body of source material in the National Archives is complemented by the holdings of the Naval Historical Center and a number of other repositories. The staff of the navy's historical program will continue to provide assistance to officials, as well as to scholarly researchers, who seek to use such materials in their work.

NOTES

1. Adams to Stoddert, 31 March 1800, in *The Works of John Adams, Second President of the United States,* ed. Charles Francis Adams (Boston: Little, Brown, 1854), 9:47.
2. Unless otherwise indicated, information in this paper on the history of the Office of Naval Records and Library is based upon J. W. McElroy, "Office of Naval Records and Library, 1882-1946," manuscript (Washington, D.C.: Naval Historical Center, 1946).
3. This relationship continued until 1900. Between 1919 and 1946, the library again was associated with the Office of Naval Intelligence.
4. See William C. Heimdahl and Edward J. Marolda, *Guide to United States Naval Administrative Histories of World War II* (Washington, D.C.: Department of the Navy, 1976).
5. U.S., Department of the Navy, Office of Naval Records and Library, *Official Records of the Union and Confederate Navies in the War of the Rebellion,* 30 vols. (Washington, D.C.: Government Printing Office, 1894-1922).
6. Idem, *Naval Documents Related to the Quasi-War between the United States and France,* 7 vols. (Washington, D.C.: Government Printing Office, 1935-38); and idem, *Naval Documents Related to the United States Wars with the Barbary Powers,* 6 vols. (Washington, D.C.: Government Printing Office, 1939-44).

7. See, for example, Philip K. Lundeberg, "The Challenge of the Museum Dimension," *Military Affairs* 37, no. 3 (1973): 105-7.

8. A more detailed discussion of this program is in Dean C. Allard, "The Navy's Operational Archives," photocopied (Washington, D.C.: Naval Historical Center, 1970).

9. Quoted in Dudley W. Knox, "The Navy's History Program," *U.S. Naval Institute Proceedings* 69, no. 9 (September 1943): 1199.

10. Ibid., p. 1197.

11. A number of these histories are described in U.S., Department of the Navy, Naval History Division, Operational Archives, *Partial Checklist: World War II Histories and Historical Reports in the U.S. Naval History Division* (Washington, D.C.: Defense Printing Service, 1973).

12. U.S., Department of the Navy, Office of Naval Records and Library, Manuscript Section, "War Diary," manuscript (Washington, D.C.: Naval Historical Center, 1943).

13. These oral histories are described and listed in Elizabeth Mason and Louis M. Starr, *The Oral History Collection of Columbia University* (New York: Columbia University Press, 1973), and John T. Mason, Jr., "An Interview with John T. Mason, Jr., Director of Oral History," *U.S. Naval Institute Proceedings* 99, no. 7 (July 1973): 42–47.

14. See U.S., Department of the Navy, Naval Historical Foundation, *Manuscript Collection: A Catalog* (Washington, D.C.: Library of Congress, 1974).

15. Dean C. Allard and Betty Bern, *U.S. Naval History Sources in the Washington Area and Suggested Research Subjects* (Washington, D.C.: Government Printing Office, 1970). For more recent and detailed descriptions of marine holdings, see Charles Anthony Wood, *Marine Corps Personal Papers Collection Catalog* (Washington, D.C.: Marine Corps History and Museum Division, 1974), and Benis M. Frank, *Marine Corps Oral History Collection Catalog* (Washington, D.C.: Historical Division, U.S. Marine Corps, 1973).

II

THE UNITED STATES NAVY
IN INTERNATIONAL RELATIONS

Group of officers, including Rear Adm. Mark Bristol (second from right) *standing on the steps of Naval Headquarters, Constantinople.* (U.S. Navy photograph.)

Naval Diplomacy
in the Interwar Years

In considering the scope and content of this paper, it became evident that readers would lose interest in a detailed recitation of the titles and holdings of the Naval History Division and National Archives record groups dealing with the navy and international relations. Actually, the best source for such information can be found in the pamphlet *U.S. Naval History Sources in the Washington Area and Suggested Research Subjects,*[1] which was published in 1970 by the Naval History Division of the Office of the Chief of Naval Operations. Along with this, of course, the researcher must start with the same office's 1972 publication of its sixth edition of *United States Naval History: A Bibliography.*[2] These two tools, plus the *Guide to the National Archives of the United States,*[3] published by the National Archives, and various "preliminary inventories" to the many record groups in the Archives should inundate the average researcher with source materials. Most researchers in naval history know of these sources, so this paper is defined in a way that would both add to the stock of information about the navy in international relations and also perhaps open the door to further research by prompting scholars to see parallels in other times and places.

Because my own area of maximum interest and expertise lies in the years 1913 to 1941, I will discuss United States naval officers and international affairs in these years. And if my mission is accomplished, it should inspire interest in later generations of naval diplomats, such as William D. Leahy in France; William H. Standley in Russia; Alan G. Kirk in Belgium, Russia, and China; Jerauld Wright in China; Raymond A. Spruance in the Philippines; George W. Anderson in Portugal; and Horacio Rivero in Spain.

World War I and America's late participation in it as an "associate" of the Entente powers, again brought the navy into diplomatic affairs. From the first week of the war, the navy participated by supplying two of the three members on the Joint State and Navy Neutrality Board. Because President Wilson had established neutrality as the official policy of the United States toward the warring states, and most questions were anticipated to be maritime in nature, it was natural to make naval officers the majority on the board. These men understood naval warfare and, as was the case with most senior officers, they had more than a passing acquaintance with international law. The thousands of pages of analyses and opinions, generated by Capts. H. S. Knapp and J. B. Oliver, provided steady guidance to Secretaries of State William Jennings Bryan and Robert Lansing as they attempted to hold England and Germany to "strict accountability" for their infringements of America's neutral rights. The records of the Neutrality Board, while used occasionally by scholars, like Charles Tansill, Daniel Smith, and Arthur Link,[4] deserve closer analysis by those interested in the navy's contributions to the field of international law. As might be expected, the bound volumes of correspondence and reports of the Joint State and Navy Neutrality Board rest comfortably in the National Archives Building.[5]

After more than two and one-half years of avoiding involvement in the conflict, principally by trying to bring it to a negotiated settlement, President Wilson, in early April 1917, asked Congress for a declaration of war. A few days before, Rear Adm. William S. Sims, and his aide, Comdr. J. V. Babcock, had sailed for England as a special liaison officer between the Navy Department and the British Admiralty. Anticipating that America would soon be at war, the department concluded that it should learn more about British naval operations and plans so that the American naval effort would be better coordinated with Royal Navy operations.

Many scholars have written at length about Sims's work. Dr. Elting Morison's biography of Admiral Sims still stands unchallenged as the finest study of the testy admiral.[6] Dr. David Trask's 1973 book, *Captains & Cabinets: Anglo-American Naval Relations, 1917-1918,*[7] is the most recent work that pays considerable attention to Sims—it is excellent in research and writing. And two fine research papers have been written by Dr. Dean C. Allard and Dr. Paolo Coletta, which deal with the notorious conflict between Sims and Secretary of the Navy Josephus Daniels.[8] I mention these works to suggest that Admiral Sims was so important and so controversial that his work during World War I still requires steady analysis and explication.

In terms of the survey, Sims was not an accredited diplomat acting in the name of the Department of State, yet much of what he did was vital to the relations of the United States with its wartime associates. If war is simply international politics carried on by other means, it was important that U.S. naval relations with Great Britain and France be entrusted to a person who understood those nations and could command their respect. Sims fit the billet nicely. He admired the English, was very familiar with the ways of the Royal Navy, and was a good friend of the first sea lord, Adm. Sir John Jellicoe. In

addition, he had studied in France, was fluent in its language, and later established an easy-going friendship with the leaders of the French navy.

It is not the purpose of this paper to examine Admiral Sims's views on the
proper American approach for winning the war, but it can suggest that his
strict adherence to a line strategy did have important consequences in terms of
Anglo-American relations. Within a few days after his arrival in England, the
admiral saw that America's principal role in the war would be the reinforce-
ment of England and her Allies, at first with supplies and later with troops. This
mission required security of the lines of communication; such security could
only be obtained through defeating Germany's submarines. Despite having
been advanced to vice admiral and given the title of commander, United
States Naval Forces Operating in European Waters, the admiral realized that
unity of command with British and Allied forces was absolutely necessary. To
achieve a satisfactory level of unity, it was evident to Sims that the mistrust of
America's new associates had to be overcome if operations were to be successful. By the end of 1917 he had accomplished this much: the destroyer force at
Queenstown, while administratively under his control, was operationally commanded by Vice Adm. Lewis Bayly of the Royal Navy. The use of convoys,
long resisted by the admiralty and questioned by the Navy Department, was
now an accepted tactic in the war against the submarines. A division of five
battleships had been detached from the Atlantic Fleet and, under the command of Rear Adm. Hugh Rodman, was serving with the Grand Fleet as the
Sixth Battle Squadron. To achieve these measures, Sims had had to convince
the Navy Department and President Wilson that the British grand strategy was
sound; that the British were trustworthy Allies who did have a will to win; that
the Atlantic Fleet should be stripped of its destroyers and patrol craft; and
that it was safe to change American naval construction policy from an emphasis on capital ships to one that stressed building destroyers and merchant
vessels. While Sims was not the only person responsible for informing the
United States about its British associate, I must conclude that he did play the
most important part.

The admiral's contribution to naval diplomacy, and the reason for his inclusion in this paper, came from his demonstrated ability to advance America's
understanding of her wartime associates. Because of the trust he inspired in
the admirality, the British were able to accept the less than cordial extension of
American naval assistance. Though writing Sims off as a hopeless anglophile,
Chief of Naval Operations William S. Benson and Secretary Daniels did have
to respect his integrity and clear line of strategic logic.

Admiral Sims, of course, was *sui generis*. He evidently recognized that he
was making history, and he kept his personal papers and official records intact
to help document his role. A good deal of the story of Anglo-American naval

relations can be found in the manuscripts of President Wilson, Edward M. House, and Sims.[9] Additional insights, as I found in writing the biography of Adm. William V. Pratt (a close friend of Sims), can be gleaned from the papers of Pratt and Adm. William S. Benson, the wartime CNO.[10] Fortunately for historians, the two decades between the wars also permitted the Office of Naval Records and Library to assemble special collections from the war for its own use and later to assist the National Archives in getting its Navy Department holdings into usable shape. It goes almost without saying that all studies of naval diplomacy must rest on a foundation supplied by the State Department's manuscripts in the National Archives.

Possibly because he was unpopular with the Wilson administration, Admiral Sims was not called upon to help end the war through participation in the Versailles Conference. On the other hand, the navy, in late December 1918, was asked by the State Department to provide an officer of flag rank to look after American interests in the Eastern Mediterranean as the victorious Allies set about dismembering the Ottoman Empire. Chosen for this work was Rear Adm. Mark Lambert Bristol, who at the time was commandant of the United States Naval Base, Plymouth, England. A month later, following briefings by Admiral Sims and Secretary of State Lansing in Paris, Bristol arrived at Constantinople. He was to remain at his post until mid-1927 and, therefore, served longer in a diplomatic capacity than any naval officer in American history.

The admiral's orders designated him as "Senior United States Naval Officer Present, Turkey" with his area of responsibility to be bounded on the west by the twenty-first meridian and on the east that area then known, somewhat imprecisely, as the Near East. Bristol simplified the limits of his command to mean the whole prewar Ottoman Empire and its boundary seas. He established his headquarters in Constantinople and flew his blue flag on *Scorpion*, the station ship. As senior U.S. naval officer present, the admiral was ordered "to keep in close touch with the American commissioner in Constantinople, with a view to keeping as fully informed as possible regarding all matters affecting American interest." He was to "cultivate the most cordial relations and cooperate to the fullest extent with all Allied representatives at Constantinople." Above all he was to "safeguard and assist American citizens and interests whenever possible."

In view of the length of his stay and the nature of his duties as they evolved, the most unusual thing about Admiral Bristol's assignment to Constantinople was that he was the person selected to go there. From graduation with the class of 1887 at the Naval Academy until his arrival in Turkey, nothing had prepared him for this duty. Of thirty-two years since graduation, twenty-one had been spent at sea and none of them in the Near East. In personal manner he was conservative, very conscious of rank and status, a good but dull public speaker, an almost compulsive letter writer, and a very difficult person to jar loose from a preconception or commitment. He was ambitious and expected to fly four stars before retirement. He shared most of the prejudices of the "white Anglo-Saxon Protestant" of his day, and he displayed very consistently an anti-British viewpoint. A strong nationalist, a bit chauvinistic, he really was not very different from the average flag officer of the 1920s.

Upon arrival in Turkey, Bristol found the country occupied by the British, French, and Italians, with the Russians and Greeks ready to join in dividing the remains of "the sick man of Europe." Though America had broken relations with the Ottoman Empire in 1917, it had not declared war. American policy toward the Near East was vague at best. It seemed to call for dissolution of the Ottoman Empire; the creation of several national states, based upon the concept that peoples of the same culture and language should live together; the opening of the Bosphorus and Dardanelles to the free flow of international traffic; and recognition of an "open door" principle in terms of equal access by all nations to the opportunities available throughout the region.

During his first six months in the Near East, the admiral waged a shrewd war to improve his diplomatic status. Because the United States commissioner was ill most of the time, Bristol took on his duties without his title. In working with the other powers, represented by high commissioners, Bristol believed his awkward naval title left him at a tactical disadvantage. On August 12 the State Department surrendered; Admiral Bristol was officially named United States high commissioner. All diplomatic personnel were under his command as were those units making up the United States Naval Detachment in Turkish waters.

Between 1919 and 1923, France, Great Britain, and Italy, with the United States as an interested and active observer, labored to draft a treaty which the Turkish government would sign. Their efforts were complicated by their own conflicting economic and territorial interests; the insistence of Greece that she have a substantial enlargement of her territories at the expense of Turkey; the desire of the Armenians to have their own nation carved out of territories in eastern Turkey; and, most importantly, the rapid growth of a vigorous young Turk nationalist movement, which rejected the old Ottoman Sultanate in Constantinople and refused to honor previous settlements made between the Sultanate and the victorious powers. The Wilson administration recognized and supported, in spirit, the Armenians and the Sultanate. When asked by the Allies to accept a mandate over Armenia, or possibly Turkey, and to back the Greeks in their desires, Wilson was willing but could not get congressional backing. Given this situation, the admiral laid out and steered his own course. Though he requested instructions and guidance regularly, the State Department normally only acknowledged that his cables had arrived. This meant that until a short time before the Lausanne Conference met in November

1922, the high commissioner had to interpret American policy as best he could, try to match his orders to that policy, and then act as he thought best for American interests.

From the beginning of his mission, Admiral Bristol worked to preserve a neutral position for the United States in the diplomatic struggle between the Allies and the "young Turks" led by Mustafa Kemal and Ismet Pasha, his foreign minister. To Bristol, the Allies, particularly the British, were attempting to prop up the sultan's government because of economic concessions they had gained. He believed the Angora government of Mustafa Kemal truly represented Turkey and that the United States should plan eventually to recognize it. Because the Nationalists were absolutely opposed to the creation of an Armenian state out of Turkish territories, and the United States could not possibly act as a guarantor for Armenia, the admiral could see no value in attempting to support the Armenians.

At the root of Bristol's approach was concern for long-term American interest in Turkey. As a naval officer, for decades working to support and protect his nation's commerce, the admiral believed the investment and trading interests would be best served by a neutral but friendly posture toward Mustafa Kemal's Nationalist government. He recognized that the British had a dominant position in the region because they had developed a large economic stake. His goal, then, was to do all he could to see that Americans developed their own stake in Turkey. This required, above all, that other nations not be granted exclusionary rights that would leave Americans on the outside looking in. To protect an American future in Turkey, Bristol steadfastly urged that friendly relations be maintained with the Nationalists and that Allied dealings with the sultan's government be opposed by the United States.

Here the Armenians complicated the picture. They were Christians and an object of great concern for the American missionary establishment in Turkey. One reason for a high commissioner in Turkey was to protect American missionaries, their mission property, and the two colleges established by them in the Ottoman Empire. Given prewar and wartime propaganda about the "Terrible Turk," spread principally by the missionaries and those seeking funds for the relief of oppressed Christian minorities in the Near East, it was difficult for Bristol to have believed any information or advice contrary to this stereotype. Yet after the Greek invasion of Turkey in May 1919 and the two years of bloody warfare that followed between Greeks and Armenians on one side and the Nationalist Turks on the other, Bristol did report that the Greeks were the aggressors and had done their share of massacring troops and noncombatants alike. He believed, and so stated officially to Washington, that peace would return to Turkey only after the Greeks withdrew and Armenia disappeared.

Bristol was able to report authoritatively because he had used his naval detachment to create an intelligence network in the Near East. He also dealt
directly, though unofficially, with the Nationalist government in Angora,
while remaining in Constantinople at the seat of the Sultanate. His destroyers
visited regularly all of the major ports in the Black Sea and the Anatolian
littoral in the Mediterranean. Their officers sent back by radio a steady stream
of on-the-spot reports about fighting, relations between Turks and the Allied
powers, political conditions, and the health and well-being of the populations.
These ubiquitous destroyermen also reported on economic conditions, shortages
of consumer products, and the readiness to receive American goods.

Armed with this economic intelligence, Bristol urged American businessmen
in the area to invest, develop, and market their wares—in short, to do all they
could to develop an American commercial stake in Turkey that would rival
the British and Greeks. His destroyers transported businessmen from port to
port and, frequently, carried cargoes from Constantinople to other port cities.
Detachment radios not only carried intelligence back to the high commissioner,
they also provided a means of placing orders for goods. When trouble erupted
in the ports, destroyers protected Americans or evacuated them.

Protecting Americans, promoting trade, and establishing an informal but
working relationship with the Kemal Nationalists constituted Bristol's most
important work in Turkey. He did participate in an investigation of Greek and
Turkish atrocities in Smyrna in 1919 and won perpetual condemnation from
Greeks for finding them more culpable than the Turks. His recommendation
that America not assume a mandate or protectorate over Armenia won him
another group of enemies. By favoring the Nationalist Turks, and thus most
directly aiding the American trading community, the admiral earned a large
measure of animosity from the missionaries and Near East relief people. He sat
in as an official observer at the first session of the Lausanne Conference in
1922-23, and later urged acceptance of the newly negotiated Turkish-American Treaty by the United States Senate. Though considered carefully by most
senators, his advice was not followed and the treaty failed. Despite the large
measure of ill will he earned, the State Department and Presidents Wilson,
Harding, and Coolidge asked that he be kept at his post.

For those who are interested in further studies of Bristol's diplomacy, there
are a number of sources available to researchers. Bristol's personal papers,
housed in the Manuscript Division of the Library of Congress, are an
enormously detailed and rich source. He kept a daily diary and saved copies of
most of the letters he sent or received. When these papers, plus State Department and Navy Department records are used, it becomes reasonably simple to
see the inside story of his labors. It should also be noted that there is an excellent doctoral dissertation written by Peter M. Buzanski[11] at the University of

California at Berkeley in 1960, which deals with Bristol's naval and diplomatic activities up to the Lausanne Conference. Another dissertation, also with a rich bibliography, is that of Howard M. Sachar, "The United States and Turkey, 1914–1927," completed at Harvard in 1953.[12] Finally, from published literature, two excellent studies are Lawrence Evans, *United States Policy and the Partition of Turkey, 1914–1924*, published in 1965, and Roger R. Trask, *The United States Response to Turkish Nationalism and Reform, 1914–1939*, published in 1971.[13]

Whereas Sims was on a naval mission with serious diplomatic consequences, and Bristol headed a diplomatic mission with considerable naval activity, several naval officers, after World War I ended, participated directly in diplomacy which concerned the future status of the navy. Adms. Hilary P. Jones, William V. Pratt, Arthur J. Hepburn, and William H. Standley, between 1926 and 1936, held high positions in American delegations that worked for international limitation of naval armaments. These were years that have been described (a bit too simply) as "isolationist," a period in which the United States eschewed treaties of alliance, collective defense arrangements, and advance commitments in most fields of international political relations. Because of these aversions, the major exception in which the nation did commit itself to serious negotiation (even in Geneva, the home of the League of Nations) and did sign treaties was to accomplish limitation and reduction of naval armament. Given the importance of the navy for the defense of the country, it was natural that its representatives would serve as delegates or advisers in the groups sent abroad to Geneva and London to join other nations in pursuit of that eternal dream of arms reduction and possible abolition.

Between 1922 and 1930 the names of two naval officers, Adms. Hilary P. Jones and William V. Pratt, were consistently associated with the subject of naval limitation. Both rose to the top of their profession to become commander-in-chief, United States Fleet (CINCUS), and Pratt continued upward to chief of Naval Operations. Each had his own loyal legion of supporters within the Navy Department, but there the similarities cease and differences between them become very significant.

Admiral Jones, a Virginian, was five years Pratt's senior and a graduate of the class of 1884 at the Naval Academy. After wartime service with the Atlantic Fleet[14] and as commander, Newport News Division of the Cruiser and Transport Force, Jones headed the Naval Overseas Transport Service during the first half of 1919 and then "fleeted up" to vice admiral to command the Second Battle Squadron, Atlantic Fleet. In mid-1921 he assumed command of the Atlantic Fleet. For more than a year, while awaiting publication of an order reorganizing the forces afloat, Admiral Jones was actually CINCUS, but he did not use his title publicly until December 1922, when he became the first

Portrait of Adm. William Veazie Pratt. (Naval War College painting; U.S. Navy photograph.)

officer to use it. Well liked, almost beloved, by the navy, Jones was known for his fierce devotion to the service and absolutely unshakable integrity. With Admiral Sims and one other officer, Admiral Jones refused, in 1919, to accept the Distinguished Service Medal for wartime achievements because he disagreed so strongly with the awards list published by Secretary Daniels.

William Veazie Pratt,[15] a native of Belfast, Maine, graduated in 1889 from the Naval Academy and until 1917 followed the normal career pattern of his generation of naval officers. As America entered World War I in 1917, Pratt graduated from the Army War College and was immediately assigned to duty in the office of CNO. In a few months he was designated assistant CNO and was held to that duty until January 1919. He then escaped to sea to command the battleship *New York* and in November 1920 assumed command of the Destroyer Force, Pacific Fleet. In June 1921 he was promoted to rear admiral and assigned to the General Board in Washington. Because of his reputation as a superb staff officer, in the fall of 1921 Admiral Pratt was assigned as a technical adviser to the American delegation of the Washington Conference for the Limitation of Armament.

As a result of Pratt's duty at the Washington Conference, he became the navy's principal expert on the Five-Power Naval Treaty, which emerged from the conference. During the next five years he published articles and spoke regularly in defense of the Five-Power Treaty itself and the concept of naval limitation. In espousing these views, Pratt stood very definitely outside the mainstream of naval thinking and laid himself open to the charge that he had become a service "politician." Many believed that he hoped to move ahead, and in fact did, because he had tailored his ideas to coincide with those of Presidents Harding, Coolidge, and Hoover. I do not accept these allegations as being valid but leave it to others to examine the evidence in my biography of the admiral.

While the Washington Conference and its Five-Power Treaty of February 1922 had done much to limit capital ships and aircraft carriers, both quantitatively and qualitatively, and in a separate treaty had closely regulated submarine warfare and outlawed the use of poisonous gases, nothing had been done to regulate construction of naval combatant auxiliaries (such as cruisers, destroyers, and submarines), armies, air forces, or the materials of war.[16] From its first sessions in 1920, the league had begun to grapple with the limitation of all armament, and it continued its work after the Washington Conference closed. At first the United States ignored these deliberations, but in 1924 President Coolidge authorized the minister to Switzerland, Joseph Grew, to attend as an observer the league's commission dealing with traffic in armaments. A year later, after finding that the American public would tolerate limited participation in league activities, Coolidge now agreed that the country could send a delegation, in 1926, to sit with a subcommission of the League Preparatory Commission for the General Disarmament Conference. Because the Preparatory Commission itself was an arm of the league and took up political questions like France's continuing insistence upon a security treaty, a special subcommission was created that would deal only with naval, land, and air armaments. Coolidge was now satisfied that the subcommission was sufficiently free of political taint that Minister Hugh Gibson and his staff could actively assist in the creation of a draft general disarmament treaty. At the head of the naval staff was Rear Adm. Hilary P. Jones. [17]

From his appointment to the Preparatory Commission delegation in early 1926, Admiral Jones served on American naval arms limitation delegations until February 1930. When meeting with the Preparatory Commission, Jones was the chief naval adviser for the United States group. In the summer of 1927 he served as a codelegate, with Minister Gibson, at the head of the American delegation to the ill-fated Geneva Naval Conference. In 1930, along with Admiral Pratt, Jones was appointed as an adviser to the American delegation attending the London Naval Conference. His assignment in London was due principally to the insistence of the General Board and its senior member, Admiral Bristol. The General Board desired that there be available to the civilian delegates a senior officer experienced in naval disarmament matters who represented a viewpoint different from Admiral Pratt and those he had selected to serve on the technical staff.

The differences between Admirals Jones and Pratt, [18] which were highlighted by the London Naval Conference, represented two fundamentally different attitudes toward international affairs and navies. Admiral Jones spoke not only for himself, but for the General Board and the overwhelming majority of the flag officers in the navy. He really did not believe that naval reductions or disarmament were possible and that only naval limitation was practical. He saw navies and their sizes as being directly reflective of national needs and ambitions. Recognizing that the United States would not enter into political or naval alliances, he then believed that America's navy should be of a size and quality that would unilaterally support the nation's foreign policy objectives and defensive requirements. As a military officer, he was conservative to the extent that he would not take risks based upon another nation's good faith. He was not an anglophobe; he simply recognized that British interests and needs were different from America's and that decision on navies should not be made on the assumption that there was a community of interests between the two powers. While not anti-Japanese, the admiral agreed with the General Board in believing that eventually the clash of interests between Japan and the United States in the Far East would lead to war. Because of this assumption, he was unwilling to see the Japanese naval ratio of 60 percent improved over where it stood in the Five-Power Treaty. Finally, having observed the unwillingness of Congress and the president to actually build the navy up to equality with Great Britain, and maintain the five-to-three ratio toward Japan, he was adamant against any change in the ratio which might be based upon an assumption that a construction program would follow.

Admiral Pratt, not surprisingly, felt differently on almost all of these points. When helping to prepare the navy's views for the Versailles Conference, the admiral had urged the creation of a League of Nations navy which would have equal representation from the United States and Great Britain. Because of his friendship with Sims and his own personal convictions, he was willing to trust the British and to work with them in the postwar years. Following several tours of duty in the Far East, considerable reading about Japan, and the development of friendships with many Japanese naval officers, Pratt tended to trust Japan and believed that most political-economic problems with that nation could be solved amicably. He did believe in collective security and, from his private correspondence, one can see that he believed that Britain and America would always be working together, should the Japanese get out of hand. In defending the Five-Power Treaty, and later the London Treaty of 1930, he discounted the General Board's concern about treaty details and emphasized the advantages of now having a full naval construction plan toward which the Congress could appropriate funds. Having observed the unwillingness of President Harding, President Coolidge, and the Congress to authorize construction of cruisers, destroyers, and submarines when they were not limited by treaty, he believed that Hoover's administration would do better by the navy with the London Treaty, which spelled out numbers for each category. Admiral Jones and the General Board did not believe this and, unfortunately for Pratt's reputation, they were right. The most thorough writing on these naval conferences, in published monographic form, has been by Thomas H. Buckley and John Chalmers Vinson on the Washington Conference and Raymond O'Connor on the London Conference of 1930. Captain Stephen Roskill and I have written books on the American-Japanese-British naval policies of the 1920s.[19] There is also a handful of fine, unpublished dissertations dealing with this period that should receive wider circulation.

Following his service with the London Conference delegation, in which he was described by Ambassador Charles G. Dawes as "a tower of strength to us, without which our difficulties might have been insurmountable," Admiral Pratt was named to succeed Adm. Charles F. Hughes as CNO. From this position the admiral was able to name the navy's representatives for the American delegation to the General Disarmament Conference, scheduled to convene in Geneva in February 1932. While the delegates were civilians, headed by Hugh Gibson, the principal adviser for the navy was Rear Adm. Arthur J. Hepburn. He had been a technical adviser at the Geneva Naval Conference of 1927 and at the London Conference in 1930. At the 1927 conference, Hepburn was head of the navy team.[20]

Without detracting from his professional qualifications, which led to his becoming CINCUS in 1936–38, Admiral Hepburn did represent rather closely the views of Admiral Pratt. An outstanding naval officer, since graduation from the Naval Academy in 1897, Hepburn had been chosen by Pratt to be his chief of staff as he moved into the highest fleet commands between 1927 and 1930. After the London Conference, when the treaty was examined minutely in the Senate, Hepburn's testimony paralleled closely that of his superior, Admiral Pratt. One might observe, cynically, that his career did not suffer from such loyalty, but he made his way to the top under a very different president and CNO following Pratt's retirement in July 1933. The General Disarmament Conference met but proved completely ineffective. Japan's activities in Asia and Germany's new assertiveness made it difficult for the rest of the major powers to work seriously toward disarmament. If any judgment might be made on Hepburn's service, it would be that he, like Pratt, showed a willingness to let the State Department set the pace while he provided the data.

The navy participated once more in a naval limitation conference, this time in London during the winter of 1935–36. This meeting had been written into the Five-Power Treaty of 1922 and convened with little hope of success. Japan had denounced the 1922 treaty in December 1934 and let it be known that she would agree to no further naval limitation unless she were granted equality in naval power with the United States and Great Britain. Neither the General Board nor Adm. William H. Standley, the CNO, was willing to consider this, but conference plans continued. As in 1927, the navy's representative, Admiral Standley, was given delegate status; and he worked very amicably with Norman H. Davis, the chairman of the delegation, and Under Secretary of State William Phillips, the other delegate.[21] With Japan laying down unacceptable conditions, and France and Italy willing to participate only as "observers," the second London Naval Conference produced little of value in the area of naval limitation. The most important result, and Admiral Standley was satisfied with it, was a new spirit of cooperation between England and America in the face of what was considered an unreasonable Japanese position. What Admiral Pratt had favored in earlier years became a fait accompli under a different CNO.

This somewhat lengthy disquisition on naval disarmament conferences was designed to suggest that the navy was an active participant in one of the most important international relations activities of the United States during the

1920s and 1930s. Thus to understand America's participation in the international arms limitation movement, a good starting point would be the records of the navy and its representatives to the various naval conferences. Between the records of the General Board, housed at the Office of Naval History, and those of the State Department in the National Archives, supplemented by presidential correspondence, it is now possible to trace the development of the United States position at each meeting. Hugh Gibson, Charles G. Dawes, Henry L. Stimson, and Norman H. Davis were the civilian heads of the American delegations to the Preparatory Commission meetings and the formal conferences, and all kept their correspondence, diaries, and journals for the enlightenment of future scholars.[22] Admirals Jones, Pratt, and Standley likewise managed to keep large bodies of personal correspondence intact and thus gave additional insights into the relationships among the civilian and naval members of the delegation. To the papers of these admirals can be added the personal logs, memorandums, and correspondence of those serving as technicians or doing the staff work in Washington. Some examples are Mark Bristol, Andrew T. Long, Frank H. Schofield, and Harold C. Train in the navy, and Jay Pierrepont Moffatt and Stanley K. Hornbeck in the State Department.[23] Through these personal papers and the official Departments of Navy and State manuscripts, one can decide what the goals were and what policies were developed to obtain them. One can also learn something of those personal traits and characteristics, civilian and naval, that make research of this sort so interesting.

Seen with hindsight, the effort to limit or reduce armaments was of critical importance to the future of all nations. Tragically, the effort was abortive. With that wonderful omniscience that comes with viewing the past, most of us who teach diplomatic history recognize that armaments were only a symptom of the malaise that lay over international affairs in the interwar years. Population explosions, maldistribution of resources, trade barriers, rising expectations, messianic ideologies, and dynamic nationalisms all need to be considered along with burgeoning armies and navies. Yet armaments were solid and quantifiable, so this is where an effort to bring international stability began. With an eye on those awesome weapons of the present, it is hard not to wish the administration godspeed as it sits down again to see if the armories of the Soviet Union and the United States might not be emptied a bit.

NOTES

1. Dean C. Allard and Betty Bern, comps., *U.S. Naval History Sources in the Washington Area and Suggested Research Subjects*, 3d ed. (Washington, D.C.: Government Printing Office, 1970).

2. *United States Naval History: A Bibliography*, 6th ed. (Washington, D.C.: Government Printing Office, 1972).
3. *Guide to the National Archives of the United States* (Washington, D.C.: Government Printing Office, 1974).
4. Charles Callan Tansill, *America Goes to War* (Boston: Little, Brown, 1938); Daniel M. Smith, *Robert Lansing and American Neutrality, 1914-1917* (Berkeley and Los Angeles: University of California Press, 1958); Arthur S. Link, *Wilson, the Struggle for Neutrality, 1914-1915* (Princeton: Princeton University Press, 1960).
5. U.S., Department of State, File 763.72111, General Records of the Department of State, Record Group 59, National Archives Building, Washington, D.C.
6. Elting E. Morison, *Admiral Sims and the Modern American Navy* (Boston: Houghton Mifflin Company, 1942).
7. David F. Trask, *Captains & Cabinets: Anglo-American Naval Relations, 1917-1918* (Columbia: University of Missouri Press, 1972). See also Mary Klachko, "Anglo-American Naval Competition, 1918-1922" (Ph.D. diss., Columbia University, 1962); Edward B. Parsons, "Admiral Sims' Mission in Europe in 1917-1919 and Some Aspects of United States Naval and Foreign Wartime Policy" (Ph.D. diss., State University of New York at Buffalo, 1971).
8. Dean C. Allard, "Admiral William S. Sims and United States Naval Policy in World War I," *American Neptune* 35, no. 2 (1975): 97-110; Paolo E. Coletta, "Over Here and Over There: Josephus Daniels, William S. Sims, and Naval Administration in World War I—As Daniels Saw It from Washington," (Paper Read before Organization of American Historians, Chicago, Illinois, 12 April 1973).
9. The papers of President Woodrow Wilson and Adm. William S. Sims are in the Manuscript Division, Library of Congress, Washington, D.C.; the papers of Edward M. ("Colonel") House are in the Sterling Memorial Library, Yale University, New Haven, Conn.
10. Gerald E. Wheeler, *Admiral William Veazie Pratt, U.S. Navy: A Sailor's Life* (Washington, D.C.: Government Printing Office, 1974). The papers of Admiral Pratt are in the Naval History Division, Washington Navy Yard, Washington, D.C.; the papers of Adm. William S. Benson are in the Manuscript Division, Library of Congress, Washington, D.C.
11. Peter M. Buzanski, "Admiral Mark L. Bristol and Turkish-American Relations, 1919-1922" (Ph.D. diss., University of California at Berkeley, 1960).
12. Howard M. Sachar, "The United States and Turkey, 1914-1927: The Origins of Near Eastern Policy" (Ph.D. diss., Harvard University, 1953).
13. Lawrence Evans, *United States Policy and the Partition of Turkey, 1914-1924* (Baltimore: Johns Hopkins Press, 1965); Roger R. Trask, *The United States Response to Turkish Nationalism and Reform, 1914-1939* (Minneapolis: University of Minnesota Press, 1971). See, also, Walter Hiatt, "Admiral Bristol, American Naval Diplomat," *Current History* 27, no. 5 (February 1928); Henry P. Beers, "United States Naval Detachment in Turkish Waters, 1919-1924," *Military Affairs* 7 (Spring 1943); Bern Anderson, "The High Commissioner to Turkey," *U.S. Naval Institute Proceedings* 83, no. 1 (January 1957).
14. Personal papers of Adm. Hilary Pollard Jones are in the Manuscript Division, Library of Congress, Washington, D.C. While no full biography of the admiral has been written, biographical articles that should be consulted are *Dictionary of American Biography*, vol. 11, supp. 2, s.v. "Hilary Pollard Jones," and *National Cyclopaedia of American Biography*, vol. 30, s.v. "Hilary Pollard Jones." Con-

siderable detail concerning Admiral Jones's activities in the field of naval limitation may be found in Ben Scott Custer, "The Geneva Conference for the Limitation of Naval Armament—1927" (Ph.D. diss., Georgetown University, 1948); Raymond G. O'Connor, *Perilous Equilibrium: The United States and the London Naval Conference of 1930* (Lawrence: University of Kansas Press, 1962); Gerald E. Wheeler, *Prelude to Pearl Harbor: The United States Navy and the Far East, 1921-1931* (Columbia: University of Missouri Press, 1963); Wheeler, *Admiral William Veazie Pratt, U.S. Navy*.

15. See footnote 10.

16. *Conference on the Limitation of Armament, Washington, November 12, 1921-February 6, 1922* (Washington, D.C.: Government Printing Office, 1922).

17. Fred Herbert Winkler, "The United States and the World Disarmament Conference, 1926-1935: A Study of the Formulation of Foreign Policy" (Ph.D. diss., Northwestern University, 1957); Merze Tate, *The United States and Armaments* (Cambridge, Mass.: Harvard University Press, 1948). The papers of Hugh Gibson are very rich concerning the work of the League Preparatory Commission. They are on deposit at the Hoover Institution on War, Revolution and Peace, Stanford University, Stanford, Calif.

18. The conflict between Admirals Jones and Pratt is fully described and analyzed in the works by O'Connor and Wheeler cited earlier.

19. Thomas H. Buckley, *The United States and the Washington Conference, 1921-1922* (Knoxville: University of Tennessee Press, 1970); John Chalmers Vinson, *The Parchment Peace: The United States Senate and the Washington Conference, 1921-1922* (Athens: University of Georgia Press, 1955); Stephen W. Roskill, *Naval Policy between the Wars: Vol. I, The Period of Anglo-American Antagonism* (New York: Walker, 1968); O'Connor, *Perilous Equilibrium*; Wheeler, *Prelude to Pearl Harbor*.

20. Except for Dr. Winkler's dissertation and biographical sketches, very little has been written about Adm. Arthur Japy Hepburn. See Winkler, "The United States and the World Disarmament Conference," and *National Cyclopaedia of American Biography*, vol. 49, s.v. "Arthur Japy Hepburn."

21. The best work on the Second London Naval Conference (1935-36) is Stephen E. Pelz, *Race to Pearl Harbor: The Failure of the Second London Naval Conference and the Onset of World War II* (Cambridge, Mass.: Harvard University Press, 1974). See, also, Gerald E. Wheeler, "Isolated Japan: Anglo-American Diplomatic Cooperation, 1927-1936," *Pacific Historical Review* 30 (May 1961); Meredith W. Berg, "The United States and the Breakdown of Naval Limitation, 1934-1939" (Ph.D. diss., Tulane University, 1966). The personal papers of Adm. William H. Standley are at the University of Southern California Library, Los Angeles, Calif.; the Norman H. Davis papers are in the Manuscript Division, Library of Congress, Washington, D.C.; the William Phillips papers are at the Houghton Library, Harvard University, Cambridge, Mass. See, also, William H. Standley and Arthur A. Ageton, *Admiral Ambassador to Russia* (Chicago: Henry Regnery Company, 1955); *National Cyclopaedia of American Biography*, vol. F , 1939-42, s.v., "William Harrison Standley"; William Phillips, *Ventures in Diplomacy* (London: John Murray, 1955); Thomas Casey Irvin, "Norman H. Davis and the Quest for Arms Control, 1931-1938" (Ph.D. diss., Ohio State University, 1963).

22. Charles G. Dawes and Norman H. Davis deposited their personal papers with the Manuscript Division, Library of Congress, Washington, D.C.; the Henry L. Stimson

papers are in the Sterling Memorial Library, Yale University, New Haven, Conn.; the Hugh Gibson papers are in the Hoover Institution on War, Revolution and Peace, Stanford University, Stanford, Calif. See, also, Charles G. Dawes, *Journal As Ambassador to Great Britain* (New York: Macmillan Company, 1939); Henry L. Stimson and McGeorge Bundy, *On Active Service in Peace and War* (New York: Harper and Brothers, 1947).

23. The personal manuscripts of Mark L. Bristol and Harold C. Train are in the Manuscript Division, Library of Congress, Washington, D.C.; Andrew T. Long, Southern Historical Collection, University of North Carolina, Chapel Hill, N.C.; and the "log" for the Geneva Naval Conference (1927) of Frank H. Schofield is in the Naval History Division, Washington Navy Yard, Washington, D.C. The personal manuscripts of Jay Pierrepont Moffatt are in the Houghton Library, Harvard University, Cambridge, Mass.; the Stanley K. Hornbeck papers are in the Hoover Institution on War, Revolution and Peace, Stanford University, Stanford, Calif.

U.S. Navy helicopter hovers over Russian submarine during Cuban "quarantine" operations. (U.S. Navy photograph.)

SALLY V. MALLISON AND
W. THOMAS MALLISON, JR.

International Law and Naval History: Change and Continuity in the Juridical Doctrines of Naval Blockade

Some international law is made and developed by multilateral conventions written by conferences, such as those associated with the names of Hague and Geneva. The law concerning blockade, however, has been developed almost entirely by a customary process of decision. [1] Naval operations, in war and in peace, lead to the making and development of international law. The naval tactics and strategy of blockade, if accepted over a period of time by other belligerents and by neutrals, become the international law of blockade. The silence and acquiesence of states have typically manifested the acceptance of particular methods of blockade as legally permissible. The function of diplomatic protest is to prevent the law from being made or developed without the assent of the protesting state. The customary process of decision involves a national state acting as claimant through the use of particular methods of blockade and as a decision maker in appraising the blockade claims of other states. This duality in function is typical of the decentralized decision-making process of international law. It is so different from the highly centralized and institutionalized lawmaking processes within national states that it is frequently misunderstood. It is sometimes alleged that the duality of function is inconsistent with an objective system of law. It should be explained that the double function of states as both claimants and decision makers enmeshes them in a network of affirmative mutualities and reciprocities as well as negative reprisals and retaliations. The result is that national officials who are capable of long-range calculations of national self-interest are encouraged to advance claims which are consistent with juridical principles and expectations. If they advance claims or make decisions not justified in law, they run the real risk of being subjected to retaliations. [2]

Reprinted with permission of the U.S. Naval Institute from *U.S. Naval Institute Proceedings* 102, no. 2 (February 1976): 44-53.

The basic principles of the law of war are traditionally stated to be military necessity and humanity.[3] Military necessity is designed to promote military efficiency, subject to the prohibitions of the law of war. Humanity reflects basic humanitarian objectives which are operative even in war and hostilities. Both principles must be considered together because neither, standing alone, can be effective in conserving values. These fundamental principles share the objective of minimizing the unnecessary destruction of both human and material values. "Unnecessary destruction" means that destruction which is not directly related to a lawful military objective. This value-conserving conception is fundamental throughout the law of war, including the doctrines relating to blockade.[4]

The purpose of the present inquiry is to examine the juridical doctrines of blockade in modern history through the use of selected examples. It would be difficult to understand the significance of the examples if they were to be considered in isolation from the main currents of naval history. It is necessary, consequently, to give some consideration to the context of historical time, place, and relevant circumstances, including technological developments.

HISTORIC DEVELOPMENT
OF THE DOCTRINES OF BLOCKADE

Blockades in modern history have encompassed both a naval operation directed at the enemy and a method of curtailing neutral seaborne commerce with the enemy. The law of blockade is, consequently, closely connected with other parts of the law of naval warfare, including contraband and neutrality. The modern law of blockade is regarded as dating from 1584 when the Dutch government declared that all the ports of Flanders under Spanish control were blockaded.[5]

The Napoleonic Wars

The Royal Navy's blockades of France and its allies during the Napoleonic wars were relatively close-in blockades by later standards. The distances of the blockading vessels from the blockaded ports were determined more by considerations of naval tactics than of law. On occasion, small ships of the Royal Navy blockading forces sheltered from storms in French harbors near to the main blockaded ports. Sometimes, as convenient, the blockading ships dropped anchor and at other times they cruised slowly back and forth.[6] The blockades were aimed at French war and merchant vessels as well as at neutral commerce with France.

The naval tactics and strategy just summarized provided a significant basis for the doctrines concerning the international law of blockade and contraband control. Blockade was required to be close and, consistent with the naval practice, applied uniformly to the ships of all states. In the view of some lawyers, a stationary cordon of warships was required, but this was inconsistent with the naval practice, and a more enlightened view stressed the necessity for the blockade to be effective. It was widely accepted that a blockade must be officially proclaimed in order to provide notification to neutrals.

The legal principles concerning contraband, although doctrinally distinct from the blockade principles, performed an analogous function in restricting neutral commerce with the enemy. Belligerent warships carried out visit and search of neutral merchant vessels anywhere on the high seas, with the objective of contraband control. The cargoes of such vessels were classified in terms of their relation to the military power of the enemy. The category of "free goods" consisted of articles such as foods which were deemed unrelated to the enemy's military capacity. "Absolute contraband" comprised goods which were specialized to military uses and, following visit, search, and capture by a vessel of the blockading force, were subject to condemnation by a prize court. "Conditional contraband" covered goods which could be used for military or civilian purposes, and it was usually necessary also to show its military destination and prospective use before it could be condemned in prize. [7] Under the international law of naval warfare, a belligerent state was entitled to employ either blockade or contraband control or both.

The American Civil War

Although the American Civil War was a domestic war for many purposes, the entire international law of naval warfare, including particularly the doctrines concerning blockade and contraband control, was applied to it. President Lincoln's Proclamation of Blockade of the Confederacy provided the government of Great Britain with a juridical basis for both the British Neutrality Proclamation and for its recognition of the belligerent status of the Confederate States. One immediate result of the United States Proclamation of Blockade was the conferring of belligerent rights, as well as the imposition of belligerent duties, upon the Confederate States.

In 1856 the principal European states had agreed to the Declaration of Paris, which is the only doctrine of blockade directly formulated by convention. Its fourth article, which was substantially declaratory of the existing customary law, provides:

Blockades, in order to be binding, must be effective: that is to say, maintained by a force sufficient really to prevent access to the coast of the enemy. [8]

Although it is clear that at the beginning of the Civil War the U.S. Navy had nothing like an adequate number of ships to enforce the blockade, with time it became increasingly efficient. As a result, there was diminishing disposition upon the part of neutrals to allege its ineffectiveness and consequent legal invalidity. The quoted provision of the Declaration of Paris was thus amended by the customary law of the Civil War to provide that if an initially ineffective blockade later meets the requirements of effectiveness, its legality will be held to exist *ex post facto* and *nunc pro tunc*.

As the effectiveness of the blockade increased, the ingenuity of neutral merchants with contraband goods for sale to the Confederacy increased proportionally. After it became too hazardous to ship contraband goods directly from the British Isles to a Confederate port in a single voyage, a different procedure was developed. The contraband goods would be sent to a neutral port, for example one in the Bahamas, and there the goods would be unloaded and transshipped to a fast blockade runner which would sail directly to a Confederate port. There is no doubt but that the goods could have been captured during the second voyage and condemned by the prize court for the attempted breach of the blockade. The U.S. Navy, however, developed the practice of intercepting the goods before the cargo reached the neutral port and asked for condemnation in the prize court on the ground that the first voyage was, in fact, a part of a single continuous voyage to a blockaded port. The United States Supreme Court viewed this as a reasonable application of the previously established doctrines concerning blockade and contraband control and thereby further developed the doctrine of continuous voyage.

Following the initial and most famous Civil War prize cases in which the Supreme Court upheld the legality of the blockade of the Confederacy, there were important subsequent prize cases involving the doctrines of continuous voyage and continuous transportation.[9] Three of the cases on this subject were particularly important and will be considered briefly. It should first be mentioned, however, that the doctrine of continuous voyage was applied earlier during the Napoleonic Wars and has indeed been traced to the War of 1756.[10]

In the case of *The Bermuda,* that ship left Liverpool for Bermuda and then proceeded to Nassau in the Bahamas. From Nassau, its cargo was apparently to be transshipped to another vessel to run the blockade to a Confederate port. *The Bermuda* was captured en route between Bermuda and Nassau. The Supreme Court looked beyond the appearance of separate voyages and held that the voyage from Liverpool to the blockaded port was actually a single continuous voyage, and the vessel was condemned. An analogous situation arose in the case of *The Springbok*, which was a British ship sailing from Great Britain to Nassau that was captured before its arrival there. The voyage to Nassau was undertaken in good faith, but the Supreme Court found that, unknown to the owners of the ship, the cargo was to be transshipped to another vessel after being landed in Nassau and then run through the blockade. The decision was that the ship was restored to its owners, but the cargo was condemned.

A factually different situation existed where a neutral merchant ship carried contraband goods directly to the neutral Mexican port of Matamoros from whence the goods were transported inland to the nearby belligerent port of Brownsville, Texas, across the Rio Grande River. Matamoras rapidly became a commercial center of considerable practical importance to the Confederate war effort, but as a neutral port, it could not be blockaded under the existing principles of international law. The case of *The Peterhoff* involved a British ship carrying a cargo to Matamoros which was intended to be transported inland to the Confederate states. The ship, however, was captured en route to that port. The Supreme Court held that the contraband portions of the cargo were condemned, but that the remainder of the cargo and the ship must be restored to the owners since the cargo was to reach its ultimate destination by land and by inland navigation and that, consequently, there was no violation of the blockade.

British merchants were distressed by the unreasonable burdens which, in their view, the newly intensified doctrines of continuous voyage and continuous transportation placed upon neutral traders. They made strong representations to the British government and asked it to take diplomatic and naval measures to uphold neutral rights. That government, after careful deliberation, declined to do so. [11] It acted in consideration of long-range British interests which included a possible future situation where it might wish to employ the doctrines of continuous voyage and transportation. Thus these doctrines, as applied in the U.S. Civil War, were accepted as a part of the law concerning blockade and contraband control with the assent of the most important neutral state.

The World Wars

Blockades enforced by surface naval power. In both World War I and World War II developments in science and technology led to changes in naval tactics and strategies. The submarine and its principal weapon, the self-propelled torpedo, along with the airplane, had started a revolution in naval warfare, which was further advanced by the incorporation of merchant ships into surface naval warfare through the convoy system. The traditional blockade was replaced by a long-distance blockade, accompanied by a comprehensive contraband list, which early in World War I swept away the distinctions between "free goods," "conditional contraband," and "absolute contraband." The development of the navicert system—providing naval clearance certificates to neutral vessels with approved cargoes, routes, and destinations—made it impossible for neutral merchant ships to operate unless they complied with Allied contraband control regulations. The rationing of neutrals was employed to limit neutral importation of various commodities to the same amounts that had been imported in peace time. [12]

As a neutral during the First World War, the United States protested vigorously against the principal measures associated with the long-distance blockade. As a belligerent in both world wars, it helped to improve the long-distance blockade as a comprehensive method of economic warfare and thus weakened its claims as a neutral.

The long-distance blockade of the Second World War may be summarized as transferring effective control "from the seas to the quays." The task of obtaining information concerning the relevance of particular cargoes to the enemy's war effort was transferred from boarding officers at sea to ministeries and boards of economic warfare on shore. They exercised comprehensive controls over all neutral commerce which could possibly be of benefit to the enemy. The function of economic warfare went far beyond capturing and condemning in prize unauthorized cargoes. It was rather conceived as making arrangements so that no ship or cargo would be allowed to go to sea unless it received the authorization of the Allied economic warfare authorities in advance. [13] The ship warrant system was used to compel the participation of neutral shipping in the Allied economic warfare. [14]

The long-distance blockade and its associated contraband control measures were not adopted by Great Britain as a claim of right. In both world wars the comprehensive blockade was stated to be in reprisal for alleged unlawful methods of warfare, particularly submarine warfare, conducted by Germany. The late Prof. Hersh Lauterpacht attempted to look beyond form to substance in formulating the doctrinal basis of the long-distance blockade:

[M]easures regularly and uniformly repeated in successive wars in the form of reprisals and aiming at the economic isolation of the opposing belligerent must be regarded as a development of the latent principle of the law of blockade, namely, that the belligerent who possesses the effective command of the sea is entitled to deprive his opponent of the use thereof for the purpose either of navigation by his own vessels or of conveying on neutral vessels such goods as are destined to or originate from him. [15]

In summary, although the long-distance blockade was deplored, it was accepted as a legally permissible expansion of the preexisting doctrines of blockade in the circumstances of total war manifested by the two world wars. This is not to say that such a blockade would be either rational or lawful in the context of a limited war. The adaptation and development of the preexisting doctrines in the light of the new technologies of the two world wars allowed law to continue its historic function as a limitation upon violence. If the law of blockade had not been susceptible to development and change, the far more likely outcome than the repetition of the close-in blockades of the Napoleonic wars would have been a situation where blockades were subject to no legal limitations whatsoever.

Blockades enforced by submarine naval power. The German unrestricted submarine warfare used against the Allies in World Wars I and II has not usually been characterized as a blockade enforced by submarines. Its function, however, to stop the enemy's commerce in enemy ships and neutral commerce with the enemy, was the same as that of the long-distance blockade. [16] In asking Congress to declare war against Germany in 1917, President Wilson claimed that the German submarine warfare violated the elementary humanitarian principles of international law, including the right of neutral nationals to sail unmolested on belligerent merchant ships. [17] The ultimate sanction of the surface naval blockade, if the intermediate sanctions of comprehensive contraband control failed, was gunfire from surface warships. The ultimate sanction of the submarine naval blockade, if the intermediate sanctions of establishing and notifying a submarine operational area failed, was torpedoes from submarine warships. It is doubtful that one of the ultimate sanctions was more destructive than the other. The U.S. government, however, persisted throughout the First World War in viewing the submarine blockade as a violation of international law.

The U.S. government has probably changed its position concerning the lawfulness of such blockades, since it conducted a blockade of Japan during the Second World War which was enforced by submarines and mines. [18] The significant juridical difference between the submarine blockade conducted by the United States and the ones conducted by Germany is that the former had no neutral vessels to contend with. It is difficult to deny the lawfulness of blockades enforced by submarines under the criteria which uphold the lawfulness of similar blockades enforced by surface warships. [19] Some scholars have taken the contrary view and have emphasized the failure of submarines to carry out the traditional procedures of visit and search. [20] They appear to have overlooked the fact that visit and search is equally impractical for surface warships where enemy submarines or aircraft may be present. In any event, the claim of the illegality of submarine blockades is no longer open to the United States since its use of such a blockade against Japan.

DEVELOPMENT OF THE DOCTRINES OF BLOCKADE SINCE 1945

Traditional Blockades

The Korean War. The Korean War was a limited war in the sense that there was a common interest of the great powers in avoiding nuclear warfare. The naval aspects of the Korean War were characterized by the relative overwhelming superiority of the United States-United Nations naval forces. The North Korean government had no significant naval forces at the beginning of the war, and it had acquired none at its termination. This situation permitted the unopposed use of seapower for logistic supply of the U.S.-U.N. armed forces ashore as well as the use of a relatively close-in blockade of the east and west coasts of North Korea.

It was stated in the blockade announcement of July 4, 1950, that all merchant ships were barred from North Korean ports and that all warships, except North Korean ones, would be allowed to go through the blockade to such ports. The blockade on the east coast excluded the port city of Rashin, which the Russian navy continued to use as a warmwater port throughout the Korean War.[21]

Thus, the tactical characteristics of the naval blockade of North Korea made it somewhat similar to the traditional close-in blockades of the Napoleonic wars which provided doctrinal authority for it.

The Indo-Pakistan War. For a period of two weeks immediately preceding the collapse of the Pakistan military forces in Bangladesh, the Indian navy maintained a blockade of the coast of Bangladesh. It was only a distance of 180 marine miles from the western extremity of the blockade (the border with India) to the eastern extremity (the border with Burma), although the sinuosities of the coast made the coastline much longer. The objectives of the blockade were the prevention of the resupply of the Pakistan army and the frustration of any attempt it might make to escape to seaward, particularly along the eastern border with Burma. The task was successfully accomplished because of the relative overwhelming surface naval power of the Indian navy combined with the airpower from its single aircraft carrier. The blockading force captured six large merchant ships that attempted to escape, along with numerous small craft. It was reported that the small craft which did not obey orders to surrender were sunk. [22]

The Indo-Pakistan War was limited both in time duration and in the quantum of the naval forces involved. The traditional law of blockade as it was developed prior to the First World War provides an adequate basis in legal doctrine for the naval blockade which was employed.

The Soviet ship Volgales *heading toward Cuba (1962). On the foredeck is a partially uncovered missile with clearly visible skin-tight protective casing; on the afterdeck are other canvas-covered missiles. The U.S. Navy radar picket ship U.S.S. Vesole has come alongside. The wing of a navy P2V patrol plane is shown overhead. (U.S. Navy photograph.)*

Special Function Blockades

Some of the diverse uses of naval power since the end of the Second World War may be characterized as special function blockades.

The quarantine-interdiction or limited naval blockade of Cuba. The principal facts of the Cuban Missile Crisis of October 1962 may be summarized briefly. The attempted emplacement in Cuba of Soviet missiles capable of carrying nuclear warheads would, if successful, have brought about a great change in the nuclear balance of power. The emplacement was being carried out secretly and was discovered by photo reconnaissance aircraft. The limited naval blockade, which was employed to have the existing missiles removed and to prevent the bringing in of additional ones, was a very restrained use of power. The alternative courses of action being considered included an air strike at the missile sites combined with an invasion of Cuba.

President Kennedy's proclamation of October 23, 1962, entitled "Interdiction of the Delivery of Offensive Weapons to Cuba," described missiles and bomber aircraft along with warheads and supporting equipment as "prohibited materiel." The proclamation also stated that the secretary of defense could provide for the establishment of prohibited or restricted zones around Cuba as well as for prescribed routes for vessels and aircraft not carrying the prohibited material. The ensuing "interception area" was defined as within two overlapping circles, each with a radius of 500 nautical miles, with one circle centered at Havana and the other centered at the eastern tip of Cuba. It was contemplated that ships entering the interception zone would be visited and searched and those with prohibited material allowed to return to the Soviet Union. Vessels leaving Cuba with prohibited material aboard en route to the Soviet Union were visually observed and photographed by vessels of the blockading force and allowed to proceed. Procedures were developed for the issuance of clearance certificates, termed "clearcerts," for vessels which were not carrying prohibited material. This terminology was based upon the navicert procedure involved in the long-distance blockade of the two world wars. The specified items of prohibited material may be regarded as a very selective type of contraband control. [23]

In making a doctrinal appraisal, it should be conceded that this limited naval blockade does not fit easily into the preexisting doctrines of the law of blockade. There are, however, other doctrines of international law which are relevant. Under customary international law which is preserved as "inherent right" in article 51 of the United Nations Charter, responding coercion must meet the tests of actual necessity and reasonable proportionality in order to be lawful. The attempted emplacement of missiles involved the most severe threat to the basic values of the United States, the Latin American republics, and Canada. In these circumstances, there can be no serious doubt

Inter-American quarantine imposed upon Cuba in 1962. Warships of the Argentine, Venezuelan, and United States navies leave Trinidad, West Indies, on the history-making first patrol of the combined Latin American-United States quarantine task force. The force consists of the flagship U.S.S. Mullinex, the Argentine destroyers A.R.A. Rosales and A.R.A. Espora, and the Venezuelan destroyers A.R.V. Zulia and A.R.V. Nueva Esparta. (U.S. Navy photograph.)

concerning the actual necessity for a type of responding coercion which would tend to deescalate the nuclear confrontation and also to eliminate the new nuclear threat in the Americas. Because the limited naval blockade was probably the least amount of force that would have been effective, it should be upheld as meeting the most stringent conception of proportionality in responding coercion.

On October 23, following the unanimous decision of the Organ of Consultation of the Organization of American States, the quarantine was proclaimed as both national self-defense for the United States and as collective self-defense for the Organization of American States. The action of the Organization of American States, although not amounting to international law authority standing alone, is significant in that it provides an appraisal by an additional independent decision maker concerning the actual necessity of the quarantine and its proportionality as responding coercion. Other states in the world community signified their acceptance of the legality of the limited blockade measure by their failure to protest its use. The most significant appraisal of the quarantine was the Kennedy-Khrushchev agreement, which accepted and implemented its objectives.

Operation Market Time in the Vietnam War.   One of the problems confronted by the government of South Vietnam in the course of the hostilities with North Vietnam was the infiltration by small craft of enemy personnel, weapons, and supplies through the territorial waters of South Vietnam. Operation Market Time, which was started in 1965, was a naval operation utilizing high-speed and well-armed small craft of the U.S. Navy and Coast Guard as well as of the Republic of Vietnam. Consistent with the "Vietnamization" program, the U.S. craft were later transferred to the Vietnamese navy. The task was to prevent infiltration; this required surveillance, including visit and search and, on occasion, capture or destruction of enemy vessels. Operation Market Time was conducted in a contiguous zone, prescribed by the government of South Vietnam as being twelve miles in width along the South Vietnamese coast. [24]

From the standpoint of the traditional doctrines of blockade, it is anomalous for South Vietnam to conduct a blockade of the coasts of South Vietnam even though its purpose was to blockade or interdict enemy infiltration. There is, however, adequate legal authority for a state to prevent military infiltration through a contiguous zone extending twelve miles from its coast. This may be described in law as an invocation of municipal police power, which is consistent with international law. It may also be maintained, *a fortiori,* that since a belligerent state has authority to conduct blockading operations in the territorial waters and contiguous zone of an enemy state, it has ample authority to do the same thing in its own waters to preserve national integrity and security.

The mining of North Vietnamese internal and territorial waters. The mining of North Vietnamese ports and territorial waters in May 1972 took place in the context of ongoing hostilities in Vietnam, including a large movement of land forces from North Vietnam to South Vietnam. The purpose of the mining, carried out mainly by aircraft, was to interdict the delivery of seaborne weapons and supplies to North Vietnam. By limiting the mining to the twelve-mile extent of claimed North Vietnamese territorial waters, the United States greatly reduced the risks to neutral shipping on the high seas. Three daylight periods were allowed after the mining took place for the vessels of other states then in North Vietnamese ports to depart before the mines automatically activated. Notice of the mining action and its location was provided and, in addition, the United States and South Vietnamese naval forces undertook to warn away all vessels that might enter the area because of unawareness of the danger. [25]

The purpose of the mining, to interdict seaborne weapons and supplies, was the same purpose which a blockade described as such could have performed. Given the situation of international conflict and hostilities, there is no doubt that the traditional law of blockade would have provided authority for a blockade conducted on the high seas and enforced by naval vessels and aircraft. The interdiction measures carried out in the smaller area of North Vietnamese territorial and internal waters may be regarded as at least as lawful. In addition, the enforcement of the interdiction by mines rather than exclusively by ships and aircraft is similar to the techniques of blockade used by the Allies in both World War I and World War II. Mines are passive weapons which are not exploded until a ship passes nearby. There is no reason why they should be treated differently in law in this factual context than gunfire from ships, which is the traditional legally permissible ultimate sanction applied to a persistent blockade runner.

The blockade of Eliat at the Straits of Bab el Mandeb. The Egyptian claimed blockade of Eliat and the Gulf of Aqaba at the Straits of Tiran near Sharm Al-Shaykh in May and June of 1967 was a traditional close-in blockade. It is interesting that the Egyptian blockade of the Bab el Mandeb Straits during the intense hostilities of October 1973 is less well known although it was much more effective. The blockade at the southern end of the Red Sea was approximately twelve hundred miles from the Straits of Tiran. It was imposed with the apparent assent of Ethiopia to the west and of Yemen and South Yemen to the east. The blockade, along with the continuing closure of the Suez Canal, resulted in preventing seaborne access to the Israeli port of Eliat at the north end of the Gulf of Aqaba. [26]

While the blockade of the Straits of Bab el Mandeb was dissimilar to the traditional close-in naval blockade, it had some similarities to the long-distance blockades employed in World Wars I and II. Its considerable distance from the port of Eliat as well as its strategic characteristics are roughly similar to those of the long-distance blockades. In the same way that such an Allied blockade during the First World War left the German Baltic ports open, this blockade left the Israeli Mediterranean ports open. A significant feature is that it was considerably less destructive of human and material values than the massive military measures which have been frequently employed in the Middle East. In comparison with such measures, the blockade is a very limited type of coercion, and this characteristic provides additional persuasive evidence of its lawfulness. There were no significant protests, other than from the Israeli belligerent, against its use.

RECOMMENDATIONS CONCERNING ANALYSIS OF THE DOCTRINES OF BLOCKADE IN THE RELEVANT CONTEXTS

It would be presumptuous to make recommendations to historians concerning the importance and necessity of historical study. Such recommendations, however, may be made to lawyers with some degree of assurance. Many years ago, Justice Oliver Wendell Holmes said that a page of history is worth a volume of logic in understanding the juridical decision-making process. Those lawyers who attempt to act on this advice should not underestimate its hazards. For example, an American looking into the naval history and international law of the Second World War might start with the inaccurate assumption that German submarine officers in general, and Admiral Dönitz in particular, were engaged in the systematic violation of the well-established humanitarian law of naval warfare. If such a scholar persists in his inquiries, he may be led to consider Captain Roskill's detailed accounts which demonstrate that Admiral Dönitz was the only naval commander involved in the Second World War who established a rescue zone of immunity on the high seas. [27] This was done in 1942 following the sinking of the British troopship *Laconia* in the South Atlantic. Admiral Dönitz's humanitarian endeavors involved reassigning a wolf pack of five submarines from a war patrol to a rescue operation. It was terminated by attacks on the submarines by a U.S. Army Air Corps Liberator bomber operating from Ascension Island. The central point for lawyers is that the recourse to naval history requires one to deal with the actual facts of naval warfare to which international law is applicable rather than with the generalizations, clichés, and prejudices which are often used to obscure such facts.

One of the most significant features of some of the blockades employed since 1945 is the relatively low quantum of coercion involved. It should be recognized, in consequence, that "blockade" is not a unitary concept or doctrine, and that it encompasses uses of naval power ranging from slight to intense degrees of coercion. It is also appropriate to question the validity of some of the historic doctrines associated with blockade. The following statement, for example, should be questioned:

> In connection with a proposal that the Allied Governments blockade Bolshevist Russia, the Department of State telegraphed to the American Commission to Negotiate Peace:
> . . . A blockade before a state of war exists is out of the question. It could not be recognized by this Government. [28]

The State Department's view at that time appears to have been based on the assumptions that a "blockade" involves a single type of naval operation and that there is an invariable connection between it and "a state of war." Neither assumption is consistent with the juridical doctrines of blockade as they have developed to the present time.

The contemporary legal doctrines of naval blockade are the outcome of a comprehensive process of decision. This on-going process is not likely to end until international hostilities and war are ended. The process involves not only the value-conserving use of the historic legal doctrines, but consideration of those doctrines in relevant historical context, including a consideration of the relation between the naval tactics and strategy of blockade and the stage of technological development of naval warfare. The naval historical context permits many distinctions to be made for particular purposes. In ascertaining the contemporary relevance of the juridical doctrines of blockade, it is essential, at the minimum, to make a distinction between the doctrines developed in situations of total war, typified by World Wars I and II, and those developed in limited wars. In the present advanced naval technology it would be disastrous to attempt to apply the comprehensive naval blockade measures of the world wars to a situation where one of the overriding objectives is avoiding a resort to nuclear weapons.

The difficulties which lawyers have had in understanding the contemporary legal doctrines of blockade at a particular time have been largely because of a failure to consider the entire context which gives meaning to the doctrines. In the view of Thomas Baty, writing during the First World War, all of the alleged illegalities of naval warfare should be traced to the Civil War decisions of the U.S. Supreme Court which developed the doctrines of continuous voyage and transportation. [29] Prof. E. G. Trimble denounced the long-distance surface blockade as illegal because it did not adhere to all of the juridical doctrines which have been applied in earlier wars. [30] Prof. James W. Garner, who understood that the long-distance surface blockade was an adaptation of nineteenth-century doctrines to the technology of the First World War, found the German submarine-enforced blockade to be illegal because it was in so many respects at variance with the practices involved in the contemporaneous surface blockade.[31] Prof. Quincy Wright, in reaching the conclusion of the unlawfulness of the quarantine-interdiction or naval blockade of Soviet weapons to Cuba, argued that under the international law of peace a contract for the sale of any article whatsoever was lawful.[32] In his view there was nothing more involved in the Soviet missile emplacement in Cuba in October 1962 than an ordinary commercial transaction. Prof. Abram Chayes reached the conclusion of the illegality of the mining of North Vietnamese territorial and internal waters in 1972 on the apparent grounds that the action was not very different from indiscriminate attacks against nonbelligerent shipping. In his view, there may have been a difference between the mining activities in North Vietnam in 1972 and the German unrestricted submarine warfare of 1917 but only, in his words, if "dropping mines is somehow cleaner than firing torpedoes."[33] In each instance, the legal opinions just mentioned could have been assisted by recourse to relevant contextual factors including the elementary differences between total wars, limited wars, and situations where the preeminent objective is to deescalate a nuclear confrontation.

In an era of weapons of mass destruction and rapid missile delivery systems, there can be no doubt that the objective of elimination of overt coercion by military means remains a primary goal on the path to world public order. Until that high objective is achieved, the overriding purpose of the laws of war, to minimize destruction of human and material values,[34] remains a valid and practically obtainable objective. The doctrines which authorize the use of blockades in some circumstances coexist uneasily with other doctrines which have been interpreted in recent years as authorizing a much greater quantum of violence directed at a much wider range of targets. The doctrines that require immediate revision and limitation are those which have been interpreted as authorizing the higher amounts of violence. The doctrines of aerial bombardment, in particular, require a revision which will, at the least, effectively protect civilians from direct aerial attacks that are unrelated to lawful military objectives.[35] Until a more adequate world public order is achieved, the juridical doctrines of blockade should be retained as a means of minimizing destruction.[36]

NOTES

1. The law of war is analyzed as a decision-making process in Myres Smith McDougal and Florentino P. Feliciano, *Law and Minimum World Public Order: The Legal Regulation of International Coercion* (New Haven: Yale University Press, 1961).

2. Ibid., pp. 39-59.
3. See W. T. Mallison, *Studies in the Law of Naval Warfare: Submarines in General and Limited Wars* (Newport, R.I.: U.S. Naval War College, 1966), pp. 16-19.
4. McDougal and Feliciano, *World Public Order*, pp. 42-43 and passim.
5. Lassa Francis Oppenheim, *International Law*, 7th ed. Hersh Lauterpacht (London: Longmans, Green, 1952), p. 769.
6. The blockade tactics employed by the Royal Navy in the Napoleonic wars are described in Alfred T. Mahan, *The Influence of Sea Power upon History, 1660–1783*, 25th ed. (Boston: Little, Brown, 1916), pp. 525-28.
7. The categories are considered in Oppenheim, *International Law*, pp. 799-813.
8. Ibid., pp. 460-61. The text of the declaration is in Carlton Savage, *Policy of the United States toward Maritime Commerce in War* (Washington, D.C.: Government Printing Office, 1934), 1:381, n. 2.
9. *The Prize Cases*, 2 Black 635 (U.S., 1862) were the initial cases. The three subsequent prize cases considered in the text are *The Bermuda*, 3 Wall. 514 (U.S., 1865); *The Springbok*, 5 Wall. 1 (U.S., 1866); and *The Peterhoff*, 5 Wall. 28 (U.S., 1866).
10. Herbert Whittaker Briggs, *The Doctrine of Continuous Voyage* (Baltimore: Johns Hopkins University Press, 1926), analyzes the named doctrine from 1756 through the First World War. S. L. Bernath, *Squall across the Atlantic: American Civil War Prize Cases and Diplomacy* (Berkeley: University of California Press, 1970) is a valuable history of the Civil War cases.
11. John Bassett Moore, *A Digest of International Law* (Washington, D.C.: Government Printing Office, 1906), 7: 723-25.
12. On the World War I blockade, see Louis Guichard, *The Naval Blockade, 1914–1918*, trans. and ed. Christopher R. Turner (New York: Appleton-Century-Crofts, 1930); Malkin, *Blockade in Modern Conditions*, 3 Brit. Y. B. Intl. L. 87 (1923).
13. On the World War II blockade, see W. N. Medlicott, *The Economic Blockade*, History of the Second World War, United Kingdom Civil Series (London: H. M. Stationery Office and Longmans, Green, 1952 and 1959).
14. See Catherine B. Behrens, *Merchant Shipping and the Demands of War*, ibid. (London: H. M. Stationery Office and Longmans, Green, 1955).
15. Oppenheim, *International Law*, pp. 796-97.
16. See Mallison, *Law of Naval Warfare*, pp. 62-84 and passim.
17. *Foreign Relations of the United States, 1917*, Supp. no. 1 (Washington, D.C.: Government Printing Office, 1931), p. 195.
18. See Elmer B. Potter and Chester W. Nimitz, eds., *Sea Power: A Naval History* (Englewood Cliffs, N.J.: Prentice-Hall, 1960), pp. 796-812; Elias A. Johnson and David A. Katcher, *Mines against Japan* (Washington, D.C.: Government Printing Office, 1973).
19. See Mallison, *Law of Naval Warfare*, pp. 87-91 and passim.
20. See e.g., Robert Tucker, *The Law of War and Neutrality at Sea* (Washington, D.C.: Government Printing Office, 1955), pp. 55-73.
21. Malcolm W. Cagle and Frank A. Manson, *The Sea War in Korea* (Annapolis: U.S. Naval Institute, 1957), pp. 281-373; D. Rees, *Korea: The Limited War* (New York: St. Martins, 1964), pp. 364-84.
22. Ravi Kaul, "The Indo-Pakistani War and the Changing Balance of Power in the Indian Ocean," *U.S. Naval Institute Proceedings* 99, no. 943 (Naval Review Issue, May 1973): 172, 189.

23. The textual statements of fact and law are based upon Mallison, *Limited Naval Blockade or Quarantine-Interdiction: National and Collective Defense Claims Valid under International Law,* 31 Geo. Wash. L. Rev. 335 (1962).

24. The factual statements are based upon R. L. Schreadley, "The Naval War in Vietnam, 1950-1970," *U.S. Naval Institute Proceedings* 97, no. 819 (Naval Review Issue, May 1971): 180, 186-92.

25. The factual statements are based in part on Department of State Bulletin no. 66 (Washington, D.C., 29 May 1972). An evaluation of other legal issues of the Vietnam War, including the role of the United States, is beyond the scope of the present inquiry.

26. The factual statements are based in part on *Middle East Monitor* 3, no. 21 (Washington, D.C., 15 November 1973): 1-2.

27. Stephen Wentworth Roskill, *White Ensign: The British Navy at War, 1939-1945* (Annapolis, Md.: U.S. Naval Institute, 1960), pp. 224-25; idem, *The Period of Balance,* vol. 2 The War at Sea, 1939-1945 (London: H. M. Stationery Office, 1956), pp. 210-11.

28. Green H. Hackworth, *Digest of International Law,* vol. 7 (Washington, D.C.: Government Printing Office, 1943). So-called "pacific" blockades have not usually been associated with a state of war.

29. Baty, *Naval Warfare: Law and License,* 10 Am. J. Intl. L. 42 (1916).

30. Trimble, *Violations of Maritime Law by the Allied Powers during the World War,* 24 Am. J. Intl. L. 79 (1930).

31. James W. Garner, *International Law and the World War* (London: Longmans, Green, 1920), 1:354 and passim.

32. Wright, *The Cuban Quarantine,* 57 Am. J. Intl. L. 546 (1963).

33. Abram Chayes, "Mr. Nixon Avoids Use of 'Blockade.'" *Washington Post,* 14 May 1972, p. B6, cols. 3-4.

34. The centrality of the minimization of destruction of values is emphasized in McDougal, *World Public Order,* pp. 59-96 and passim.

35. See U.S., Congress, House, *Problems of Protecting Civilians under International Law in the Middle East Conflict, Hearing before the Subcommittee on International Organizations and Movements of the Committee on Foreign Affairs of the House of Representatives,* 93d Cong., 2d sess., 4 April 1974; Air War Study Group of Cornell University, *The Air War in Indochina,* rev. ed. (Boston: Beacon Press, 1972).

36. See Robert D. Powers, "Blockade: For Winning without Killing," *U.S. Naval Institute Proceedings* 84, no. 8 (August 1958): 61.

Commentary

I n this commentary on the navy and international relations, it is my purpose
to make observations on points raised in the presentations, on the navy as
a political factor, on naval officers as representatives abroad, on international law, and on archival materials.

The navy was established by the Continental Congress in response to a
military need as the revolt escalated in intensity and aims and the colonists
vied with the Mother Country in taking steps to induce the other side to
capitulate. Much of the obfuscation about the origins of the navy and the
American maritime effort in the War for Independence is being eliminated
by the monumental series *Naval Documents of the American Revolution,*
edited by William Bell Clark and William J. Morgan, being produced by the
Division of Naval History [Washington, D.C.: Government Printing Office,
1964–]. What needs to be emphasized in the context of this session is the
great breadth of coverage. These volumes encompass not only technical,
tactical, and strategic activities, but most specifically they include materials
concerning the instructions and conduct of naval commanders and the captains
of privateers in their relations with enemy and neutral vessels and representatives
of other nations. The Congress, anxious for assistance or cooperation from
neutrals, adopted rules of behavior consistent with those of a weaker seapower,
rules that were in the process of evolution, that had been incorporated into
many treaties, and that were shared by most nations who had been victims
of Great Britain's supremacy at sea. For example, provisions of the congressional
"Plan of 1776" were included in the Treaty of Amity and Commerce with
France in 1778 and in the Declaration of Catherine II of Russia in 1780, a
declaration that formed the basis for the Armed Neutrality. This organization
of European neutrals was modestly successful in coercing Britain into modifying
a search-and-seizure policy that worked a hardship on them and was even
more distressful to the struggling Americans. Just what role the navy played
in formulating the doctrines approved by the Congress in regard to neutral
or belligerent rights is beyond my ken, although most delegates to this august

body were familiar, directly or vicariously, with past procedures and pontifi-
cations on the subject by governments and learned jurists. We look forward
to further elucidations on these and other matters as additional volumes in the
Naval Documents series appear, matters such as the correlation between the
diplomatic and romantic achievements of John Paul Jones in Paris and the
naval activities of commissioners and agents abroad.

While lauding the contributions of the Division of Naval History and, of
course, almost any other publisher of documents, we are aware that editing
involves selection and that editors are limited by their own criteria and by
the imperatives of space. Few, if any, printed series contain all of the documents
pertaining to even one dimension of a topic that a scholar wishes to investigate,
so we are obliged to consult the collection from which materials have been
chosen. Here we are at the mercy of the archivist, who controls our access to
the data and determines what is there and how it is organized. The researcher,
occasionally overwhelmed by the meticulous cataloguing and even calendaring
of the material, often finds many people well informed on the subject matter
under investigation. This shattering experience to the ego of the scholar is not
confined by any means to the Division of Naval History. Staff members in
the National Archives and at other depositories have pointed out items that
I have overlooked or ignored; calling my attention to the work of others who
have preceded me has proved invaluable.

Still, even the archivists are not aware of all the valuable materials over
which they preside. Some years ago while going through the Franklin D.
Roosevelt Papers at Hyde Park, I ran across the original of Adm. H. R. Stark's
letter presenting options available to the United States, all listed in lettered
subparagraphs. The one prefaced by "D" was selected by the president, and,
subsequently known as "Plan Dog," it became the basis for the "defeat-Germany
first" strategy in World War II. Interestingly, this original document was
covered with penciled comments. Excitedly thinking they might be Roosevelt's,
my enthusiasm was diluted by Herman Kahn, then director of the library,
who determined to his satisfaction that the scribblings were those of Secretary
of the Navy Frank Knox.

Moving to the diplomatic exploits of naval officers, Professor Wheeler has
described characteristics and circumstances that made them useful and even
essential in representing the United States overseas, especially in dealings with
recalcitrant and so-called undeveloped nations. Naval vessels constituted the
only official contact with most of these distant countries; and the commanding
officer or squadron commodore was assigned the tasks of showing the flag,
protecting American citizens and property, establishing relations, and conducting the negotiations designed to reach an agreement consistent with what
the government wanted. A significant and less familiar aspect of these ventures

is the how, why, and where the directives came from that guided these emissaries in their missions. Evidently, Matthew Calbraith Perry drafted his own instructions for the Japan expedition, profiting by his experience with other nations and that of his predecessor, Commodore James Biddle. Consistent with the president's wishes, they were issued by the secretary of state and delivered in the form of orders by the secretary of the navy.[1] Charles O. Paullin mentions nothing of this somewhat elaborate interdepartmental cooperation.[2] While I do not pretend to be knowledgeable on recent studies of naval officers as diplomats in the nineteenth century, it does seem important to discover their function in the formulation of policy as well as in its execution. To what extent was their advice followed by statesmen, and what were the factors that determined their position? Also, what sort of latitude did they enjoy in carrying out their orders?[3] Time and distance were compelling restraints in the days of sail and early steam, restraints that would encourage an admonition of initiative exceeding the limitations imposed by written instructions composed for congressional scrutiny and public approbation. Adm. Mark Bristol seems to have had a free hand in the eastern Mediterranean in part because, in the chaos of World War I settlements, few if any people in Washington knew or cared about what happened to the defunct Ottoman Empire. Sifting through some of the documents would lead one to suspect that at times two sets of written instructions — one formal and one informal — might have been issued, along with a bit of oral exhortation from the civilian authorities at various echelons in the governmental hierarchy.

Then there was the vexing problem of what to do about the man on the spot who, for whatever reason, placed the government in an embarrassing and delicate situation. An overzealous commander who realized his error could make amends on his own, as did Commodore Thomas Jones when he occupied Monterey in 1842. Comdr. Robley Evans could survive asserting the right of American sailors to get drunk at the True Blue Saloon in Valparaiso in 1891 because President Benjamin Harrison seized on the incident to demonstrate Yankee machismo. Differing substantially from the aforementioned cases was the episode at Tampico in 1914 when Rear Adm. Henry T. Mayo, in retaliation for the arrest of some American crewmen, demanded an apology, a disavowal of the act, the punishment of the officer responsible, and a twenty-one-gun salute. Assuming that the territorial integrity of the United States had been violated by removing the sailors from a whaleboat and that honor was at stake, what possible authority did Admiral Mayo have for issuing his ultimatum? Fortunately for the admiral, he was supported by President Woodrow Wilson, possibly because the president did not want to repudiate the action of a ranking American official; more likely because the president attached great importance to national honor; and most probably because it offered the president an excuse to further his efforts to remove the government of Victoriano Huerta.

Throughout our history, navy diplomats have been successful in negotiation — in negotiation with the threat of force, and in the use of force followed by negotiation. At times "gunboat diplomacy," in any form, has not worked at all. But many of us would like to know more about how and why ships were assigned to foreign stations (such as the establishment of a European squadron following the outbreak of the Spanish Civil War) or sent on goodwill visits (such as detailing a cruiser in 1939 to return the body of the Japanese ambassador who had died in Washington). A good deal of work has been and is being done on the subject although it appears that materials are lacking. Recently a scholar, Prof. William N. Still, Jr., studying the American Navy in European waters, 1865–1940, was sufficiently desperate to write me for information about my experience in Squadron 40-T. Everyone was able to speculate on whether these vessels were there to evacuate refugees, to signify an American commitment to European affairs, or to intimidate the dictators by the presence of an obsolescent six-inch gun cruiser and two World War I destroyers. Being at the time a signalman and not a messcook, I could supply Professor Still with little substantive data, and his gratitude for the scuttlebutt I did provide further illustrates the paucity of sources in the area of the peacetime projection of American naval power.

While as diplomats naval officers have not always been successful, it must be remembered that some of them, like their civilian counterparts, are human beings. They have convictions, they make errors in judgment, they do not always win, and, contrary to much of what is dispensed through the communication media, not all fit the popularized stereotype. The image so often portrayed of the gruff, unsophisticated old seadog, crude in behavior and coarse in speech, is a case of the exception becoming the rule. Much, too, has been made of the "military mind," a sort of robot mentality that embodies not only those characteristics noted by Paullin and Wheeler — namely, an addiction to the use of force and straight-forward dealings — but a rigidity and regimentation of beliefs that make for inflexibility and conformity and stifle imagination or creativity. The exceptions in discretion and innovation, such as William S. Sims and Hyman Rickover, are cited as examples that merely prove the rule. Yet Wheeler indicates that there was considerable disagreement among naval officers as to the merits of the disarmament treaties as well as the battle effectiveness of six-inch versus eight-inch gun cruisers. And we are all familiar with the controversies that have preceded and accompanied the introduction of any new type vessel or weapons system. Perhaps these altercations can be dismissed as the kind of family squabble that occurs among most professionals and only reflect differences of opinion over technical issues.

To carry the analysis a little further, Paullin states "The sailor-diplomat . . . is a stranger to the devious and tortuous methods of procedure which so long disfigured international statecraft."[4] Just how Paullin could say this, after having written his articles on naval administration, is beyong me. From my limited exposure to the real worlds of the navy and academia, and vicariously through reading and observing the rarefied atmosphere of "international statecraft," I conclude that persuasion, manipulation, coercion, and compromise are common methods for accomplishing anything in the realm of interpersonal relations. A perusal of naval correspondence, minutes of meetings, diaries, recollections, reports, interviews, transcriptions of courts of inquiry and courts martial, from the period of the American Revolution through Adm. Thomas Moorer's explanation of the circulation of National Security Council material and Adm. Elmo Zumwalt's interview in an issue of *Playboy* magazine, provides sufficient evidence to convince me that a naval officer who attains high rank is not a stranger to those attributes so vastly prized in statecraft. He may be more principled and less flexible when it comes to the national interest, and his concept of the vital interests of the nation usually includes a strong and conceivably aggressive military posture. This attitude reflects the nature of his professional obligation, namely, to support by force any policy the government decides to follow.

Here, then, is the perennial problem in what are now called civil-military relations: a conflict in the responsibilities of the serviceman and the statesman. This conflict, in my opinion, is most visibly demonstrated in disarmament negotiations, where the statesman can view national security in a perspective that embraces more than armed preparedness—a luxury, if you will, denied to the serviceman. One can discern an almost adversary relationship between the civilian and uniformed segments of the government in the planning, preparation, and negotiation of arms limitation agreements. As Wheeler noted, after the Washington Conference for the Limitation of Armament both the United States and Great Britain agreed to exclude naval officers from the delegations. They should be advisers only, "on tap not on top," and Adm. Hilary Jones was one of those accused of "viewing the world through a porthole." Actually, this was not too inaccurate a charge in light of the admiral's professional responsibility and his understandable skepticism of naval parity with Britain, whose huge merchant marine and world-wide bases gave her such a maritime advantage.

The adversary component in civil-military relations is well depicted in, but not confined to, disarmament conferences. Going back to the Continental Congress, one finds disputes over budget, pork-barrel legislation, political influence, appointments, seniority, construction, defense posture, and strategy, whether in war or peace. Most senior naval officers have been prepared for and have participated in the Washington arena, and dealing with an American politician or a member of another branch of the armed forces, much less coping with the system itself, is sufficient training for negotiation with the most astute or unscrupulous of foreign dignitaries. So, in my opinion, the "average" naval officer possesses certain attributes as well as limitations in functioning as a diplomat, and we need more in-depth studies of their successes and failures while serving in this capacity.

To be more specific about points raised in Wheeler's paper, to what extent were the differences in opinion in the navy hierarchy due to an altercation over technical issues, such as the relative merits of six-inch and eight-inch gun cruisers; the myopic approach of Admiral Jones versus the broader and more comprehensive vision of Admiral Pratt, who could embrace the political realities involved; or a basic disagreement, to which Professor Wheeler has alluded, as to the capabilities and intentions of potential enemies. Certainly, both of these men were aware of commercial rivalries and of the distinct possibility, perceived by President Wilson and Secretary of the Navy Josephus Daniels, that the Royal Navy might be used to enforce League of Nations decisions, even in the Western Hemisphere, and that Japan, dissatisfied with the allocation of the spoils at Versailles, controlled the Pacific-mandated islands and had not forgotten her twenty-one demands that abridged the Open Door and American rights in China. Some authorities contend that the United States was stupid by insisting on naval parity with Great Britain instead of allowing her to build what she wanted. Aside from areas of existing and potential Anglo-American friction, Japan was adamant in demanding that her ratio be based on that of the strongest naval power, and the American position vis-á-vis Japan was tied to that of Britain.

Professor Wheeler has rejected the charge that Pratt's views were "tailored" to those of the administration because of "political" considerations. But in dealing with this problem we are back to the question of where the ultimate responsibility of the serviceman happens to lie. A detailed exposition of the reason for Admiral Pratt's disagreement with the majority of his colleagues over the provisions of the disarmament treaties is contained in Wheeler's 1974 biography. Nevertheless, the issue of primary loyalty will remain, and the studies that have appeared on the German military high command in the framework of a Nazi regime are illustrative of what needs to be done in the civil-military field in the history of this country. If clarification of this volatile topic is to be made, it will only be found in those documents that reside, unfortunately, in too many scattered depositories.

To digress for a moment on the subject of the proliferation of holdings, in 1967 at the Naval War College I discovered, to my dismay, that records pertaining to this institution were spread with abandon from Boston to Washington, with what might be called a sprinkling of material at Newport. Granting that the physical burden of stowage is overwhelming, it did seem desirable and feasible to have an inventory of existing sources relating to the Naval War College and a record of their location. Discussions, in which the National Archives participated, eventually led to the appointment of an archivist to organize and collate holdings and provide a more orderly approach to the availability of these invaluable documents. The various sophisticated devices for reproduction and information retrieval have reduced the need for expensive and time-consuming travel by impoverished scholars, and I look forward to continued progress in expediting and simplifying the availability of materials.

The sources emanating from the Naval War College bear directly on the political-military and international law dimensions of naval history, for while the curriculum has varied from the broad principles of strategy derived from past examples as instituted by Luce and Mahan to nuts and bolts tactical instruction, the course content has usually stressed international relations. The published "Blue Books" have long had a well-deserved reputation for their exposition of international law topics, situations, decisions, and documents. To reiterate, however, it is not just naval officers as diplomats that we need to know more about. We must understand the political philosophy and concept of world-power relationships of those who participated in the formulation and execution of naval policy. To do so one has to go beyond the official documents to discover the premises and assumptions on which planning, recommendations, and actions were based. After all, a defense posture is not created in a vacuum, and the "most probably enemy" concept emerges from an assessment of existing or anticipated clashes of interests. Most senior naval officers have been discretely reluctant to pontificate publicly on foreign affairs while on active duty, and some of us, justifiably, have been suspicious of "after-the-fact" autobiographical versions. Oral interviews, too, are suspect, and their reliability reminds me of the law of gravitation in that it varies inversely with the square of the distance from the event. Moreover, the interviewer does not have the questionable advantage of examining the subject under oath. The future holds the prospect of interviewing a computer, which may be the most reliable witness, provided it has been suitably programmed and has been fed the proper information.

As of now we have to rely on three indispensable major sources for ascertaining the contemporary political and ideological beliefs that determined the strategic and armament views espoused by admirals: first, private correspondence and diaries; second, the papers written while students at the Naval War College; third, the minutes and preliminary studies of the Navy General Board. In regard to the first source, both Wheeler and I had some trouble gaining access to Rear Adm. Frank H. Schofield's diary of his experiences at the

General Naval Conference of 1927 and then getting certain notes cleared. The issue was not so much a question of security classification as it was of the confidentiality of candid observations. But I, at least, found the diary an invaluable adjunct to other information and especially helpful in understanding Schofield's attitude toward the negotiations and the negotiators. On the second source, Fleet Adm. Ernest J. King has said that his education at the Naval War College prepared him for the intricate dealings with his British colleagues and the global problems he faced during World War II, and the theses written by those who later became naval leaders are quite illuminating.[5] To comment on the third source, the Navy General Board was appointed in 1900 to serve as a "brains' trust" to succeed the moonlighting "think tank" assignments of the Navy War College, and its members researched and reported on virtually every phase of international and naval activity. It is the investigatory work and the uninhibited exchanges that preceded the submission of an official report that provide the most complete exposition of the factors, including political, economic, and ideological, and the assessments of foreign capabilities and intentions, upon which the final report was based. Opinions, expressed freely and frankly, orally and in writing, are recorded, and they provide insights into the "navy mind" that reveal the rationale behind the recommendations and decisions.

As examples of naval involvement in international affairs, in 1900 the General Board recommended that the harbors of Guantanamo and Cienfuegos be acquired as permanent naval bases. The following year it advocated the acquisition of the Danish West Indies. In 1909 it considered Easter Island "not of sufficient strategic importance to warrant its purchase by the United States." And in 1910 it urged "that the United States should obtain control of all the Galapagos Islands, by lease or otherwise, so as to effectively prevent any other power establishing a base in that locality."[6] Among other things, this advisory group determined the width of the locks in the Panama Canal.

To reiterate, however, it is necessary to understand the assumptions on which the board based its recommendations. Again resorting to examples, this body on April 21, 1909, defined "its duty as a military board to advise clearly as to the strength necessary to meeting contingencies, probable or possible, and to point out the Naval force which it deems indispensable to maintain the traditional policy of the United States with respect to the Monroe Doctrine, and the inevitable new policies which the possession of the Philippines entail, with or without the consent of powers whose interests run in a contrary direction." Escalating its premises the following year, on September 28, 1910, the General Board felt "compelled to consider the obligations of the United States to uphold not only its traditional policy of the Monroe Doctrine, but also a later one, that of the 'Open Door,' and still a third, the preservation of the neutrality of the Panama Canal." By 1915 the board had added Asiatic exclusion and no entangling alliances, i.e., no assistance could be anticipated in the event of war, in addition to the admonition, "History shows that wars are chiefly caused by economic pressure and competition between nations and races." The aftermath of the First World War found the board concerned about the disposition of the German Pacific islands and continuing to add to the list of American policies that must be defended, including a specific warning about Great Britain in the Atlantic and Japan in the Pacific, the only nations militarily capable of threatening American interests. Both, the board concluded, had embarked on aggressive trade policies, and both were linked in an alliance that made it "reasonably certain" the two would be allies in any conflict with the United States.[7]

Continuing with Japan for a moment longer, an example of a statesman and a naval officer being hoist by their own petard may be found in 1932. Secretary of State Henry L. Stimson as head of the American delegation to the London Naval Conference shared, along with Admiral Pratt, some of the responsibility for the compromises that made agreement possible. When the Manchurian crisis erupted in 1931, Stimson made fruitless efforts to halt the fighting and then to persuade Great Britain and the League of Nations to exert pressure on Japan. By February 18, 1932, Stimson was writing in his diary: "The whole situation is beginning to shake me up and get me back to a little bit nearer my old view that we haven't yet reached the stage where we can dispense with police force; and the only police force I have got to depend upon today is the American Navy. Pretty soon I am going to tell the President so."

Meeting with Admiral Pratt, then chief of Naval Operations, eleven days later on February 29, 1932, Stimson recorded: "Admiral Pratt came in this morning and gave me a careful and not altogether encouraging summary of our naval strength." After conferring with the president on March 8, 1932, Stimson wrote: "I told him that I had been very much alarmed about the present situation of the Navy; that I had had occasion to go into it, and it was more unequal than I had thought, to meeting Japan . . . I said I wasn't talking about an offensive but a defensive Navy. After the Cabinet Meeting was over I went into his room and showed him the figures that Pratt had given me, and repeated very earnestly that I thought we were down to the danger point, and that one of our first things to do would be to build up the Navy."[8]

More than a year later, Chief of Naval Operations William H. Standley wrote to Adm. David Foote Sellers, commander in chief, United States Fleet, posing the following question: "Suppose an enemy fleet were to appear off Santa Barbara Islands tomorrow morning. Have you men enough on the various types of ships to go out and give battle to the enemy? In other words, with the men you have on board can you go into action at once and use every weapon of offense or defense on board and make the necessary speed to give highest battle efficiency?" In his reply, by letter of October 9, 1933, Admiral Sellers stated categorically that he could not, that the crews would have to be increased from the peacetime allowance to 100 percent of wartime complement.[9]

A similar disconcerting experience took place in December 1937, when the Japanese attack on the U.S.S. *Panay* created apprehension about war. Although the Japanese government offered apologies and reparations for the incident before the United States could lodge a formal protest, apparently Chief of Naval Operations William D. Leahy suggested a blockade of Japan to enforce contemplated American demands; and Secretary of the Navy Claude A. Swanson stated that the fleet would be prepared to carry out this assignment within two weeks. Yet at a conference of top level officials, it was revealed that the United States was not capable of dispatching sufficient naval forces to the Far East to intimidate the Japanese.

The point I am trying to make is that the navy has played a significant role in American foreign policy through its ability or inability to permit the government to pursue a desired course of action—to provide, as it were, that margin of credibility to impress other nations sufficiently to induce them to mend their ways and behave the way our government wanted them to. The hands of the statesman are tied at times of crisis when an appeal to the threat or actual use of armed force is required, and it is incumbent upon both the civil and military authorities to understand and reach agreement on policies that must be supported and promoted in order to avoid what can be a catastrophic disparity. Fortunately for the United States, geographical isolation and other factors have prevented grievous harm resulting from an improper juxtaposition of aspirations and capabilities. The secretary of the navy could report in 1885, "At the present moment it must be conceded that we have nothing which deserves to be called a navy," and at the time it did not seem to make any difference. Then a "new navy" was created, and there is some argument as to whether it was merely the instrument of imperialism or its instigator. Actually, the navy has been a means, not an end, in regard to the fulfillment of national aspirations. On the other hand, by its very existence it has, on occasion, contributed to, and possibly acted as a catalyst for, the adoption of an aggressive policy. It seems unlikely that President William McKinley and the Congress would have been so arbitrary over Cuba if the modern American Navy had not replaced the fleet so bluntly depicted in 1885. To what extent, then, have statesmen been encouraged to embark upon dangerous ventures because, to paraphrase Theodore Roosevelt, they have had the means to back them up? Or, to reverse the perspective, would the existence of a powerful navy have prevented belligerents from violating our concept of neutral rights in 1798, 1812, and 1917, or from ignoring our interests in 1940 and 1941?

In this context, the London Treaty of 1930 established an equilibrium of naval power designed to prevent either of the Big Three—the United States, Great Britain, and Japan—from being able to launch an attack on the other with a reasonable expectation of success. This balance did not, however, deter Japan from infringing on the interests of the other two signatories, and her leaders had to weigh both capabilities and intentions in anticipating the response her actions might provoke. Admiral Zumwalt, in his *Playboy* interview, claims that, "as long as one side is clearly superior and both sides know it, one side will back off. It's during that period of uncertainty, as the trend lines cross, that we have to be very uncomfortable."[10] Thus he dismisses the validity of parity in arms control negotiations. But it seems unlikely that even the civil authorities of a major power will accept an arrangement that places their nation's security at the mercy of another unless compelling circumstances prevail. These circumstances, as Oliver Wendell Holmes, Jr., said, can alter cases, and it is in this area of political and economic realities that the defense posture is determined, an area where the professional and the statesman must conjoin. Further analysis of our past experience in cooperation, or the lack of, and differences between these two components of government will help clarify the steps our country has taken in its emergence from national liberation to a great world power, and, one hopes, serve to illuminate the present and plan for the future.

Getting back to the cloudy firmament of international law, much of the American concern has been with the rules that regulate the conduct of vessels on the high seas, both warships and merchant ships, in war and in peace. Most of us are aware that the basic question in time of war is often not what a neutral will agree to but how much the neutral will tolerate. Many of us are less familiar with the multifarious precepts governing maritime warfare that proliferated as nations "looked outward," the naval mission expanded, and technological change made old tenets obsolete. A traditional general commitment to principles embodied in the "Plan of 1776" and the Declaration of Catherine of Russia, which included a definition of "effective" as distinct from a declared or "paper" blockade, helped involve the United States in a quasi war with France, war with Great Britain, and World War I. The latter conflict found both Britain and Germany willing to resort to drastic measures, however distasteful to neutrals, in order to prevent supplies from reaching the enemy. Over the years, refinements of doctrines evolved and precepts were added covering the rights and duties of belligerents, cobelligerents, nonbelligerents, and neutrals. Recent incidents have spurred a search for the formulation of rules to cover situations arising in the limbo between "conventional" peace and war; and the exploitation of the ocean waters and seabed for commercial and military purposes has created problems undreamed of by experts from Grotius to Hackworth.

It is not my intention to present a capsulated and superficial summary of the American interpretation of the law of the sea or the rules of maritime warfare. What I want to stress is the fact that these positions taken by our government directly affected naval activities, and that they were often formulated by, or in consultation with, the navy. Although I say "often," I do not know the extent of navy responsibility or the occasions on which it was consulted. One does find, for example, evidence in the General Board papers that it was asked for recommendations on matters that arose at the International Maritime Conference held in London in 1909, including questions relating to continuous voyage and contraband, and the board did meet with the solicitor of the State Department, Dr. James B. Scott. The same year the board advised that submarines be employed solely for coastal defense, thereby avoiding any sensitive problems over commerce raiding. [11] The highly esteemed Blue Books, issued periodically by the Naval War College, have been cited repeatedly to verify points or interpretations of law, and naval officers have served as delegates or advisers to maritime conferences. [12]

While many historians have only an elementary knowledge of international law, those of us in naval history can provide an invaluable service to colleagues and students by incorporating it to a greater extent into our studies and teaching, relating it to naval activities and indicating the role the navy has played in its formulation and execution. The law of the sea conferences will undoubtedly stimulate more interest in the subject, and whether international law is in the process of disintegrating or codifying a new world order, we can elucidate on what it has been and why and how it has affected the nation.

The dimensions of navy involvement in international relations certainly extend beyond diplomacy and international law. The navy has been global in its orientation and has, in the words of Sen. Albert J. Beveridge, made other lands contiguous. It has shown the flag in distant seas, to the gratitude of some and the distress of others; it has ruled islands, supported or suppressed revolutions, been an emissary of good will and of destruction, displayed an image of Americans ranging from chivalrous to uncouth, and brought the Yankee dollar into every corner of the globe. It has been a vehicle for humanitarianism and imperialism, a reflection of and a contributor to what the nation represents; and for good or ill, it has had a direct or indirect impact on the lives of Americans and most other peoples of the world.

Our task is to clarify the navy's role and reveal its inner workings for the benefit of scholarship, the nation, and the world. It is to those records that have been gathered so assiduously, preserved and organized, that we must go in order to understand our naval policy and the functions the navy has performed on the international scene.

NOTES

1. Samuel Eliot Morison, *"Old Bruin," Commodore Matthew C. Perry, 1794–1858* (Boston: Little, Brown, 1967), pp. 270–89.
2. Charles Oscar Paullin, *Diplomatic Negotiations of American Naval Officers, 1778–1883* (Gloucester, Mass.: Peter Smith, 1967), pp. 253–57.
3. Perry's instructions included the following provision for contingencies: "It is proper that the Commodore should be invested with large discretionary powers and should feel assured that any departure from usage or any error of judgment he may commit will be viewed with indulgence." Morison, *"Old Bruin,"* p. 285.
4. Paullin, *Diplomatic Negotiations,* p. 7.
5. Ernest J. King and Walter M. Whitehill, *Fleet Admiral King: A Naval Record* (New York: W. W. Norton, 1952), pp. 235, 236, 242; Raymond G. O'Connor, "Reflections on the Characteristics of a Commander," *Naval War College Review* 21 (October 1968): 37–43.
6. General Board No. 91, 17 December 1900, Letterbook I, Classified Operational Archives Branch, Naval Historical Center (hereafter records of the Naval Historical Center are cited as NHC), p. 123; General Board No. 187, 12 November 1901, Letterbook I, NHC, pp. 374–78; General Board Endorsement No. 414, 30 September 1909, Letterbook VI, NHC, p. 138; General Board Endorsement No. 414-1, 1 October 1910, Letterbook VII, NHC, pp. 92–93. In 1900 the board recommended "diplomatic steps" to prevent the "cession or leasing of all or a part of the Island of Hayti [sic] to any European country," and in 1906 it urged abrogation of the agreement of 1817 with Great Britain restricting the size and number of armed vessels to be maintained on the Great Lakes. General Board No. 87, 10 December 1900, Letterbook I, NHC, pp. 109–10; General Board No. 420-2, 28 February 1906, File 420, NHC.
7. General Board No. 420-2, 21 April 1909, Letterbook VI, NHC, pp. 22–26; General Board No. 420-2, 28 September 1910, Letterbook VII, NHC, pp. 58–62; Memorandum Adopted by the Executive Committee, clipped to copy of General Board No. 420-2, 30 July 1915, Letterbook VI, NHC; General Board No. 438, Serial 1088, 12 September 1921, Washington Conference Files, Box 14, General Records of the Department of State, Record Group 59, National Archives Building, Washington, D.C.
8. Henry L. Stimson Manuscript Diary, Yale University Library, New Haven, Conn.
9. Standley to Sellers, 4 October 1933, and Sellers to Standley, 9 October 1933, David Foote Sellers Papers, Manuscript Division, Library of Congress, Washington, D.C. In 1935 the secretary of the navy wrote: "At the present time the Navy Department contemplates no change in its policy with respect to base development in the Pacific, even should the prohibition against the development of bases in the Western Pacific be terminated by the expiration of the Treaty Limiting Naval

Armaments." Claude A. Swanson to Senator Ernest W. Gibson, 7 August 1935, SecNav File (SC) A15-1 to A16-1/QM, General Records of the Department of the Navy, 1798–1947, Record Group 80, National Archives Building, Washington, D.C. By 1940 the secretary of the navy, in an endorsement of a General Board report of thirty-five pages with a twenty-one-page supplement, said: "The attached report indicates that a satisfactory state of readiness of the Navy to meet a major emergency does not now exist." SecNav to CNO, 8 July 1940, SecNav Files (SC) A16-1, ibid. Naval and foreign affairs continued to be out of phase.

10. *Playboy,* June 1974, p. 80.
11. General Board No. 438, 25 January 1909, Letterbook V, NHC, pp. 389–90; Proceedings of the General Board 19 February 1909, III, NHC, p. 295; General Board No. 407, 27 January 1909, Letterbook V, NHC, pp. 396–403.
12. For a fine example of the Naval War College "Blue Books," see W. T. Mallison, Jr., *Studies in the Law of Naval Warfare: Submarines in General and Limited War* (Newport, R.I.: U.S. Naval War College, 1968). In reference to Professor Mallison's paper and his observation on the article in the 1856 Declaration of Paris defining "blockade," a case was discussed in a 1935 Blue Book of a ship protesting the illegality of a blockade because it was not maintained by a sufficient force. An amusing comment was to the effect that "It would be difficult for a vessel which has been captured by a blockading force to maintain that the blockade was not effective." *International Law Situations with Solutions and Notes, 1935* (Washington, D.C.: Government Printing Office, 1936), p. 86. Obviously, this assessment misses the letter and spirit of the formulated doctrine.

III
TECHNOLOGY AND THE NAVY

Rear Adm. Bradley A. Fiske. (U.S. Navy photograph.)

PAOLO E. COLETTA

Bradley A. Fiske: Naval Inventor

There is nothing in the antecedents of Bradley A. Fiske to indicate either great motivation toward the navy or the mysteries of invention. His father was a Protestant minister. His own first meeting with military discipline, at a private military school he attended when twelve years of age, was sad, for he was so slight physically that at drill he carried a wooden gun while the other boys carried real ones. At maturity he weighed about 130 pounds. His decision to become a naval officer resulted from a visit by a maternal uncle wearing a resplendent naval uniform and telling rosy tales about life at the U.S. Naval Academy. Though the uncle was killed in the Civil War, Fiske did not change his mind.

The earliest evidence of Fiske's interest in inventing things is found during his high school days, when he concerned himself with distilling freshwater from saltwater by evaporation. But for the next dozen years the "invention bacillus" lay dormant.[1] When he attended the Naval Academy, from 1870 to 1874, he was taught by a number of distinguished officers and civilians. Among the latter was William Chauvenet, but none of the instructors was an inventor.[2]

Fiske's class contained some men who would gain fame as leaders and scholars, such as Austin M. Knight. Much more the researcher, theoretician, and inventor was Washington Irving Chambers, while the prizewinner on campus was Albert Abraham Michelson. Fiske believed Michelson to be a "real genius," a cogent conclusion because Michelson went on to become one of the foremost physical scientists of the world. But instead of learning something from him, and although Michelson was two years older and the welterweight champion at the academy, during an argument the peppery Fiske cast aspersions upon his Hebraic origin—and spent eight days on the sick list.[3] In any event, Fiske left the academy with about as good a technical education as that offered in any engineering school of his day.

The status of the navy Fiske served after graduation was extremely poor. In exercises in the Caribbean in 1874, its ships proceeded at four knots on auxiliary steampower, their smoothbore guns unable to hit a target more than six hundred yards away.[4] Soon thereafter there reawakened in Fiske the spirit of investigation and the capability that made him the most innovative, inventive, and scientific-minded naval officer of his generation.

A revolution of coal and iron had metamorphosed European and American life between 1780 and 1850. Fiske was born at the beginning of a second revolution, of steel and electricity, that occurred between 1850 and 1914. As the Philadelphia Centennial Exposition of 1876 revealed, the United States was still largely a natural resource area awaiting transformation into an industrial giant by technological power. Dynamos were quite new. Only a few cities had their streets illuminated, by arc lights. Thomas Edison's practical incandescent bulb would not appear until 1879, and the telephone was not yet a proven instrument. Neither private nor public systems of research and development existed. No school offered a formal course in electrical engineering. The American Institute of Electrical Engineers would not be founded until 1884. By that time such corporate giants as Thompson-Houston and Westinghouse could well afford to support such pioneer inventors as Elihu Thompson, William Stanley, and Nikola Tesla. But the navy, just producing the first of its modern ships, had no research and development program and had few contacts with the civilian world of science. However, in the succeeding generation, Fiske's friend, Elmer A. Sperry, would evolve from scientist and engineer to entrepreneur, providing goods and services not only for the civilian economy but for the navy as well. On the other hand, Fiske, while performing all the duties required of a line officer, would turn to private industry, especially the Western Electric Company, to help him develop instruments that would improve the habitability, efficiency, and especially the fighting qualities of naval ships.[5]

Not trained as a scientific researcher, Fiske sometimes failed to read the literature in the field. Only after he had invented a typewriter and telegraphic printer did he learn that both were already being marketed.[6] Then, having heard about Thomas Edison, he decided to study electricity. While he did so, he put together a breech-loading musket on the same principle as a gun that he thought improved upon the Gatling. The Bureau of Ordnance found that it was no better than guns already in use.[7] Nonplussed, Fiske worked on a boat-detaching apparatus by which a boat could be lowered from a ship and hoisted in again quickly and safely and a motor torpedo boat carrying electrically fired mortar shells. An insight into how things were done in the late 1870s is gained by noting that the chief of the Bureau of Equipment told Fiske to have his boat device built by a private firm so that he could enjoy some profit from it and stimulate other officers to invent things.[8]

During a course taken at the Newport, Rhode Island, torpedo station,

Fiske's interest in electricity was excited by lectures delivered by the civilian professor Moses F. Farmer. That interest was further stimulated in talks with Park Benjamin, a Naval Academy classmate who had resigned and at the age of twenty-eight years was editor of the *Scientific American*. [9] With funds provided by the Bureau of Navigation, Fiske began experiments with an "electric log," a device whereby a ship would tow a small propeller by an electric wire which would actuate a mechanism on board ship and indicate each turn and every tenth of a mile traveled. [10] Next came a sounding machine, or fathometer — a small metal plate secured at a particular angle to a towline that was made to signal an alarm on board ship when it struck bottom. Although Fiske dabbled with both the electric log and sounding machine for several years, he lacked the interest or funds to develop them; he abandoned the projects, only to see others perfect and make profits from them. [11] For many years, too, he tried to measure the altitude of the sun where the horizon could not be seen. [12] One device that worked well, and was eventually adopted, was his signaling lamp. Intership communications at night had depended upon the waving of oil-burning lamps or the firing of "stars" or rockets. These were unsatisfactory. Fiske placed a lamp behind an aperture which could be opened and closed by a shutter according to a code. [13] "Flashing light," fixed and portable, has become an integral and important part of intership communications.

In 1879, Fiske invented two mechanical lead pencils and had them marketed by Eberhard Faber. Again, however, he had failed to survey the literature in the field. Sued by the American Lead Pencil Company for infringement of patent, he sold out. [14]

In 1882, Fiske verged upon leaving the navy. As he put it, with some lack of modesty, "the Navy was an extremely uninteresting place for a man who had already learned virtually all there was about the naval profession, and who could see no prospect ahead except a tiresome alternation of monotonous cruises at sea and profitless tours on shore." [15] Three things happened that changed his mind. The first was the building of the cruisers *Atlanta, Boston,* and *Chicago,* and the dispatch boat *Dolphin.* The second and third were the illimitable prospects that electricity and the telephone promised for naval use. [16] In 1882, for example, the U.S.S. *Trenton,* fitted with an Edison plant, became the first warship in the world to be electrically lighted. Taking a year's leave, Fiske studied electricity and soon became a double-threat because he knew not only theory but could handle mechanical apparatuses as well. He realized there was much to invent or to improve with respect to dynamos, lights, and telephones. He earned some money by improving electrical insulators used on telegraph poles and some from a textbook on electricity that eventually ran through ten editions in twenty-two years. [17] Upon his return to duty, now with the Bureau of Ordnance, he designed electric primers for firing the modern guns on the largest of the new cruisers, the *Chicago*.[18] Experiments with megaphones ten feet wide and three feet long as a method of intership communication failed because they carried unwanted sounds.[19] After attending the International Exhibition held under the auspices of the Franklin Institute in Philadelphia, in the fall of 1883, he reported to the chief of the Bureau of Ordnance that the time had come to use electric motors for steering ships, hoisting projectiles and powder from magazines, working the yards and stays, hoisting articles from holds, and indicating whether a ship's engines were going forward, backward, or were stopped.[20]

Made responsible for adapting electricity to the ordnance of the new cruisers, Fiske also worked with torpedoes and gun mounts. Finding that a heeling over of a cruiser by only ten degrees would make it impossible for the two men at the training gear to move their gun "uphill" because they had handpower only, Fiske ran a shaft down from the gun carriage, gearing it to a steam engine in a compartment below.[21] More important, he noted that the ships were not fitted with rangefinders and decided to invent one, a decision that kept him hard at work for many years.[22] In 1886, he also began to experiment in "signalling by induction," or wireless telegraphy; helped conduct the acceptance trials of the "dynamite cruiser" *Vesuvius*, which had pneumatic guns; and obtained patents on an idea that used the exhaust gases from a machine gun to operate the gun, the same principle used in the later Browning Gun.[23] Much more important was a patent for an apparatus whereby the motions of an electric motor could be made to follow those of an operator's hand in both speed and direction, which made possible, among other things, the ammunition hoist, electrical ship steering, and electric gun training. Ammunition hoists built for the *Atlanta* by the Sprague Electric Motor Company worked perfectly, as did an electric gun training system. An electrical after-steering mechanism would follow and a rudimentary but revolutionary fire control system.

Because firing through open sights was accomplished either by firing successive shots until one reached the target or by bracketing it, few captains would fire at a target much more than five hundred yards distant. By 1888, however, warships proceeding at twenty knots toward each other caused a change in relative position of about six hundred eighty yards a minute. Guns of different sizes required different elevations, and the rolling and pitching of the ship added to the problem of sighting the guns. By 1890, using a Fiske rangefinder, the *Chicago's* fire at 1,500 yards was within nine yards of the point aimed at, thus easily hitting along the length or even across the breadth of an ordinary battleship. There were, of course, optical rangefinders, but these did not become really accurate until about 1907. Fiske solved the problem of triangulation by having the ship serve as a base line. He had two telescopes, one forward and one aft, run along electrical wires calibrated to represent distance to target and a galvanometer to point an arrow toward a range scale. The system was admirably adaptable for electrical firing from forts and was also useful for piloting. That the system was good for short-range work only was unimportant because open gunsights gave only dismal results. [24]

One day in 1890, when Fiske was looking at some schooners through one of his rangefinder telescopes, he noticed how its crosshairs moved across their sails as his own ship gently rolled and pitched. The genesis of broadside fire came to him. As he put it, "anybody could fire all the guns in the broadside . . . and hit the target every time, by setting the telescope at the angle of depression equal to the proper angle of elevation of the guns, leaving the guns parallel to the deck, and firing when the roll of the ship brought the crosshairs on the target." He patented the idea. [25] He then went ahead and developed a range and position finder that permitted all guns in a fort to fire simultaneously at a target. To get all the guns on a ship to do so was another matter, but by 1893 Fiske had received a patent for a telescopic gunsight. According to the chief of the Bureau of Ordnance, he had "changed naval gunnery from a game of chance into a science." [26] By providing telephonic communication between the telescope watchers and range readers, he also was the first to install telephones on board ship. If the American Navy did not think too highly of his rangefinders and the British preferred a simpler optical arrangement, they were nevertheless purchased by the French, who also put them on ships they built for Chile.

Fiske's idea was to produce a complete gunnery system whereby he could measure ranges with a rangefinder, telegraph these to the guns with a range indicator, and use the ranges for hitting the target by a gun rigged with an absolutely accurate telescope sight. By the time he had overcome objections to having instruments that measured range on targets only on one side of a ship, other men with better ideas had come along, and he abandoned his project. Nevertheless, by using a telescope he had provided an exactness with respect to the location of a target heretofore denied a gunner and greatly enlarged his field of view. Because the telescope did not recoil with the gun, the pointer could keep his eye constantly at the eyepiece. By 1895, the accuracy of fire permitted by his gear was one-half of 1 percent per 1,000 yards. By 1913, when gun-elevating motors were in use and rangefinders had been installed atop tall cage masts, a single gun or a whole battery could be fired by electricity when the roll of the ship brought the telescope sight on target, thus accomplishing director firing.

Fiske should have been detailed to duty in a laboratory where he could perfect electrical and gunnery gear. The principle prevailed, however, that all naval officers were the same except in the matter of rank, that one could solve a mechanical design problem as well as the other, and that they should be rotated every three years between sea and shore. In consequence, the navy's foremost electrical engineer and master of mechanical contrivances saw service during the explosive situation in Valparaiso Harbor during the Chilean civil war of 1891–92, chased pelagic sealers in the Bering Sea, and protected American lives and property during an insurrection in Brazil before returning to duty in the Bureau of Ordnance and proving that electricity could turn turrets better than steam or hydraulic methods. In part because of his work, central electrical powerplants were installed in two battleships laid down in 1896, the *Kearsarge* and the *Kentucky*, to turn turrets, drive ammunition hoists, light the ships, and run all auxiliary machinery, except the windlass and steering gear. Similar installations were made in the even newer *Illinois* and *Alabama,* and telescopic sights were fitted to all four-, five-, and six-inch guns issued the fleet. In addition, Fiske invented the stadimeter and what have been called "the nerves of a warship"—the engine-order telegraph, helm indicator, engine speed and direction indicator, and steering telegraph. As his friend Park Benjamin put it, Fiske's rangefinder enabled a captain to determine distance to target. If the rangefinder were shot away, Fiske's stadimeter could be used. While gunners sighted through Fiske's telescopic sights and fired with Fiske's electrical primers, engines and helms were controlled by his engine-order telegraph and helm indicator, and speed was indicated by an improved version of his speed indicator log. Fifty thousand ingenious Americans asked for patents every year, none of them for equipment useful to the navy. What had been done to improve the fighting qualities of warships had been done by Fiske. Conditions between two ships being otherwise equal, the ship containing his inventions should win in battle.[27]

Because flag-hoist signaling was often undependable, Fiske developed an electrical keyboard that would move four huge revolving arms placed on a mast. The system resembled semaphore but transmitted coded letters. By the time he perfected it, wireless telegraphy displaced it.[28] Still, by the age of forty-two years Fiske had enough inventions in his name to secure a favorable niche in the history of naval inventors.

Following attendance at the Naval War College in 1896, Fiske was sent to be the navigator on the *Petrel* and from a platform rigged high up on her mast took ranges with his stadimeter during the Battle of Manila Bay. Subsequently assigned as executive officer of the old battleship *Massachusetts,* in 1903, he had little time for invention. He, nevertheless, obtained a patent on a combined rangefinder and turret; that is, he placed an optical rangefinder inside the turret, with only its glasses exposed, so that it could revolve with the turret toward a target. He also improved upon the "Morris tube," or sighting machine, for gunnery practice and helped devise a superheater that greatly extended the range of torpedoes.

From 1906 to 1910, Fiske commanded the speedy cruiser *Minneapolis,* a cruiser division, and a monitor. In 1908 he suggested two ideas that were eventually adopted. A gunnery plotting room below deck was approved by a fire control board in 1910.[29] His idea that the navy establish a Board of Invention and Experiment similar to the research laboratories used by large industrial concerns was adopted in 1915.[30] Noting that a conning tower could be shot away, Fiske saw the need to control a ship from below deck in emergencies. By managing to make a magnetic compass work in a room completely enclosed in iron, he developed an after-steering room, which functioned much better after Elmer Sperry invented and developed the gyroscopic compass.[31]

Although he had important duty on the General Board of the navy, in 1910 Fiske decided to study aeronautics, saying that "there was not much to learn for a man who had the knowledge of mechanics that I had gradually acquired in my experience as an inventor and navy officer; in fact, I was surprised to find out how little there was to learn, and how little had been done ... especially by our army and navy."[32] In a philosophical vein, in 1911 he dwelled upon the problems faced by inventors and made an eloquent plea for more liberal treatment of inventors by the navy. As he well knew, the navy preferred that an inventor demonstrate a working model than sponsor invention through navy-funded development. "Does anyone deny," he asked, "that our electric lights, torpedoes, guns and engines were invented before they were developed?" It was the duty of the navy, he asserted, to encourage not merely engineering skill and mechanical ingenuity but real invention, a matter he believed as important as progress in strategy, tactics, and engineering.[33]

Although busy as commander of a cruiser division and then of a battleship division, Fiske thought about having Elmer Sperry provide gyroscopes for mechanisms used for gunfire control.[34] He also conceived the idea of building aircraft large enough to enable them to launch torpedoes. Upon obtaining a patent for a torpedo plane in 1912, he concluded that he had invented not just a new weapon "but a NEW METHOD OF WARFARE."[35] Pending provision of a plane powerful enough to carry a 2,500-pound torpedo, he invented "check fire" by putting a small glass prism before a telescope. Because the prism deflected light rays entering it a number of degrees to the right or left, target practice could be carried on against ships in company and towed targets were made unnecessary.[36]

From February 1913 until he retired in May 1915, Fiske was the equivalent to today's chief of Naval Operations. He nevertheless somehow found time to perfect an automatic gun-pointing device with Elmer Sperry and to obtain a joint patent for it. [37] Although he hoped that following his retirement he might head the Naval Consulting Board, Thomas Edison was chosen instead. Because the board was directed "to originate within the Navy proper machinery and facilities for utilizing the natural inventive genius of Americans to meet the new conditions of warfare as shown abroad," it institutionalized the relationship between civilian inventors and the navy that officers like Fiske, on the one hand, and civilians like Sperry, on the other, had long demanded. [38]

Because Fiske had long supported a reformation of the Navy Department in which naval officers rather than civilians would direct it, he was persona non grata to Secretary of the Navy Josephus Daniels, who served from 1913 to 1921. Therefore, Fiske turned to the Aero Club of America and private sources for support in developing a torpedo plane. By the end of the Great War, both British and German planes fitted with his release mechanism had successfully used torpedoes. The refusal of the navy to help Fiske, however, delayed the production of an effective American torpedo plane for many years after the war. [39] In recompense, when he was sixty-four years of age, he received recognition from the Aero Club as a pioneer in the field of naval aviation and inventor of the torpedo plane and in an editorial in the *New York Herald*, in what will well serve as a penultimate closing remark, that "Rear Admiral Fiske has probably invented more successful naval and military inventions than any other man in history." [40]

Whatever Fiske did in the way of invention during his forty-five years of naval service was accomplished "on the side," for he was a line officer who went from midshipman to rear admiral; and as aide for operations, he served in the highest professional navy post. That the navy's most prominent electrical engineer should have been given some of the seagoing assignments he suffered can be understood only by those who can fathom the mystery of the procedures followed by personnel detailers. Largely unsupported by the navy either before or after the creation of the Naval Consulting Board, he had obtained about sixty patents. He had greatly eased the physical burden of work on board ship; improved intra- and inter-ship communications; devised mechanisms still in use in modern pilothouses, gun mounts and turrets, fire directors, gunplotting rooms, and after-steering; and revolutionized both gunnery and naval aviation.

Fiske is not listed in the *Biographical Memoirs* published by the National Academy of Sciences; in *American Men of Science: A Biographical Directory*, edited by the Jacques Catell Press and published by the R. R. Bowker Co.; in McGraw-Hill's *Men of Science;* nor in the popular Bernard Jaffe, *Men of Science* (1944, 1958). He is unknown to the general public, which will recognize the names of Charles Goodyear for vulcanizing rubber; Elias Howe for inventing the sewing machine; Richard M. Hoe for the rotary press, Elisha G. Otis for the elevator; perhaps George Westinghouse for the automatic airbrake; Alexander G. Bell for at least the telephone; possibly Nikola Tesla for developing the alternating current motor; and Charles P. Steinmetz, who acquired more than two hundred patents in motors and electrical equipment. Nevertheless, as he sat occasionally on a rocking chair on the porch of his Jamestown, Rhode Island, hotel in the year of his death, 1942, at eighty-eight years of age, Fiske may have thought that the ships that passed by from Newport were equipped, except for their sonar and radar, with basic electrical and optical equipment of his invention, which made them the effective ships that they were.

NOTES

1. Bradley A. Fiske, *From Midshipman to Rear-Admiral* (New York: Century Co., 1919), pp. 3-38.
2. From 1870 to 1874 the superintendents of the Naval Academy were John Worden, of *Monitor* fame, and Christopher Raymond Perry Rodgers, one of the ubiquitous Rodgers clan. Among the officer instructors were Robley D. Evans, French Ensor Chadwick, Caspar F. Goodrich, Henry D. Taylor, Winfield Scott Schley, and William T. Sampson. Among the civilians were William Chauvenet and James R. Soley. Chadwick and Soley wrote on international law, diplomacy, and naval history. Sampson was a good engineer and would be the victor in the naval battle of Santiago during the Spanish-American War. Chauvenet was an excellent teacher of mathematics and navigation.
3. Fiske, *From Midshipman to Rear-Admiral*, pp. 14-16; John Henry Wilson and Albert A. Michelson, *America's First Nobel Prize Physicist* (New York: Julian Messner, 1958), pp. 38-40; Marcus Benjamin, "Prof. Albert A. Michelson: The New President of the American Association for the Advancement of Science," *Scientific American* 101 (7 January 1911): 8.
4. *Annual Report of the Secretary of the Navy, 1874* (Washington, D.C.: Government Printing Office, 1974), pp. 5-6; Walter Herrick, Jr., *The American Naval Revolution* (Baton Rouge: Louisiana State University Press, 1967), pp. 9-10, 14-15; John R. Wadleigh "1873 — The Best Was Yet to Be," *U.S. Naval Institute Proceedings* 99 (November 1973): 56-70.
5. Thomas Parke Hughes, *Elmer A. Sperry: Inventor and Engineer* (Baltimore: Johns Hopkins University Press, 1971); David Woodbury, *Elihu Thompson: Beloved Scientist, 1853-1937* (Boston: Museum of Science, 1960); "The Industrial Corporation and the Inventor," *Scientific American* 105 (18 November 1911): 448-49. The archives of the Western Electric Co. contain records of Fiske's patent applications for the wireless control of torpedoes, of his direct-reading rangefinders, and other inventions. (Young Hi Quick, Historical Research Librarian, Western Electric Co., to the writer, 27 September 1973.)
6. Fiske, *From Midshipman to Rear-Admiral*, pp. 38-39.
7. Ibid., pp. 39-40.

8. Ibid., pp. 40, 45, 61–62.

9. Ibid., p. 49.

10. Ibid., pp. 48–49.

11. Ibid., pp. 49–50.

12. Ibid., pp. 410–11, 575, 581, 620,; Bradley A. Fiske, "The Horizometer," *U.S. Naval Institute Proceedings* 32 (September 1906): 1043-55, and "Navigating without Horizon," ibid. 33 (September 1907): 955–57.

13. Fiske, *From Midshipman to Rear-Admiral,* pp. 54–56.

14. Ibid., pp. 60–61.

15. Ibid., p. 71.

16. Ibid.

17. *Electricity in Theory and Practice, or, the Elements of Electrical Engineering* (New York: D. Van Nostrand, 1887).

18. Fiske, *From Midshipman to Rear-Admiral,* p. 85. There was actually little saving of time between pulling a lanyard to fire a gun or pushing a button by which a battery would energize an electric primer. Reports from various ships over the years to the Bureau of Ordnance either praised the electrical system or, if they had had trouble with it, condemned it. (Conclusion based upon reports contained in Ordnance and Gunnery, BG, Box 109, Naval Records Collection of the Office of Naval Records and Library, Record Group 45, National Archives Building, Washington, D.C. [Hereafter records in the National Archives Building are cited as RG __, NA.])

19. Fiske, *From Midshipman to Rear-Admiral,* p. 86. Shortly thereafter, about 1884, Fiske had an improved model patterned after Edison installed on top of the pilot-house of the cruiser *Atlanta.* Out of these beginnings grew the "bull horn" carried by most ships.

20. Ibid., pp. 89–90, 117–19.

21. Ibid., pp. 82–84.

22. Ibid., chaps. 7–12.

23. Ibid., pp. 111–26. Problems encountered in testing and installing pneumatic guns are described in BG, Box VIII, No. 8, RG 45, NA, and in Seaton Schroeder, *A Half Century of Naval Service* (New York and London: Appleton, 1922).

24. Fiske, *From Midshipman to Rear-Admiral,* pp. 111–26; Elting L. Morison, *Men, Machines, and Modern Times* (Cambridge, Mass.: M.I.T. Press, 1966), pp. 17–44. Target practice scores by calibre of guns on board all ships are filed in Guns and Gunnery RG 45, NA. Fire control matters are in RG 19, NA. The great improvement made in target practice scores while William S. Sims was director of target practice may be followed in Record Group 19 and, in beautiful fashion, in Elting T. Morison, *Admiral Sims and the Modern American Navy* (Boston: Houghton Mifflin Co., 1942). For the mathematics involved in merely adjusting a range-finder, see U.S., Department of the Navy, "To Adjust Range Finders before Battle. By Captain Bradley A. Fiske, U.S.N.," General Order No. 5, 6 February 1909, in *U.S. Navy Department Special Orders, 1909-1911* (Washington, D.C.: Department of the Navy, 1911).

25. Fiske, *From Midshipman to Rear-Admiral,* pp. 124–25. In the argument over whether Fiske or Adm. Sir Percy Scott, R.N., was first to develop director firing, I would give Fiske chronological precedence even though further investigation must be made to reach a definitive conclusion. For Scott's contentions, see his memoirs,

Fifty Years in the Royal Navy (London: J. Murray, 1919), and the biography of him by Peter Padfield, *Aim Straight: A Biography of Admiral Sir Percy Scott* (London: Hodder and Stoughton, 1966). It may well be, as C. P. Snow has suggested, that "societies at about the same level of technology will produce similar inventions" (*Science and Government* [Cambridge, Mass.: Harvard University Press, 1961], p. 70).

26. Fiske, *From Midshipman to Rear-Admiral,* pp. 177-78.
27. Royal B. Bradford, Chief of Bureau of Equipment, Memorandum for the Bureau of Navigation, 12 January 1899, EL, RG 45, NA; Park Benjamin, "The Nerves of a War-ship," *Harper's Monthly Magazine,* March 1896, pp. 631-36.
28. Rear Adm. A. S. Crowninshield, Chief of Bureau of Navigation, to Western Electric Co., 28 November 1899, EL, Box 1, RG 45, NA; Fiske, *From Midshipman to Rear-Admiral,* pp. 129, 218-19.
29. Report of Board on Fire Control, 15 January 1910, Box 84-2, RG 19, NA. The senior member of the board was Capt. Templin M. Potts. Particularly after the world cruise of the Great White Fleet, 1907-9, the Navy Department frequently called upon special boards to advise it on the best kind of conning tower for battleships, the best location for ship and fire controls, telescope and master pointer locations, and similar questions. See President, General Board of the Navy [George Dewey], to Secretary of the Navy, 6 January 1909 and 19 February 1910, GB Letters; Senior Member Present, W. L. Rodgers, General Board of the Navy, to [John] Hood, [W. R.] Shoemaker, [S. S.] Robison, and [W. S.] Sims, 11 March 1916, GB Study, Serial No. 491; Josephus Daniels, Secretary of the Navy, to President, General Board, 10 February 1916, on the subject of revising the report of the 1915 Fire Control Board; Board on Fire Control [of which Capt. C. P. Plunkett was senior member], to Secretary of the Navy, 27 January 1916, on the same subject; President, General Board, to Secretary of the Navy, 27 April 1916, GB Study No. 420-11, Serial No. 491, advising the retention of the conning and fire control tower used on the *Pennsylvania*-type battleship rather than reverting to the *Virginia*-type (GB Records, Operational Archives Branch, Naval Historical Center, Washington, D.C.). By 16 July 1915, fire director control installations had been made on eleven battleships of the Atlantic Fleet and plans had been made to install similar systems on all other turret ships in commission (Joseph Strauss, Chief of Bureau of Construction and Repair, to Secretary of the Navy, 16 July 1915, Box 84-1, RG 19, NA). For instructions on using fire control systems, see Commander in Chief, Atlantic Fleet, to Atlantic Fleet, less Battleship Force, 7 December 1916, Box 84-13, ibid. By using the gyrocompass as a basic component, Sperry's gunfire control system was a great improvement over Fiske's (Hughes, *Elmer A. Sperry,* pp. 230-33, and Bradley A. Fiske, "Sperry's Contributions to the Naval Arts," *Mechanical Engineer* 49 (1927): 111-12).
30. Of the vast amount of material written about the Naval Consulting Board, see, particularly, Lloyd N. Scott, *Naval Consulting Board of the United States* (Washington, D.C.: Government Printing Office, 1920); Hughes, *Elmer A. Sperry,* pp. 290-309; and idem, "Early Government Research and Development: The Naval Consulting Board during World War I" (manuscript, University of Pennsylvania, 1973).
31. Fiske, *From Midshipman to Rear-Admiral,* pp. 443-45.
32. Ibid., p. 478.

33. Bradley A. Fiske, "Naval Power," *U.S. Naval Institute Proceedings* 37 (September 1911): 718, and *Invention: The Master-Key to Progress* (New York: E. P. Dutton and Co., 1921). Before the House Naval Affairs Committee in December 1914, Secretary of the Navy Daniels was asked, with particular respect to aircraft, if it would not be wise to help inventors perfect their inventions instead of waiting to be shown working models. Daniels answered that "We ought not to enter on that, as it would cost a great deal of money." Had he the money, he could fund the private development of aircraft, "but where we got one good one we would spend thousands of dollars on worthless machines" (U.S., Congress, House, *Hearings before the House Naval Affairs Committee*, 63d Cong., 3d sess., 1915, pp. 711-15. See also "The Navy and the Inventor," *Scientific American* 105 [18 November 1914]: 444).

34. Hughes, *Elmer A. Sperry*, pp. 139-42; "The New Navy Gyroscopic Compass," *Scientific American* 106 (29 June 1913): 588-89.

35. Fiske, *From Midshipman to Rear-Admiral*, pp. 504-5; Park Benjamin, "The Flying Fish Torpedo: A New and Terrible Form of Attack on the High Seas or in Harbors," *Independent* 80 (2 November 1914): 164-66; "Fiske Torpedo Plane," ibid. 90 (12 May 1917): 281-82.

36. Fiske, *From Midshipman to Rear-Admiral*, pp. 519-21.

37. Hughes, *Elmer A. Sperry*, p. 215.

38. Ibid., pp. 257-74; Fiske, *From Midshipman to Rear-Admiral*, p. 634. The board was comprised of twenty two members, two from each of eleven technical societies enrolling a total of 36,000 engineers. Among the members Fiske knew were Frank Julian Sprague, American Institute of Electrical Engineers (who was one of four Naval Academy graduates on the board); Hudson Maxim, American Aeronautical Society; and Henry Wise Wood and Elmer A. Sperry, American Society of Aeronautics. The board differed from Fiske's vision of it only by having a civilian instead of a naval officer as its director. See Thomas Commerford Martin, "Frank Julian Sprague: Inventor and Engineer," *Scientific American* 105 (21 October 1911): 363, 377, and "Navy Experts Picked," *Independent* 83 (20 September 1915): 387.

39. Fiske, *From Midshipman to Rear-Admiral*, p. 684. Late in 1926, Fiske brought suit in the Supreme Court of the District of Columbia against the government for $198,500 for infringement of the patent on his torpedo plane. The suit raised a number of interesting questions. Could a naval officer or enlisted man sue the government? To what extent could such a person profit from inventions conceived and developed while in the employ of the Navy? Was the material at issue so confidential that it must be tried in camera rather than before a jury? Fiske sued Secretary of the Navy Curtis D. Wilbur and his successor, Charles Francis Adams; the chief of the Bureau of Aeronautics, Rear Adm. William A. Moffett; and the chief of the Bureau of Ordnance, William D. Leahy. The trial was held in camera. On 7 October 1929, after Fiske had won his suit, the attorney general of the United States, who had represented the government, appealed the case to the Court of Appeals for the District of Columbia. On June 29, the court decided that Fiske's patent was "invalid for inoperativeness," i.e., he had never provided a working model of it. The refusal of the Supreme Court, on October 26, 1931, to review the case meant that Fiske's case was dead. Fiske's attorney was Ernest Wilkinson, author of the interesting article "The Legal Rights of Naval Officers and Enlisted Men and Their Inventions," *U.S. Naval Institute Proceedings* 50 (August 1924): 1266-77.

40. Fiske, *From Midshipman to Rear-Admiral*, p. 684.

Fig. 1. *A contemporary illustration depicting the loss of the* Monitor. *Although somewhat inaccurate in detail the engraving presents an excellent contrast between the traditional architecture of the* Rhode Island *and that of the* Monitor. (*Reprinted from* Harper's Weekly, *January 24, 1863.*)

JOHN G. NEWTON AND GORDON P. WATTS

The Role of Archival Records
in the Search and Discovery
of the Wreck of the U.S.S. *Monitor*

Less than ten months after her historic encounter with the Confederate ironclad ram, C.S.S. *Virginia*, the Union's celebrated "Cheesebox on a Raft" floundered in a gale off the North Carolina coast. The *Monitor* separated from her towship, the powerful side-wheel steamer *Rhode Island*, and disappeared at approximately 1:30 A.M. on the morning of December 31, 1862 (fig. 1).[1] The vessels, accompanied by the steamer *State of Georgia* towing the newly commissioned *Passaic*, were en route to the Union-held port of Beaufort, North Carolina.[2] This, the *Monitor's* second sea voyage, was to have been the first leg of a cruise that would take the ironclads to Charleston where they were to participate in an assault on Confederate fortifications defending the harbor.[3]

In spite of extensive repairs and alterations completed at the Washington Navy Yard during October and November, the *Monitor* was no more capable of operating in a heavy sea than she was on her first sea voyage from Sandy Hook to Cape Charles the preceding March.[4] The addition of a large telescoping stack and higher fresh-air intakes failed to keep out water in the heavy seas. With the deck awash, water still found its way under the turret. While releasing the anchor succeeded in bringing the vessel into the sea, the action carried away the hawsehole packing, providing water with an additional unobstructed passage. For the second time, water-soaked blower belts failed, eliminating power for both engines and pumps. Powerless, the already sluggish vessel offered no alternative. The *Monitor* was abandoned with a loss of four officers and twelve of the crew.[5]

In August of 1973, an interdisciplinary scientific party aboard the Duke University research vessel *Eastward* located the heavily damaged remains of the sunken ironclad approximately fifteen miles south-southeast of Cape Hatteras. The expedition, sponsored by the National Science Foundation and National Geographic Society, with the cooperation of the United States Army Reserve, was designed to accomplish dual objectives. The first of these was a geologic investigation into the origins of a ridge and swale feature located on the continental shelf south of Ocracoke Inlet. This work was carried out under the direction of Dr. Robert Sheridan, a geologist from the University of Delaware, whose specialty is the movement of sediment on the sea floor. The second objective was to carry out an electronic search for the remains of the *Monitor*.

Using a sophisticated array of remote sensing, navigational, and photographic equipment, much of which was designed by the project's remaining coinvestigator, Dr. Harold Edgerton of the Massachusetts Institute of Technology, the *Eastward* located a total of twenty-two shipwreck sites. Each of these was carefully examined to determine its similarity to an electronic signature which had been developed for the *Monitor*. Those sites which conformed to the *Monitor's* signature were examined further using oceanographic cameras and closed-circuit television. Only two of the sites warranted examination in this manner, and both were conclusively identified.

The electronic search made by the *Eastward* was preceded by a full eight months of comprehensive historical background research. The objective of this systematic examination of the existing contemporary records was to determine, as accurately as possible, the most probable location for the target and to identify sufficient reliable criteria to make positive identification of the *Monitor* possible. Since ship time was limited, isolation of the search area was a critical factor in determining a functional and effective search pattern.

While contemporary historical records consistently indicated that the *Monitor* was lost south of Cape Hatteras, several previous attempts to locate the vessel had been conducted in an area immediately north of Diamond Shoals.[6] Although work in this area resulted in several claims of having located the site, no evidence to confirm these discoveries was ever presented. The impetus of this activity seems to have been based upon the existence of an obscure nineteenth-century diary which noted sighting the "yankee cheesebox" in the surf north of Hatteras light.[7] The rumored existence of the graves of several members of the crew whose bodies were reported to have washed ashore in the same area possibly added credence to the theory.

If we assume that the diary account is genuine, it is worthwhile to consider that the author may well have mistaken the remains of another steam-powered vessel for those of the *Monitor*. For example, the vertical cylinder engine of the wooden steamer U.S.S. *Oriental*, which went aground and broke up north of the shoals in 1862, is still visible today (fig. 2).[8] From the beach the wreck distinctly resembles the profile of a turreted vessel. It is conceivable that this or other similar sites may have deceived both the diarist and later investigators. Our research revealed no evidence to substantiate either the sources or the claims, and the area was eliminated as a potential location for the site.

Fig. 2. *The steam cylinder of the* Oriental *in the surf off Bodie Island. From the beach the remains might be mistaken for the turret of a monitor-class vessel. Aerial photographs of the site reveal that the wooden hull has deteriorated leaving an outline similar to that of the* Monitor's *armor platform.*

In spite of numerous inconsistencies and frequent navigational discrepancies, Civil War naval records preserved at the National Archives provided the only credible source of data related to the loss of the *Monitor*. Of those available, the deck logs of the *Monitor's* towship, *Rhode Island*; the steamer *State of Georgia*; and the monitor *Passaic* proved to be the most valuable. These logs contained the basic information regarding speeds, bearings, and occasional positions, which allowed replotting of the vessel's courses. Equally important, they contained a meticulous record of wind direction and velocity, barometric pressure, depth, and water temperature. This information made it possible to reconstruct critical environmental conditions during the voyage. Additional useful information was found in the records and correspondence of the *Monitor's* captain and crew.

By combining the information available in archival sources with current bathymetric data and knowledge of the influence of the Gulf Stream, it was possible to calculate a maximum and minimum potential effect for each of the variables suspected of having been responsible for the frequent time, distance, and position discrepancies in the logs. While it is possible that some of these contradictions were related to strong local magnetic disturbances in the Hatteras area, no satisfactory method for gauging their influence could be determined. Reconstruction of environmental conditions made it possible for "set" and "drift" to be estimated during the critical period after the *Monitor* and *Rhode Island* separated. After making adjustments for the natural annual variation in magnetic north and establishing the correct position of the mid-nineteenth-century Hatteras light, the data were plotted on a current Coast and Geodetic Survey Chart of the North Carolina coast. The result was a five-by-fourteen-mile rectangle (fig. 3), hypothetically the area of highest probability. Although new information on the area currents gathered during the

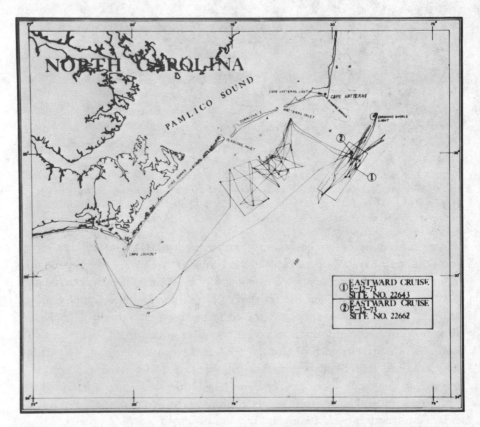

Fig. 3. *Chart of the North Carolina Coast showing the R/V* Eastward *(E-12-73) cruise pattern during both the geomorphic and archeological investigations. The northeast extension of the search pattern in the area of the search rectangle illustrates the effect of revised calculations concerning the currents in the area. Bottom contours are indicated in fathoms. Taken from U.S. Coast and Geodetic Survey Chart No. 1110, now No. 11520. (Map by David Bunting, courtesy of the Duke University Marine Laboratory.)*

cruise made revisions necessary, the technique proved to be invaluable in isolating the search area.

Archival records proved to be as critical in identifying the *Monitor* as they had in isolating the search area. Although a wealth of published data concerning the details and specifications of the *Monitor's* construction was found, extensive contradictions made it immediately apparent that relying on these sources alone would be extremely hazardous. To insure that the comparative data used in the identification process were as accurate as possible, an intensive effort was made to locate and evaluate any primary sources of information related to the vessel's construction. By relying on those sources either directly involved in the construction or actively engaged in the operation of the vessel, it was possible to establish an acceptable framework within which significant comparison could be made. The existence of several photographs of the ship's exterior assisted greatly in the process of evaluating the credibility of some of the questionable sources.

While specifications of the *Monitor* were the subject of almost continuous adjustment during construction, the general design and basic features of the vessel remained essentially unaltered. Detailed analysis of available marine architectural sources confirmed that the *Monitor's* prototype design remained unique (fig. 4). Although many of the characteristics which combined to make the *Monitor* unique were utilized in later classes of turreted, heavily armored and low freeboard vessels that were built in the United States, their design was unquestionably altered from its original form. Through comparative historical analysis, a series of distinguishing characteristics which could be considered reliable criteria for identifying the *Monitor* were isolated. To increase the accuracy of this method of identification, as many of the specifications pertaining to these features as possible were determined.

Perhaps the most obvious of those characteristics determined to represent reliable indicators of the *Monitor's* identity was the turret, which Ericsson designed to house the vessel's ordnance. In spite of the fact that this was one of the most frequently reproduced aspects of the vessel, this first turret remained unique in both design and specifications. Similarly, the pilothouse located slightly aft of the bow was determined to be another of the *Monitor's* identifying characteristics. Unlike the turret, the pilothouse designed for the first ironclad was never reproduced, due to deficiencies in its location and design. The armor belt which overlapped the lower hull of the battery comprised a third identifying feature. Because of their massive construction, these portions of the vessel were anticipated to be readily identifiable regardless of physical deterioration at the site.

Under the bow a unique anchor well, which penetrated the projecting armor platform, and the distinctive four-fluked anchor were singled out. It

Fig. 4. *One of the more detailed and historically accurate of several existing plans of the U.S.S. Monitor. (Courtesy of the Naval History Division, U.S. Navy.)*

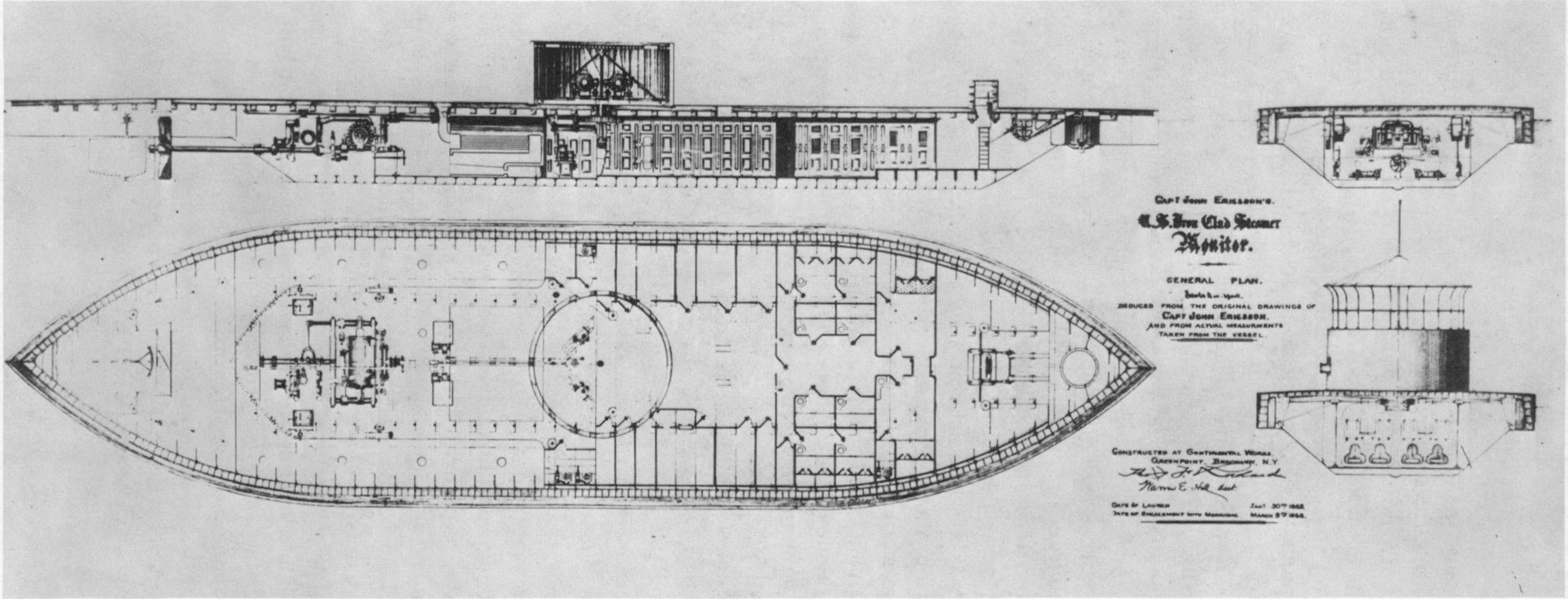

was also felt that the unusual configuration of the lower hull would prove to be a useful factor in the identification process. In an effort to save both construction time and expenses, Ericsson designed the lower hull with a virtually flat bottom, extremely hard chine, and flat sides which rose to the inside of the bottom of the overlapping lip of the armor belt. The extremely blunt bow and stern were plated vertically while the plating of the lower hull ran athwartships rather than longitudinally, as had generally been the custom. This configuration and plating technique eliminated the expensive and time-consuming necessity for bending plates to obtain a more sea-kindly and conventional hull design. In the stern the unusual propeller, skeg, and rudder arrangement were considered to be reliable keys to the *Monitor's* identity. Although there were additional details, these criteria formed the nucleus for the visual evaluation of the sites with the photographic and television equipment.

Because almost all of the data collected at the site during the *Eastward* cruise were in the form of random photographic or television-tape records, identification of the heavily damaged *Monitor* proved to be a difficult and time-consuming process. In order to correlate the data from and location of each individual camera pass, small photomosaics of significant features were constructed. These were carefully related to drawings of the remains, which were also produced with the assistance of the video and photographic data. This technique tied the random camera passes together in the form of a composite picture.

Measurements of significant features were scaled from a series of references of known size which had been suspended at known distances below the various camera pods. When these references came in contact with features on the wreck it was possible to accurately compute their size. Once this had been accomplished, it was possible to calculate both the sizes and locations of other features which did not come into direct contact with the references yet existed in the same horizontal plane. Identification was made possible by comparing these data with a series of features and specifications which the most credible historical records revealed were unique to the *Monitor*.

While the accuracy of this method was relative to the reliability of the historical sources and the accuracy of the system of recording and measurement, correlations between archival documents and the actual remains proved to be enough to quickly eliminate the first site visually examined and positively identify the second as that of the *Monitor*.

The first site visually examined was found in 320 feet of water, nineteen miles south-southeast of Cape Hatteras. Aside from a light coat of marine fouling organisms, the vessel was found to be in an excellent state of preservation. A composite drawing of the site (fig. 5) produced from the photographic and television-tape records revealed that a semicircular feature, which had

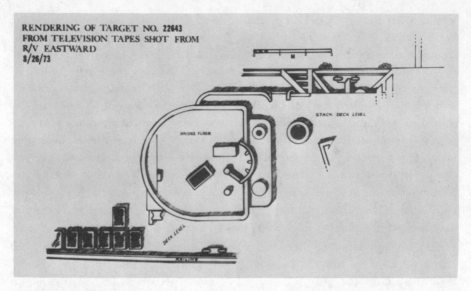

Fig. 5. *A composite rendering of the first site examined with photographic and closed-circuit television equipment. The configuration of the hull and the existence of a well-defined superstructure and bridge eliminated the wreck as possibly that of the* Monitor. *Note the modern winch head on the portside of the bridge. (Courtesy of the Division of Archives and History, North Carolina Department of Cultural Resources.)*

previously offered some encouragement, was the remains of the ship's bridge. The conventional hull configuration, with its soft contours and permanent bulwark—the presence of a well-defined superstructure—was sufficient to eliminate the wreck. This evidence and the presence of modern deck machinery indicated that the vessel was of twentieth-century origin.

The second site was located fifteen miles south-southeast of Cape Hatteras in 220 feet of water. In spite of heavy structural damage and marine fouling, detailed analysis of the data collected at the site revealed that the distinctive features of the capsized vessel corresponded with those which historical research indicated could be considered reliable criteria for identifying the *Monitor* (fig. 6).

The most obvious of these was the presence of the displaced turret. Although fully three-quarters of this feature was obscured by the port quarter of the vessel's hull, sufficient data were found for comparative purposes (fig. 7). Measurements of the thickness of the turret wall, scaled from the references in

Fig. 6 (facing page). *Complete photomosaic of the* Monitor *site prepared by naval photographic experts and a scale drawing of the remains produced to assist in the evaluation of the photographic data from both the* Eastward *and Alcoa Seaprobe cruises. (Mosaic, courtesy of the Naval Photographic Reconnaissance Center, U.S. Navy; drawing by Steve Daniels, courtesy of the Office of Marine Affairs, North Carolina Department of Administration.)*

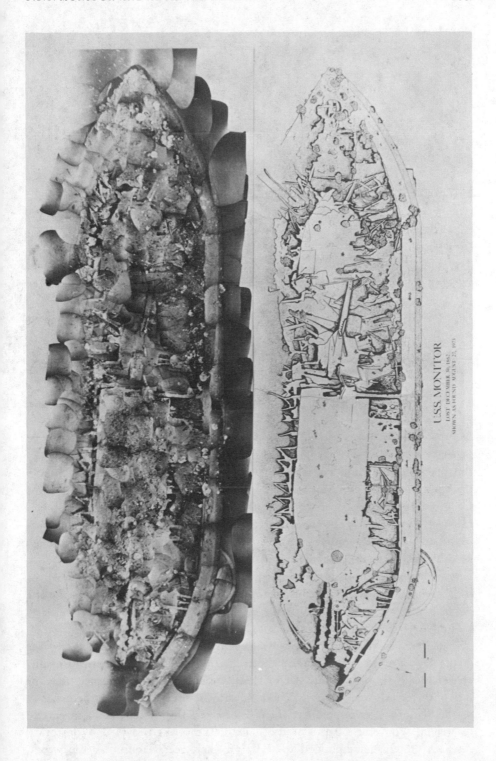

U.S.S. MONITOR
LOST DECEMBER 30, 1862
SHOWN AS FOUND AUGUST 22, 1973

Fig. 7. *The displaced turret, partially obscured by the port quarter armor belt. The heavy wrought iron transverse support which formed part of the turret suspension can be seen in the lower right corner of the frame.* (*Photograph by Glenn Tillman*, Alcoa Seaprobe *136–074, courtesy of Alcoa Marine Corporation.*)

the photographic data collected at the site, confirmed the eight-inch wall thickness indicated by historical sources.[9] By extending the exposed arc of the turret the full 360 degrees and using the wall thickness as a scale, a diameter of twenty-two feet was obtained. This figure corresponded with the twenty one-foot-four-inch exterior diameter indicated by historical research.[10] Although vertical measurement was considerably more difficult, an approximate height of seven feet six inches was determined. The inconsistency between the nine-foot height[11] indicated by the historical research and the actual height at the site may be partially resolved by scour settling and the accumulation of sand around the base of the turret.

While concretions and the growth of fouling organisms have obscured the distinctive exterior rivet pattern of the turret, several other distinguishing characteristics were evident. All of these indicated that the turret, like the hull of the vessel, was inverted. The most convincing evidence was the presence of the distinctive crossmember which intersected the turret base and carried its weight. The recess depth of the floor of the turret provided by historical research closely corresponded to the eight-inch recess found at the wreck.

Also apparent was the absence of the remains of the chest-high, one-inch-thick rifle armor which was added to the top of the turret following the encounter with the *Virginia*.[12] This, and the absence of evidence of either the canopy stanchions or their sockets, which were located inside the top of the turret wall, adds credibility to the conclusion that the turret was upside down.

Finally, it was significant to compare the distinct difference in the fouling organisms found on the horizontal surfaces of the armor belt with those on the horizontal surface of the turret wall. A corrosion and marine-fouling specialist from the Francis L. Laque Corrosion Laboratory, a subsidiary of International Nickel, interpreted the absence of heavy fouling on the upper turret wall as evidence that the top of the structure was covered with a layer of nonferrous metal. Since the turret was to have rested on a machined brass ring recessed into the deck, it is logical to assume that a similar ring was secured to the bottom of the turret to reduce wear and provide the watertight seal required by the contract with the navy.[13] While no direct historical evidence has been found to support this, it can be documented that the technique was being utilized in the later turreted vessels constructed during the Civil War.[14]

Although no evidence of the gunports can be found in either the photographic or television-tape data, this fact cannot be considered significant. It is reported that the guns were mounted perpendicular to the crossmember, which intersects the floor of the turret. Considering the present orientation of the turret, this would place the ports either directly under the hull of the vessel or under the armor belt on the port quarter. While possibly exposed in the latter position, none of the random camera passes covered the turret wall in this area. Even with adequate camera control to inspect the area, the possibility exists that nothing conclusive could be found because the ports were fitted with iron covers which were dogged down and caulked during foul weather. It is more than reasonable to assume that this was the case during the *Monitor's* last voyage. In this condition it would be only a matter of time before fouling organisms obscured all surface evidence of their location.

With the exception of extensive damage to the stern and starboard quarter, the armored "raft," with its distinctive overlapping armor belt, was found to be in very good condition (fig. 7). Because the port quarter rests on the displaced turret, the armor belt on that side was completely exposed, almost to the bow. Measurements of the projection made above the turret produced a horizontal width of thirty inches and a vertical height of approximately five feet. Immediately inside the armor belt the four-inch angle iron used to reinforce the joint between the armor platform and the lower hull can be seen.[15] On the starboard and lower side of the hull the armor belt was almost completely obscured by the bottom.

Aft of the only substantial athwartships bulkhead, located almost amidships, the lower hull was found to be in an excellent state of preservation. Plating

Fig. 8. *Natural deterioration of the hull plating exposing the framing pattern along the starboard side of the lower hull. (Photograph by Glenn Tillman,* Alcoa Seaprobe *133– 310, courtesy of Alcoa Marine Corporation.)*

on the bottom of the hull remained virtually intact as did the vertical plating of the stern. Along the portside of the lower hull a considerable portion of the athwartships plating was found to be either missing or badly damaged. Only occasional plates and braces remained to testify to their prior existence. On the starboard side only the unreinforced areas of the plates have deteriorated, leaving the remains attached to the reinforcing iron ribs underneath (fig. 8). In spite of heavy fouling, the faint outline of the false keel could be seen near the extreme stern and the harsh chine is clearly evident.

Deterioration of the hull plating along the portside has exposed many of the interior details of the ship's construction. Immediately inside the armor belt is a series of "beam knees," which Ericsson designed to support both the inside of the armor belt and the ends of the deck beams (fig. 9). From the base of each of these brackets a diagonal brace extends down to the underside of the deck beam and connects to the top of a stanchion. This series of vertical stanchions follows the line of the vessel's chine and connects the deck beams with the transverse floor "timbers" at the bottom of the hull.[16]

Although much of the exposed interior of the hull was cluttered by the remains of the plating, one of the coal scuttles which penetrated the deck

Fig. 9. *Inboard of the port quarter armor belt* (top) *showing the exposed iron beam knees. A displaced hatch reveals one of the coal scuttles which provided direct access to bunkers located directly below.* (*Photograph by Glenn Tillman,* Alcoa Seaprobe *134–283, courtesy of Alcoa Marine Corporation.*)

slightly inboard of the port armor belt remains exposed. The chutes, sixteen inches in diameter, provided access to the coal bunkers located directly below, along both the starboard side and portside of the lower hull (fig. 9).

From the extreme stern of the lower hull, the skeg (an extension of the false keel) and propeller shaft can be traced aft some nine feet to the screw and a wrought-iron post, which contains the bearing for the aft end of the propeller shaft (fig. 10). Although heavily encrusted with marine organisms and possibly damaged, two of the four blades of the propeller are readily apparent. The unique "equipoise" rudder has been carried away by the damage to the stern but appears on the bottom, immediately under its original position aft of the propeller (fig. 11). While portions of the thin plate and wooden core of the rudder have deteriorated, its distinct outline and four-inch axle remain intact. Because of the heavy damage to the starboard quarter, little of the under-plating of the armor platform remains intact aft of the lower hull. However, it is not unreasonable to assume that these remains, like the rudder, may be located immediately below their original position.[17]

In addition, the geographical location of the site, the orientation of the hull, and the present position of the vessel must be considered significant. The site lies inside the search area isolated by historical research. Although the location is eleven miles northeast of Commander Trenchard's estimated position and eleven miles north-northeast of Commander Bankhead's estimated position of the sinking, the discrepancy cannot be considered unusual.[18] The lack of accurate positioning capability reflected in the log of the *Rhode Island*

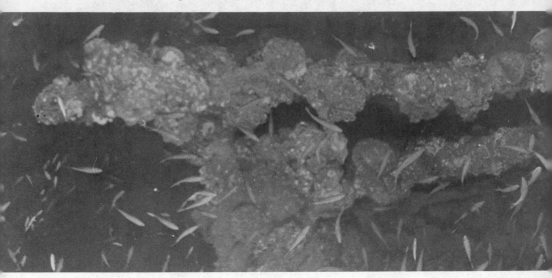

Fig. 10. *Heavy marine fouling virtually obscures the propeller located immediately below the skeg. This feature forms the highest point at the site. (Photographed by Glenn Tillman,* Alcoa Seaprobe *136–136, courtesy of Alcoa Marine Corporation.)*

has already been established. Considering the conditions at the time of the *Monitor's* sinking, it is inconceivable that they could improve appreciably. Aboard the sinking *Monitor,* Commander Bankhead's positioning capability could only have been less accurate. The disparity in their positions for the sinking tends to confirm this fact.

The orientation of the hull should also be considered in relation to the conditions at the time of the sinking. As has already been pointed out, the anchor of the *Monitor* was released in an effort to bring the bow of the powerless vessel into the seas.[19] With gale winds piling up a heavy sea from the southwest, it is reasonable to assume that the anchor would bring the bow into the southwest. This orientation is confirmed by the sonar records, which indicate that the wreck is aligned southwest to northeast with the area of

Fig. 11. *Remains of the "equipoise" rudder which Swedish-American engineer John Ericsson designed for the* Monitor. (*Photograph by Glenn Tillman,* Alcoa Seaprobe *134–085, courtesy of Alcoa Marine Corporation.*)

maximum relief at the northeast extremity. Visual analysis confirms that the highest point on the wreck is the remains of the stern.

While it is quite natural for a wood or iron ship loaded with cargo or in ballast to sink in an upright position, exactly the opposite seems to be the case for heavily armored vessels. Because its weight distribution is very similar to that of the *Monitor,* it is perhaps worthwhile to note the case of the monitor U.S.S. *Tecumseh,* sunk during the Civil War battle of Mobile Bay, Alabama, on August 5, 1864.[20] Located and examined in 1967, the *Tecumseh* was found to have capsized on sinking. Since the *Monitor,* like the *Tecumseh,* carried an excessive amount of weight on its armor platform, it is logical to assume that the vessel also capsized once sufficient water filled the lower hull.[21]

When the *Alcoa Seaprobe* visited the site in April of 1974, a complete photographic and video-tape record was made of the entire vessel. This evidence confirmed the identification of the *Monitor* and revealed the condition of the previously unseen forward portions of the wreck. Heavy sanding on the lower starboard side has not obscured the bow. The five-foot-diameter anchor well (fig. 12) located in the forward section of the upper hull was evident despite heavy marine growth.[22] The forward portions of the lower hull have suffered more damage than the stern, which has, to some degree, been supported by the heavy machinery located there. In the area of the officers' and crew's quarters, the wreck has been reduced to the level of the upper hull.

In spite of the damage, the wreck is one of the most valuable mid-nineteenth-century archeological sites available for scientific investigation. From both the historical and technological perspective, the wreck represents an invaluable source of information unavailable elsewhere. It has already been shown that while the contemporary historical records have preserved a great deal of information about the *Monitor,* they are often incomplete and frequently contradictory. Only a brief exposure to this material is necessary to confirm that relying on the historical data to answer questions about the ship is no substitute for a thorough scientific investigation of the wreck itself. This is particularly true of the details of the interior of the vessel. At best these data are extremely sketchy and has frequently been omitted entirely. Excellent plans and specifications for the later classes of monitors are available; however, generalizations cannot be drawn because of the myriad changes in their design and construction.

ADDENDUM

On January 30, 1975, one hundred thirteen years to the day after the *Monitor* was launched, the wreck site was declared the nation's first marine sanctuary, protecting it for additional scientific investigation already being planned.

Fig. 12 (facing page). *Extreme bow of the* Monitor *with circular anchor well* (arrow). (*Photograph by Glenn Tillman,* Alcoa Seaprobe *136–118, courtesy of Alcoa Marine Corporation.*)

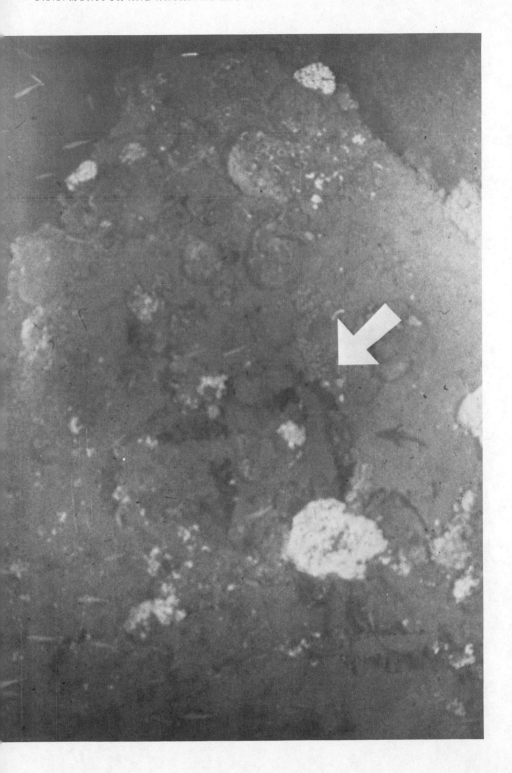

NOTES

1. Comdr. J. P. Bankhead to Acting Rear Adm. S. P. Lee, 1 January 1863, *Official Records of the Union and Confederate Navies in the War of the Rebellion*, ser. 1, vol. 8 (Washington, D.C.: Department of the Navy, 1894-1927), pp. 347-49 (hereafter this series is cited as ORN).

2. S. P. Lee to Capt. Percival Drayton, 26 December 1862, ser. 1, vol. 8, ORN, p. 341.

3. Originally the destination of the *Monitor* and the *Passaic* was to have been Wilmington. However, the lack of reliable information concerning the bars at the entrances to the Cape Fear River and the unknown strength of Confederate fortifications in the area precluded this possibility.

4. Robert W. Daly, *Aboard the U.S.S. MONITOR, 1862: The Letters of Acting Paymaster William Frederick Keeler, U.S. Navy, to His Wife, Anna* (Annapolis: U.S. Naval Institute, 1964), pp. 20-27.

5. S. P. Lee to Gideon Welles, 3 January 1863, ser. 1, vol. 8, ORN, p. 340.

6. Clay Blair, *Diving for Pleasure and Treasure* (New York: World Publishing Co., 1960), p. 348; John Broadwater, "A Search for the U.S.S. MONITOR," *International Journal of Nautical Archaeology and Underwater Exploration* 4, no. 1 (1974) 117-21.

7. Although the authors of several popular treatments of the subject (e.g. Blair, *Diving for Pleasure and Treasure*) have made reference to a diary which notes sighting the *Monitor* in shallow water north of Buxton, an extensive search by historian James Pleasants of Buxton failed to reveal any indication of the diary's existence.

8. The remains of the *Oriental* have been identified historically by the National Park Service, U.S. Department of the Interior. J. G. Newton, O. H. Pilkey, J. O. Blanton, *An Oceanographic Atlas of the Carolina Continental Margin* (Raleigh: Duke University Marine Laboratory, 1971); page 29 additionally cites the remains on Bodie Island.

9. John Ericsson to Commodore Joseph Smith, 17 October 1861, Records of the Bureau of Yards and Docks, Record Group 71, National Archives Building, Washington, D.C. (hereafter records in the National Archives Building are cited as RG 00, NA).

10. Alban Stimers to Gideon Welles, 15 November 1861, "Copies of the Letters from John Ericsson to Hon. Gideon Welles ... Commodore Joseph Smith ... in relation to the building of the original MONITOR and similar Vessels," Entry 186, Box 113, Bureau of Ships, RG 19, NA.

11. Ericsson to Joseph Smith, 27 September 1861, Records of the Bureau of Yards and Docks, RG 71, NA.

12. Paymaster Keeler makes reference to the addition of chest-high rifle armor on top of the turret following the engagement with the C.S.S. *Virginia*. Daly, *Aboard the U.S.S. MONITOR*.

13. U.S., Department of the Navy, "Letter of the Secretary of the Navy, Communicating ... Information in Relation to the Construction of the Ironclad MONITOR," *Executive Documents No. 86*, 40th Cong., 2d sess., 1868, pp. 6-7.

14. "Ironclad Vessels," *Harper's*, September, 1862, p. 441.

15. "The Ericsson Battery," *Scientific American* 6, no. 5 (February 1862): 73.

16. John Ericsson, "The MONITORS," *Century Magazine*, December 1885, p. 290.

17. "The Ericsson Battery," p. 73.

18. Both estimates of the position of the loss of the *Monitor* were made after the fact and at best were based upon questionable records.

19. J. P. Bankhead to S. P. Lee, 1 January 1863, ser. 1, vol. 8, ORN, p. 348.

20. U.S., Department of the Navy, Naval History Division, *Civil War Naval Chronology: 1861–1865* (Washington, D.C.: Department of the Navy, 1971), pp. iv–95.

21. Baker, Bolster, Leach & Singleterry, "Examination of the Corrosion Salt Contamination of Structural Metal from the U.S.S. *Tecumseh*," Naval Research Laboratory Memorandum Report, Naval Research Laboratory (Washington, D.C., 1969), p. 1.

22. Ericsson, "The MONITORS," p. 282.

Commentary

In his paper Professor Coletta has necessarily relied heavily upon Fiske's autobiography, *From Midshipman to Rear-Admiral*. The book is one of the best accounts we have of the development of the "new navy." Fiske's career spanned decades of immense technological change, and when he left the navy, he had risen to a position which was roughly comparable to that of chief of Naval Operations. The question is, how reliable is Fiske, the author? He was vigorous, opinionated, and contentious. But is he a good witness? A question so basic as this can hardly be settled in a short commentary; however, the effort may be interesting and useful. My approach will be to discuss briefly Fiske's autobiography, select a particular incident from it, and then measure his account against documentary evidence which I have come across while doing research at the National Archives.

Fiske published his autobiography in 1919. He seems to have written it largely to vindicate himself in his struggle with Secretary of the Navy Josephus Daniels over the need for a general staff. He devoted most of the book, however, to his career. He did not rely completely on his memory, for he quotes from papers and a diary. The result is a well-written, chronological mixture of professional incidents and personal anecdotes. Fiske was a proud man. He claimed credit for a large number of inventions, but he balanced his occasional stridency with a sense of humor.[1]

The incident I have selected from Fiske's autobiography which I will compare with archival evidence deals with the application of electric power to turning gun turrets. The problem is really part of a much larger issue. Those men who designed and built the ships of the new navy had to devise the means to move heavy weights and equipment which were aboard ship—to perform those jobs which, in the earlier days of sail and cannon, had been done by muscle, block, and tackle. Turning turrets that weighed several hundred tons was one of the more difficult assignments which naval architects and marine engineers faced when Fiske was a young lieutenant.

To summarize Fiske's account briefly: He stated that he reported to the Bureau of Ordnance in October 1894. The chief of the bureau was William T. Sampson, a line officer later to win fame at the battle of Santiago in the Spanish-American War. When Fiske reported to the bureau, Sampson was working on the application of electric power to turning turrets. Since Fiske already had a considerable reputation in the area of electricity, Sampson welcomed him and set him to work. Fiske turned to several electric companies, among them General Electric. Near the end of 1895 the company developed what looked like a promising system at its plant in Schenectady. Sampson visited the factory and was pleased with what he saw.[2]

The General Electric system looked feasible for the armored cruiser *Brooklyn*, which was nearing completion on the building ways of William Cramp and Sons at Philadelphia.[3] However, other bureaus took part in the design and construction of ships. Of these, the most important at this time, besides Ordnance, were the Bureau of Construction and Repair and the Bureau of Steam Engineering.[4] Two officers from Construction and Repair came to Schenectady where Fiske showed them the General Electric equipment. The two men recommended against installing the system on the *Brooklyn*. In their view, steam was superior in reliability, cost, and economy of space.

Fiske was crushed. He wrote a long letter to Sampson, repeating once again the advantages of electricity. Knowing that these arguments had been used before and had failed, Fiske searched for a new idea. The *Brooklyn* would carry four turrets. Why not, proposed Fiske, power two by steam and two by electricity? According to Fiske, Sampson was pleased and adopted the scheme as the position of the Bureau of Ordnance.

The other bureaus, however, remained obdurate. Furthermore, under the navy's procedures, it was the secretary of the navy—a civilian—who had to make the decision. To quote Fiske:

> The man who had to decide was the Secretary of the Navy, who knew almost nothing about any phase of the subject, and least of all about the most important phase, which was the applicability of any kind of system to the requirements of naval gunnery in war. Captain Sampson knew a great deal about this, whereas the Bureau of Steam Engineering and the Bureau of Construction knew almost nothing. The result was that the Secretary could not come to any decision whatever. Thus this important matter was held up *because of the lack of any one who combined the necessary authority with the necessary knowledge.*[5]

But when the secretary at last made up his mind, he accepted the Sampson-Fiske recommendation.

Now what do the records at the Archives show on the subject? Before answering this, I must give some background.

As Fiske related, steam had been the main power used to turn gun turrets since the Civil War, but it had serious drawbacks. In the first place, the system required steamlines. If these ruptured, they could scald the crew. Furthermore, the means of controlling the steam-driven, turret-turning machinery was cumbersome. The gun captain had to manipulate a long lever and, since the speed of rotation was not constant, he frequently had to move his eyes off the target. To circumvent such difficulties, other approaches had been developed but these, too, had been found wanting. Compressed air was hard to maintain and had almost the same defects as steam. Hydraulic power was superior in some respects to both steam and compressed air, but maintenance was a problem.[6] With all of its disadvantages, steam held its favored position for turning turrets because there was nothing better.

By 1890 the question of power for turrets took on new significance. In that year Congress approved the construction of the navy's first battleships—the *Indiana*, the *Massachusetts*, and the *Oregon*. In the American tradition, these were to be heavily armed ships. Each was to carry six turrets, two of which were to have pairs of thirteen-inch guns and four were to have pairs of eight-inch guns. The ships were also to have a generous assortment of smaller weapons, but these could be handled by manpower.[7] It was the six turrets that were the problem.

The navy contracted with Cramp in Philadelphia to build the *Indiana* and *Massachusetts* and with the Union Iron Works at San Francisco to construct the *Oregon*. The record is not very clear, but apparently the two Cramp-built ships were to have steam-powered turrets and the Union Iron Works battleship was to have hydraulic-powered turrets.[8]

In late 1892 or early 1893 Cramp proposed to turn the eight-inch turrets of the *Indiana* and *Massachusetts* with electric power. Sampson considered the proposal and turned it down. To the chiefs of the other bureaus he explained that no satisfactory experiments had yet been made which had proved the efficiency of electricity for turning turrets. Therefore, he believed that the original scheme for the ships should be followed.[9] Since Sampson was not proposing any changes, his recommendation provoked no reaction. This was the situation when Fiske reported for duty to the Bureau of Ordnance.

The next document I found was Fiske's report to Sampson, dated November 13, 1895.[10] It stated that the General Electric equipment had operated satisfactorily, that it was simple and rugged, that the parts were easily accessible for repair, and that the system could be controlled easily by the operator. In his book Fiske dated the report of the naval constructors as December 11, 1895. The Archives has a document of that date signed by Joseph H. Linnard, a naval constructor.[11] Linnard favored steam because of its reliability, simplicity, and savings in weight, space, and expense. Moreover, installing the electrical equipment on the *Brooklyn* might delay completing the cruiser.

Fiske in his book described the bitter and prolonged fight between the bureaus and the struggle to get the secretary to make up his mind. According to the evidence in the Archives, what happened was somewhat different.

Fiske dated his report November 13, 1895. Linnard dated his December 11, 1895. On December 19, Philip Hichborn, chief constructor of the navy, addressed the secretary, recapitulating Linnard's arguments and recommending against installing the electrical system on the *Brooklyn*. On January 4, 1896, Sampson sent his case to the secretary. Not only did he attempt to refute the arguments of the Bureau of Construction and Repair, but he recommended that two of the four turrets of the *Brooklyn* be turned by electricity and two by steam. In this way, both methods could be tried fairly. Yet to be heard from was the Bureau of Steam Engineering. On January 22, Chief Engineer George W. Melville took a position against the electrical system, arguing that steam was reliable and electricity was not. To paraphrase Melville, when a steam system failed, you could find the trouble quickly, but when something went wrong with an electrical system, all you had were dead wires and an urgent need for a skilled technician. All the different views had been submitted with Melville's memorandum.

Only three days later, January 25, 1896, the acting secretary of the navy approved Sampson's proposal. This was fast action for the leisurely days of the 1890s. There is reason to think that it would be considered fast action today in the Department of the Navy or the Department of Defense.

Why was Fiske accurate in one part of his account and not in the next? One explanation, of course, is that there is no inconsistency at all. My research on the navy between 1898 and 1917 has been going on for some time and is incomplete. Perhaps I simply failed to run across documents which show that the acting secretary's decision was held up for a few agonizing months. Although this is possible, I am inclined to doubt it. The Archives also has another memorandum written in 1915 which summarizes the steps taken in the adoption of electric power to turning turrets. The paper makes no reference to delays concerning the *Brooklyn*. It did, however, refer to delays concerning other ships, and possibly this is what Fiske had in mind.[12] Perhaps, too, Fiske's memory misled him.

Even if it was a lapse of memory, the incident is significant, for it shows Fiske's attitude toward civilian authority. He tended to be hard on civilians, particularly politicians. He liked the neatness, orderliness, and precision of military life. He liked the logic and power of engineering. He had no sympathy or understanding of the dilemma faced by a secretary who had to decide between conflicting recommendations from his technical advisers. Fiske's argument that the secretary should trust Sampson because he knew more about the problem could not have been very helpful. Although Fiske did not mention it, those bureau chiefs who opposed Sampson were men of stature and achievement.[13] Perhaps they were more qualified in their fields than Sampson was in ordnance. Curiously, Fiske does not, I think, give himself enough credit for the idea of dividing the *Brooklyn* turrets between steam and electricity. The proposal cut through all the argument by proposing such a fair test that a nontechnical individual could understand the results. It might have been Fiske's idea that solved the secretary's problem.

To conclude, I believe that Fiske is generally reliable in recounting facts, but perhaps he overstated his opinions. He saw the problems of technological innovation far too simply and he regarded them impatiently. Fiske was a man of strong character. The clash with Daniels that led to his resignation was over a matter of principle. Finally, and I hope that Professor Coletta agrees with me, the history of the navy between 1898 and 1917 needs reappraisal. For such a task, Fiske's autobiography offers a useful point of departure, but it must be used cautiously.

NOTES

1. Bradley A. Fiske, *From Midshipman to Rear-Admiral* (New York: Century Co., 1919).
2. Ibid. Fiske describes the incident on pp. 198-203.
3. The ship was well along. The keel had been laid on 2 August 1892. See U.S., Department of the Navy, *Dictionary of American Naval Fighting Ships*, vol. 1, app. 2, s.v. "Cruisers, 1882-1958."
4. The Bureaus of Ordnance, Construction and Repair and Steam Engineering were the main organizations which made up the Board on Construction. The board was established in 1889. The Bureau of Construction and Repair was given general supervision over the board in 1894. See Charles Oscar Paullin, *Paullin's History of Naval Administration, 1775-1911: A Collection of Articles from the U.S. Naval Institute Proceedings* (Annapolis: U.S. Naval Institute, 1968), pp. 380-81. The importance of the board may be underestimated. Its minutes are in Entry 179, General Records of the Department of the Navy, 1798-1947, Record Group 80, National Archives Building, Washington, D.C. (Hereafter records in the National Archives are referred to as E—, RG—, NA.)
5. Fiske, *From Midshipman to Rear-Admiral*, p. 202. The emphasis is Fiske's.
6. For brief descriptions of the approaches, see William F. Fullam and Thomas C. Hart, *Text-Book of Ordnance and Gunnery* (Annapolis: U.S. Naval Institute, 1903), pp. 201-3.
7. For armament, see *Dictionary of American Naval Fighting Ships*, vol. 1, app. 1, s.v. "Battleships, 1886-1948."
8. Reference to the original installation (but not necessarily the planned installation) is in W. C. Dean, Research Data Memorandum, 6 March 1914, vol. 2, "Research Data, 1913-29," E 118, RG 19, NA.
9. W. T. Sampson, Chief of Bureau of Ordnance, Memorandum for the Board on Construction, 27 February 1893, E 11, RG 74, NA; Minutes, Board on Construction, 27 February 1893, E 179, Box 1, RG 80, NA.

10. For convenience, this note cites all the documents on the turret recommendations. Fiske to Chief, Bureau of Ordnance, 13 November 1895; Linnard to Chief, Bureau of Construction and Repair, 12 December 1895; Hichborn to Secretary of the Navy, 19 December 1895; Sampson to Secretary of the Navy, 4 January 1896; Melville to Secretary of the Navy, 22 January 1896; Acting Secretary McAdoo, "Brooklyn: Motive Power for Operating Turrets; Two by Steam and Two by Electricity," 25 January 1896. All from Miscellaneous Correspondence and Report, 1883–1895, E 83, RG 19, NA.

11. For a biographical sketch of Linnard, see his obituary in *Transactions of the Society of Naval Architects and Marine Engineers* 43 (1935): 313–14.

12. C. M. Hamblin, Research Data Memorandum, 16 October 1915, vol. 3, "Research Data, 1913–1929," E 118, RG 19, NA.

13. Hichborn is credited with inventing the Franklin lifebuoy and the Hichborn balanced turret. Biographical data on Hichborn is hard to find. See *Who Was Who in America, 1897–1942*, vol. 1 (Chicago: A. N. Marquis Company, 1942), p. 559. Because Melville was an Arctic explorer and engineer, secondary biographical material is readily available. A useful brief article is George W. Grupp, "Rear Admiral George W. Melville, As a Man and Engineer-in-Chief of the Navy," *U.S. Naval Institute Proceedings* 74 (May 1948): 612–17.

IV

THE NAVY
IN EARLIER WARS:
SOURCES
AND RESEARCH POTENTIALS

A Selected Photographic Essay
of U.S. Navy Sailing Ships

Pictorial resources for naval history in the National Archives are abundant and rich in detail. The selection in this gallery represents rare photographic coverage of some of the U.S. Navy's sailing ships. Whereas visual representations of early sailing ships and ship-board life are most commonly depicted through paintings and drawings, they are inevitably subject to artistic interpretation and embellishment. The camera illustrates the beauty and grace of these ships and preserves a bygone era as an accurate pictorial record.

U.S.S. Bear, built in Scotland as a
sealing vessel, purchased by the
U.S. Navy on January 28, 1884.
Bear (left and above) *and the U.S.S.*
Thetis *successfully rescued Lt. A. W.
Greeley (U.S.A.) and the six other
members of his marooned Arctic
expedition at Cape Sabine in June
1884. Rear Adm. R. E. Byrd used*
Bear *on his Antarctic expedition of
1933–35. She made two more voyages
to the Antarctic before the outbreak
of World War II. (RG 19, No. 19-N-
12839 and No. 14991.)*

**U.S.S. Brooklyn, wooden screw sloop, commissioned January 26, 1859,
by Capt. David Glasgow Farragut.** Brooklyn *served in the Civil War with
the West Gulf Blockading Squadron and participated in the attacks on
Forts Jackson and Saint Philip; the capture of New Orleans; and bombard-
ments on the Galveston, Texas, and Vicksburg, Mississippi, batteries. In
August 1864 at the battle of Mobile Bay,* Brooklyn *led the fleet toward the
bay entrance but her hesitation to go through the field of floating torpedoes (mines) at a crucial moment prompted Captain Farragut to proclaim "Damn the torpedoes," and sail around* Brooklyn, *himself taking the
lead in the U.S.S.* Hartford. *(RG 19, No. 19-N-13743.)*

"YANKEE RACE HORSE"

U.S.S. Constellation, one of the first six frigates authorized by act of Congress, launched September 7, 1797, in Baltimore, Maryland. *Constellation's first cruise, from June to August 1798, was to convoy merchant ships to sea. During this cruise she showed admirable qualities, including a sailing speed that won her the nickname* "Yankee Race Horse." *Constellation saw her first action in the quasi war with France, when she captured the forty-gun frigate* L'Insurgente *on February 9, 1799. In the course of this early dispute with France,* Constellation *seized two privateers and successfully engaged two major warships. Her accomplishments proved the seaworthiness and excellent fighting characteristics of this first major type of American naval ship.* Constellation *went on to engage in the Barbary wars, the War of 1812, and the Civil War. During peacetime* Constellation *circumnavigated the globe several times and participated in many diplomatic and politico-military missions. She remained in active commission until August 1955, when she returned to Baltimore Harbor where she is currently on public display. (RG 19, No. 19-N-56D-1.)*

"OLD IRONSIDES"

U.S.S. Constitution, launched at Boston on October 21, 1797. *The Constitution is perhaps the most famous of all U.S. warships. She saw service in the quasi war with France, Barbary wars, War of 1812, Mexican War, Civil War, World War I, and World War II. Today she remains in commission as the oldest ship on the Navy List. As depicted in the photograph of her as a training ship,* Constitution *had reached such a state of disrepair that she was almost broken up. However, patriotic citizens, including Justice Oliver Wendell Holmes and the school children of Boston, refused to allow her to come to an ignominious end. Sufficient funds were collected to complete her restoration in July 1931, and today she rests in Boston Harbor as a proud and worthy representative of the navy's era of great sailing ships. (RG 19, No. 19-N-20-2-12.)*

U.S.S. Constitution in use as a receiving ship, 1882–84 *(RG 19, No. 19-N-9721.)*

OVERLEAF:

U.S.S. Dale, sloop-of-war, launched November 8, 1839, at the Philadelphia Navy Yard. *Her first cruise took her around Cape Horn to the navy's Pacific Station, where she was based at Valparaiso. She cruised the coast of South America until ordered north for duty in the Mexican War. Not only did she capture several Mexican privateers and merchantmen, but landing parties she sent ashore raised the American flag over the towns of Guaymas and Muelje. This photograph was probably taken when Dale served as a training ship at the Naval Academy between 1867 and 1884. (RG 19, No. 19-N-11467.)*

U.S.S. Cumberland (Training Ship No. 1), steel-hulled sailing bark, launched August 17, 1904, at the Boston Navy Yard. *She was commissioned as an auxiliary to the U.S.S.* Constellation *and 200 apprentice seamen were immediately quartered aboard her. She continued with this duty until November 1912 when she was assigned to the Navy Station at Guantanamo Bay, Cuba. After World War I she served as a station ship at the U.S. Naval Academy until she was decommissioned in October 1946. (RG 19, No. 19-N-13898.)*

**U.S.S. Essex, wooden screw steamer,
commissioned at Boston Navy Yard,
October 3, 1876.** Essex *patrolled off the
west coast of Africa and in the South
Atlantic from 1878 to 1879. She saw duty
with the navy's Pacific Station during
1881–82, then transferred to the Asiatic
Squadron for two years. Regarded as one of
the finest of the fleet,* Essex *was next designated as a training ship and served in this
capacity from 1893 to 1930. (RG 19, No.
19-N-12903.)*

U.S.S. Galena, wooden screw steamer, commissioned at Norfolk, August 26, 1880. *Notable among Galena's many years of service was a special mission beginning March 11, 1885, when she arrived at Aspinwall to offer protection to the lives and property of American citizens during a revolution that threatened to interrupt traffic over the Isthmus of Panama. On March 30, after some revolutionists had seized the Pacific Mail Line steamer* Colon, Galena *recaptured the steamer and returned her to her owners. The next day a landing party from* Galena *went ashore and extinguished a fire in the town of Colon which had been set by the revolutionists. The landing force saved part of the town and all the property of the Pacific mail company. On April 10 a force of 600 sailors and marines from* Galena *and the U.S.S.* Tennessee *landed at the Isthmus and enforced treaty obligations until order was restored in May. (RG 19, No. 19-N-8353.)*

U.S.S. Jamestown launched in 1844 at the Navy Yard, Gosport (Norfolk), Virginia. *Before the Civil War* Jamestown *was used chiefly in the African Squadron to suppress slave trade from Africa; in 1847 she transported food to the Irish following the potato famine; in 1848 she was dispatched to the Mediterranean to protect American lives and interests during the convulsive times of the European revolutions; during the Civil War she fought in both the Atlantic and Pacific Oceans; and while she was with the North Pacific Squadron,* Jamestown *was present for the hoisting of the U.S. flag on Sitka on October 18, 1867, after Alaska was purchased from Russia. (RG 19, No. 19-N-6809A.)*

OVERLEAF:

Main deck of the U.S.S. Hartford, screw sloop-of-war, launched November 22, 1858, in Boston and commissioned May 27, 1859. *Hartford's most notable service came during the Civil War as flagship of Flag Officer David Glasgow Farragut. She participated in the battles against Forts Jackson and Saint Philip, which culminated in the capture of New Orleans on April 25, 1862. In the battle of Mobile Bay on August 5, 1864, Hartford, as flag ship, met a formidable Confederate defense composed of the ram Tennessee, three steamers, and the powerful guns of Forts Morgan and Gaines in the bay. The battle lasted three hours, during which the Union forces suffered 335 casualties but the Confederate force and forts suffered a decisive defeat. In October 1945 Hartford was towed to the Norfolk Navy Yard and classified as a relic; however, she sank at her berth in November 1956 and was subsequently dismantled. (RG 19, No. 19-N-9655.)*

U.S.S. Kearsarge, launched September 11, 1861, at the Portsmouth Navy Yard. *Kearsarge sailed for Europe in February 1862 engaged in search for the Confederate raider Alabama. She found Alabama in Cherbourg, France, on June 14, 1864, and patrolled outside the harbor waiting for her to appear. On June 19, Alabama sailed out to confront Kearsarge. The battle was decided quickly when Alabama struck her colors one hour after she fired her first salvo. Kearsarge remained in naval service until she was wrecked on Roncador Reef off Central America in February 1894. (RG 19, No. 19-N-13842.)*

Main deck of the U.S.S. Kearsarge. *This photograph was taken the morning of the battle with the Alabama. (RG 19, No. 19-N-14160.)*

**U.S. frigate Macedonian, launched in
1836.** *In 1852 Macedonian was assigned to
the East India Squadron under Commodore
Matthew C. Perry as part of his fleet which
sailed to negotiate a treaty to open trade
with Japan.* Macedonian *was one of the six
American ships impressively arrayed off
Uraga, Japan, on February 13, 1854. This
show of strength did much to break down
Japanese resistance to negotiations, and the
treaty was signed on March 31. (RG 19,
No. 19-N-13288.)*

U.S.S. Minnesota, launched December 1, 1855. *Minnesota's first mission was to carry William B. Reed, U.S. minister to China, to negotiate a new treaty with that country in 1857. During the Civil War, in March 1862, Minnesota was blockading the Confederate port of Norfolk when she engaged the Confederate ironclad Virginia. Virginia passed up Minnesota on March 8 and first sank the U.S.S. Cumberland and forced the U.S.S. Congress to surrender. That night the U.S. ironclad Monitor slipped into Hampton Roads and tied up to Minnesota. The next morning when Virginia appeared to engage Minnesota in battle, Monitor* steamed out from behind the big wooden frigate and fought the Virginia to a draw. (RG 19, No. 19-N-9901.)

OVERLEAF:

Dressed-ship, U.S.S. Minnesota, celebrating the centennial in the port of New York. *In time-honored custom for ships of the sailing navy, signal flags have been strung from the bowsprit to the transom and sailors stand at attention along every yardarm. (RG 19, No. 19-CN-1779.)*

145

Bonhomme Richard *commanded by John Paul Jones, defeated the* Serapis *in 1779. She was an old India trade ship given to Jones by France, who named her after Benjamin Franklin's "Poor Richard's Almanac." (RG 19, No. 19-N-7873.)*

WILLIAM JAMES MORGAN

Documenting the American Navies of the Revolution: A Scattered but Fruitful Seedbed

Speaking some thirty years ago in an address entitled "A Neglected Phase of Revolutionary History," naval historian William Bell Clark noted: "Upon military and diplomatic and economic phases, I could find anything I desired from Paul Revere's ride to Yorktown, from the French Alliance to the Peace Treaty, from Tom Payne's 'Common Sense' to the inflation of the Continental dollar. But of the naval phases, printed history has had little to say except of the exploits of John Paul Jones."[1]

Clark may have been stating the case a bit too strongly, but in essence he was correct. He rectified some of the deficiency through his biographies of Continental naval officers—Barry, Biddle, Wickes, Young—and finally as the initial editor of the multivolume series *Naval Documents of the American Revolution.*[2]

More recent scholarship, including Harold Larrabee's *Decision at the Chesapeake;* Piers Mackesy's *The War for America; 1775-1783;* David Syrett's *Shipping and the American War, 1775-83;* George Athan Billias's *General John Glover and His Marblehead Mariners*; and Ira Gruber's *The Howe Brothers and the American Revolution,*[3] as well as several new and interesting dissertations—Jonathan Dull's "The French Navy and American Independence, 1774-1780," California, Berkeley, in 1972, and Frank Mevers's "Congress and the Navy," University of North Carolina, also completed in 1972—have addressed themselves to various aspects of the Revolution's war at sea.[4] Of the eight most recent doctoral dissertations on American Revolution naval topics, of which I have knowledge, five have been published by commercial or university presses.

Nevertheless, William Bell Clark's observation three decades ago calling attention to the paucity of naval/maritime coverage of this War for Independence still has validity. A 1913 work, Gardner W. Allen's *A Naval History of the American Revolution,* remains the best general coverage of the sea war, and for the overall treatment of the administrative history of the several naval components, we must turn to Charles Oscar Paullin's *The Navy of the American Revolution: Its Administration, Its Policy and Its Achievements,* published in 1906.[5] This would suggest that recent interest in the revolutionary years and, specifically, the war afloat has just scratched the surface, and that possibilities for profitable inquiry and investigation are, at this date, virtually boundless.

It is not my intent in this paper to propose specific topics but rather to highlight some areas which hold considerable promise for the researcher.

One such area is biography. John Paul Jones, who was his own best press agent and public relations man, has attracted a host of biographers, from John H. Sherburne in the nineteenth century to Samuel Eliot Morison in the mid-twentieth century.[6] But, John Paul Jones was not the entire officer corps of the Continental navy, nor was he the only one who fought the good fight. The officer list included forty-six captains (the highest naval rank) and 133 lieutenants, exclusive of marine officers. Besides Jones, the indomitable Scot, who appropriately came to his final rest in the crypt below the U.S. Naval Academy's chapel, a handful of American sea officers have been examined by modern biographers—the most notable afforded such treatment are John Barry and Nicholas Biddle.

However, the only biography of Esek Hopkins, first commander in chief of the Continental fleet, who was summarily cashiered from the service after he characterized Congress as "a pack of ignorant lawyer's clerks who know nothing at all,"[7] was written in 1898. The biography of Silas Talbot, the irrepressible army lieutenant colonel whose heroics on the sea finally won him a captaincy in the Continental navy and later in the U.S. Navy, was written in 1850, and that of John Manley, commodore of George Washington's fleet before entering the Continental navy, was written in 1915.[8] The biography of Capt. Samuel Tucker, who commanded the frigate *Boston* when it carried John Adams to France, was written in 1868.[9] It is an interesting aside that on this tumultuous voyage Adams not only left us a vivid picture of a wet and uncomfortable ocean passage but took time to evaluate Captain Tucker. He saw Tucker as "an able Seaman and a brave, active, vigilant officer, but I believe has no great Erudition."[10] Adams ridiculed the books in Tucker's small library on board the *Boston,* but concluded, "I found him after a while as sociable as any Marblehead man,"[11] From John Adams of Braintree this came close to being a compliment. Each of these older biographies is unobjective, totally deficient by modern standards, and sadly in need of redoing.[12]

Many officers who challenged the might of Britain's Royal Navy with varying degrees of success, or lack of it, have not been brought out of oblivion by full biographical treatment. Among these officers are James Nicholson, a Maryland politician and senior captain in the Continental navy; Abraham

Whipple, who, in 1772, led the band which boarded and burned the trouble-some British revenue schooner *Gaspée* and who, on one cruise, struck a British convoy, capturing ships as prizes with cargoes valued at over one million dollars; John Peck Rathbun with one small ship, the sloop *Providence,* captured and held the island of New Providence in the Bahamas; Dudley Saltonstall, first captain of the Continental navy's first ship, who later, through timidity and ineptness, turned easy victory into shattering defeat at Penobscot, Maine; and a gentleman with the unlikely name of Hoysteed Hacker, a character as interesting as his name, who seemed to be present in some capacity wherever the naval action was on this side of the Atlantic, from the first fleet cruise in 1776 to the Penobscot disaster in 1779 and the surrender of Charleston in 1780. If no ship was available for Capt. Hoysteed Hacker to command, he would readily serve on board as a lieutenant, or, barring that, he would go off privateering.

Thus far in pointing out a few prospective subjects for biographies I have confined my remarks to Continental naval officers and have made no mention of the common seamen of the Revolution. The man who sailed before the mast has left relatively few records, often he could not write and only mastered the X for his signature; but he would be well worth looking for in existing private journals (including those kept on board prison ships and in English jails), in ship logs, in muster rolls and pay rolls, in court-martial proceedings, and in pension records.

There are also the civilians who did not weather the sea or stand to the cannon's roar, but who, nevertheless, played essential naval roles. For example, those responsible for building naval vessels or converting and outfitting merchant ships and those in Congress who shaped and directed naval policy and strategy — such as Henry Laurens, Christopher Gadsden, Richard Henry Lee, Joseph Hewes, or Robert Morris, who, as agent of marine, presided over the demise of the Continental navy and the troublesome wrap-up of naval business after the war.

Departing from the biographical arena, I turn now to another quadrant of this saltwater-nurtured research seedbed — privateers — those merchant entrepreneurs who risked capital while their officers and crew, lured by the prospect of quick wealth, risked capture and possibly the hangman's noose. A privateer was a privately owned vessel, outfitted as a warship, and commissioned by a state or Congress to prey upon enemy commerce. Several thousand American privateers infested coastal Atlantic waters, the West Indies, and European seas, including the Mediterranean.

Privateers brought in captured supplies which helped to sustain military and civilian alike. They inflicted infinitely more damage on the British than the regular Continental navy; they diverted the Royal Navy from blockade to convoy duty, caused marine insurance rates to soar, and made an unpopular war even more unpopular with the English business community.

Yet, the story of privateers remains largely untold. There are Gardner W. Allen's *Massachusetts Privateers of the Revolution*; William Bell Clark's *Ben Franklin's Privateers*; and Edgar Maclay's *A History of American Privateers,* one-half of which is devoted to the Revolution and the other half to the War of 1812.[13] But here the bibliography just about dead ends. What of the privateers from New Hampshire, Rhode Island, Connecticut, Pennsylvania, Maryland, Virginia, and the Carolinas and of the exploits of particularly active and successful privateer ships or privateersmen? What was the economic impact of prize ships and cargoes on the port cities and the total effect of privateering on the outcome of the conflict? These are questions that need to be answered and await the searcher.

Every state, except for Delaware and New Jersey, organized and maintained individual navies. Regarding New Jersey, however, recent exploration in little-used state records by a Naval Historical Center researcher seems to indicate that, contrary to what has been so long accepted, New Jersey may indeed have had a navy; more research will be necessary before this can be confirmed.

Some state navies were small like those of North Carolina and New Hampshire, while others — Massachusetts and Pennsylvania, for example — were major forces, usually with more vessels operating than the Continental navy. State navies were designed for coastal and harbor defense, troop and cargo transport on demand, and enemy commerce raids. Generally, they struggled to keep sealanes open from state ports to Europe and the West Indies, but when no choice remained, they joined battle with British armed vessels.

The Navy Department Library publishes a *United States Naval History: A Bibliography,* now in its sixth edition. The bibliography section on revolutionary war literature has only one state navy title, Robert Stewart's *The History of Virginia's Navy of the Revolution.* The book is wanting, disjointed, and of interest primarily to genealogists and the first families of Virginia, but it is all there is. The state navy research prospects are quite evident.[14]

For want of a more descriptive term, the final area in this discussion of revolutionary war naval history which holds significant potential for research and writing will be called naval administration. This, admittedly, is a catchall with more facets than a well-cut diamond. Included are the several agencies which administered naval affairs for Congress — that is, the Naval Committee and its successor, the Marine Committee, and the ineffective Board of Admiralty, followed by a single naval executive, the agent of marine, who may be considered as the progenitor of today's secretary of the navy.

Congress also formed two regional boards to assist in running the navy, one in Boston, designated the Navy Board of the Eastern Department, and the other in Philadelphia, called the Navy Board of the Middle Department. The boards' duties were varied and many.

Agents were likewise appointed in the several states to handle the details of condemnation, the sale of prize ships and cargoes, and the distribution of prize money. They were charged with the purchase of all manner of supplies as well as vessels. Commercial agents in Europe and in the West Indies, such as William Bingham at Martinique and the firm of Van Bibber and Harrison in Saint Eustatius, represented the interests of Congress and individual states alike; for their trouble, incidentally, agents took a nice percentage.

The functions, transactions, and effectiveness of these various naval committees, boards, and agents are matters needing analysis and evaluation.

Accepting the premise that the naval history of the American Revolution holds broad fields ready for plowing, the next step is to determine what sources of naval documentation are available and where these materials can be found. Before delving into this area, it would seem necessary to define the term "naval document," which is not subject to as precise a definition as are the papers of an individual, such as Jefferson, Franklin, or Madison, or a single institution. For my purpose here, I will confine the word "document" to the written word and will not consider other documentary categories — contemporary prints, paintings, maps and charts, or artifacts, which could be anything from a uniform button to an entire vessel like the gondola *Philadelphia* of Benedict Arnold's Lake Champlain fleet, now so effectively displayed at the Smithsonian Institution.

My definition of "naval document" will be that which we use for compiling the *Naval Documents of the American Revolution* volumes, namely, that documentation bearing upon the regular naval forces, state navies, privateers, merchant shipping — insofar as it relates to the course of the war — the seaborne logistics of the conflict, and operations on sea, lake, bay, and river.

Within the confines of the foregoing definition, the following categories of materials are to be numbered among those which will yield naval documents:

1. Official records: proceedings, minutes, and resolutions of legislative bodies at all levels of government — congresses, councils, committees, and naval and war boards:

2. Official correspondence: reports and letters to and from executives, legislatures, foreign governments, diplomats, naval and army officers, shipbuilders and suppliers, and the numerous petitions on myriad subjects directed to central and local authorities;

3. Admiralty court records: vice admiralty court records of the interrogation of prisoners and trial and condemnation of prizes, including the British courts at Halifax, New York, Bermuda, and the West Indies;

4. Ship logs and records: muster rolls, payrolls, ship accounts, and inventories of supplies and equipment carried on board;

5. Private correspondence, journals, and diaries;

6. Records, accounts, and correspondence of merchant houses; and

7. Newspapers: ship arrivals and sailings; prize libels and sales; recruiting advertisements; and reports of actions at sea carried in extracts of letters deemed newsworthy by the printer.

If this is the stuff of which Revolutionary War naval documents are made, where is it to be found?

James Fenimore Cooper wrote in 1839: "The documents connected with the early history of the navy of the country, were never kept with sufficient method, and the few that did exist have become much scattered and lost."[15] That they were not kept "with sufficient method," and that they "became much scattered" there can be no quarrel, but they were not as "few" or as "lost" as Cooper believed.

In general, but with innumerable exceptions, official type records, official correspondence, and vice admiralty court records are housed in national and state government archives and libraries. No better illustration of this general conclusion can be found than in the National Archives, holder of the massive and indispensable Papers of the Continental Congress, which include the Marine Committee letterbook; journals of Congress; Robert Morris letterbook, as agent of marine; exchange of correspondence between naval officers and the president of Congress; privateer commissions and bonds; and a wealth of other pertinent and succulent items far too numerous to enumerate here.

Other record groups in the National Archives of particular interest are the pension records, (located in various record groups), which often contain original documentation to authenticate the wartime sea service of a claimant; records of the United States Supreme Court (Record Group 267), which include details of prize cases heard on appeal from state courts; and records of the Navy Department's old Office of Naval Records and Library (Record Group 45), containing unique copies of letters and other items, fortunately made before the originals were destroyed by the 1911 fire in the New York State Library. While the National Archives is not a prime repository for revolutionary war ship logs, there are several in Record Group 45, for example the log of the frigate *South Carolina* of the South Carolina State navy. Among the exceptions referred to earlier is the official letterbook of the Boston-based Navy Board of the Eastern Department. Rather than in the National Archives or a Massachusetts repository, this is found in the New York Public Library. Nevertheless, the general principle holds—provincial or state archives and libraries from Nova Scotia to Georgia have the official type records of concern to the researcher for the years 1775–83. These records are, of course, in varying degrees of completeness and ease of use.

The best sources for private correspondence, private journals and diaries, newspapers, and records of mercantile firms are historical societies (state and local); public libraries; private libraries, such as the Pierpont Morgan in New York City; the Marine Historical Association in Mystic, Connecticut; university libraries; and private collections. Getting back again to exceptions, if one were to seek out the commercial correspondence of the Baltimore merchants, Woolsey and Salmon, a trip to the Maryland Historical Society would be in vain; the firm's letterbook is in the Library of Congress.

Ship muster rolls and payrolls have largely found their way into historical societies and state archives. But for the most bountiful source of ship logs, which I consider one of the most informative of all operational naval documents, we must express thanks to the British for capturing so many of our ships during the war. Logs and other papers of captured American vessels were routinely sent to the admiralty, where they were maintained in an organized manner and today are available in the Public Record Office in London. If a captured "rebel" ship was deemed worthy of being added to the British navy, her lines were meticulously taken off at a royal dockyard and preserved. Thus, because of the successes achieved by George III's men-of-war, we know far more about American ships of the Revolution than otherwise would have been possible.

To illustrate the spread and variety of naval documentation and repositories, I have selected two states at random—Massachusetts and Virginia—to look at as generally representative of the type of naval resources likely to be unearthed in each of the original thirteen states.

Starting with Massachusetts, the archives in Boston houses rich holdings among the papers and correspondence of state legislative bodies, armed vessel bonds, petitions for exceptions to the trade embargo, state admiralty court records, and Board of War minutes and letters (the Massachusetts Board of War also handled naval matters).

The Massachusetts Historical Society holds individuals' papers which have naval interest, e.g., Timothy Pickering, Benjamin Lincoln, William Heath, and Robert Treat Paine, and issues of the Massachusetts newspapers *Independent Chronicle* and the *Continental Journal and Weekly Advertiser,* as well as the New Hampshire paper *Freemans Journal or New Hampshire Gazette.* The society also has a copy of the "Conduct of Vice Admiral Samuel Graves," commander of the American Station during the first year of the war. The original was held in the British Museum, but the museum's manuscript collections have been separated recently, for administrative purposes, into what is now designated the British Library.

The Boston Public Library has a log of the Massachusetts navy ship *Tyrannicide* and an autograph group, the Chamberlain Collection, which includes letters for this period and subject. Boston Athenaeum has a collection of accounts between the Continental Congress and the state of Massachusetts, some for the outfitting of ships. Harvard University Library holds the Arthur Lee Papers and Jared Sparks's transcripts of Lord Grantham's correspondence. Grantham was Britain's ambassador to Spain, and his observations on American privateers' use of Spanish ports are especially pertinent.

The Essex Institute in Salem has logs, crew lists, and journals of privateers; an auctioneer's sales book, which reveals information about the sale of prizes and cargoes; and another log of the state ship *Tyrannicide*. The Peabody Museum, also in Salem, has a complete inventory of all stores carried on board the Continental frigate *Raleigh* and an account book of Thomas Cushing, political crony of John Hancock, who had charge of building the two Continental frigates in Massachusetts.

The American Antiquarian Society has, in addition to substantial newspaper holdings, the journal of Capt. John Fisk of the *Tyrannicide*. This is the third Massachusetts repository I have mentioned that holds *Tyrannicide* materials.

A small, well-organized local society, the Beverly Historical Society, has much documentation on privateers. And across the harbor, Beverly's arch rival community, Marblehead, has a historical society run by dedicated volunteer ladies. Marblehead's holdings include a ledger book of Col. John Glover, privateer commissions, and bills for fitting out privateers sailing from that port.

The New England Historical and Genealogical Society has a private journal kept by one William Russell of Boston while a captive in England's Mill Prison. This journal includes listings of seamen prisoners and the names of ships on which they were serving when captured.

South from the Bay State to Virginia, Richmond's state library holdings embrace Committee and Council of Safety records; governors' communications; state navy board minutes, ledgers, journals, and orders; the James River Naval Office Manifest Book (1773–75); correspondence with state agents abroad; papers of the Public Ropewalk; and papers relating to cooperation with Maryland for the defense of the Chesapeake Bay.

The Virginia Historical Society has papers of various Lee family members, including William, Arthur, and the Lee who was so instrumental in having Congress name Capt. James Nicholson senior officer in the Continental navy— Richard Henry.

Lee papers are also much in evidence in the Alderman Library, University of Virginia, as well as the very valuable papers and narrative of Capt. Andrew Snape Hamond, R.N., who commanded the H.M.S. *Roebuck* and was involved with Lord Dunmore during that royal governor's marauding period in the Hampton Roads and Chesapeake Bay areas.

The College of William and Mary has a sizeable collection called the

Tucker-Coleman Papers which sheds considerable light on Bermuda's role commercially and militarily.

Colonial Williamsburg has photostats and microfilm of the British Headquarters Papers (sometimes called the Carleton Papers), which in many volumes comprise the papers of the successive British commanders in chief in America. As a gracious gesture of international good will the original papers were returned to the British government in 1957 during Queen Elizabeth's state visit.

In Newport News the Mariners Museum possesses a journal kept by a Massachusetts captain in the Continental navy, Hector McNeill, while he commanded the frigate *Boston* in 1777. The museum also has a log of the *Boston.*

If this admittedly incomplete survey tour through Massachusetts and Virginia and my earlier reference to repositories in the thirteen states have created the impression that American resources for the sea history of the Revolution are restricted to libraries, historical societies, archives, and universities east of the Hudson River or Appalachian Mountains, please allow me to dissuade you with a few examples to the west.

In the Chicago Historical Society are accounts of prize money paid to crews of the *Bonhomme Richard* and the frigate *Alliance* (February 23 to March 20, 1780). These records tell not only how much prize money was shared but how it was divided and who was serving on board during the tradition- and legend-making duel with the H.M.S. *Serapis* off Flamborough Head, England. Also in Chicago are a few papers of Caesar Rodney of Delaware.

The Clements Library of the University of Michigan has British papers of incalculable value—those of Gen. Thomas Gage, Lord George Germain, and Sir Henry Clinton. And the Detroit Public Library will yield papers of the Rhode Island State navy and Continental navy Capt. Abraham Whipple.

The Huntington Library in San Marino, California, a true treasure trove, has a collection of John Paul Jones manuscripts; a participant's account of the *Bonhomme Richard* and *Serapis* battle; a group of Vice Adm. Richard Lord Howe's orders and correspondence while he commanded British naval forces in America; and an excellent collection of French manuscripts, which include the papers of Admiral Destouches and logs of French naval vessels operating in support of the American war—some of these logs are magnificently illustrated.

In conclusion, I would hope that this highly selective overview of the "whereabouts" of revolutionary war naval documents would clearly affirm the accuracy of James Fenimore Cooper's findings voiced more than one and a quarter centuries ago—namely, they are "much scattered." But, within the past decade the Naval Historical Center of the United States Department of the Navy has taken a giant stride toward "unscattering" them. When the navy reached the decision to collect, edit, and publish the *Naval Documents of the American Revolution,* an intensive search effort was undertaken. The results today—and the collection continues to grow—are an accumulation of naval and maritime documents of the American Revolution years unparalleled anywhere in the world. We hold copies of hundreds of thousands of manuscripts; some are photocopies, but most are on about one thousand reels of microfilm from well over one hundred repositories and private collectors spanning, literally, from the state archives in Venice, Italy, to California. For example, from Britain's Public Record Office our selected materials of the admiralty, Colonial Office, state papers, and High Court of Admiralty records now number 108 reels, and we have the logs of 188 different British naval vessels operating in American waters during the war. Our newspaper holdings, foreign and domestic, account for 216 microfilm reels. From the South Carolina Historical Society we have 11 reels; the American Philosophical Society, 15 reels; the Library of Congress, more than 200 reels (including extensive French and Spanish naval documentation); the New York Public Library and New York Historical Society, 16 reels; and the Historical Society of Pennsylvania, 18 reels.

In our *Naval Documents of the American Revolution* volumes, huge as they are, averaging more than fifteen hundred pages each, we can only include a tightly selected group of manuscripts from the vast collection. But the collection as a whole has become an invaluable national resource which, as its existence becomes more widely known, is gaining markedly increased use among researchers. We welcome the student and the scholar alike to avail themselves of the untapped veins of gold to be found in the naval and maritime documents of our nation's struggle for independence—gold waiting to be mined—some will yield readily to surface scraping, and some will require deep shaft digging.

NOTES

1. Clark, "A Neglected Phase of Revolutionary History" (Paper delivered at the 162d Annual Meeting of the State Society of the Cincinnati of Pennsylvania, Philadelphia, Pa., 4 October 1945).
2. Idem and William James Morgan, eds., *Naval Documents of the American Revolution* (Washington D.C.: Government Printing Office, 1964-).
3. Larrabee, *Decision at the Chesapeake* (New York: Potter, 1964); Mackesy, *The War for America, 1775-1783* (Cambridge, Mass.: Harvard University Press, 1964); Syrett, *Shipping and the American War, 1775-83: A Study of British Transport Organization* (London: University of London, Athlone Press, 1970); Gruber, *The Howe Brothers and the American Revolution* (Williamsburg: Institute of Early American History and Culture, Atheneum, 1972); Billias, *General Glover and His Marblehead Marines* (New York: Holt, 1960).

4. The Dull dissertation has been published since this paper was presented. Jonathan R. Dull, *The French Navy and American Independence: A Study of Arms and Diplomacy, 1774-1787* (Princeton: Princeton University Press, 1975).

5. Allen, *A Naval History of the American Revolution* 2 vols. (1913, reprint ed., New York: Corner House, 1970); Paullin, *The Navy of the American Revolution: Its Administration, Its Policy and Its Achievements* (1906; reprint ed., New York: Haskell, 1970).

6. Sherburne, *The Life and Character of John Paul Jones, a Captain in the United States Navy during the Revolutionary War* (New York: Adriance, Sherman, 1851); Morison, *John Paul Jones: A Sailor's Biography* (Boston: Little, Brown, 1959).

7. Edward Field, *Esek Hopkins, Commander-in-Chief of the Continental Navy during the American Revolution: 1775 to 1778* (Providence: Preston and Rounds Co., 1898), p. 235.

8. Henry T. Tuckerman, *The Life of Silas Talbot, a Commodore in the Navy of the United States* (New York: J. C. Riker, 1850); Isaac J. Greenwood, *Captain John Manley, Second in Rank in the United States Navy: 1776-1783* (Boston: C. E. Goodspeed, 1915).

9. John H. Sheppard, *The Life of Samuel Tucker, Commodore in the American Revolution* (Boston: A. Mudge & Son, 1868).

10. L. H. Butterfield, ed., *Diary and Autobiography of John Adams* (Cambridge, Mass.: Harvard University Press, 1961), 2:274.

11. Ibid, p. 368.

12. Since this paper was presented, books about Captains Tucker and Manley have been authored by Philip Chadwick Foster Smith. See *Captain Samuel Tucker (1747-1833), Continental Navy* (Salem: Essex Institute, 1976), and *Fired by Manley Zeal: A Naval Fiasco of the American Revolution* (Salem: Peabody Museum, 1977).

13. Allen, *Massachusetts Privateers of the Revolution* (Boston: Massachusetts Historical Society, 1927); Clark, *Ben Franklin's Privateers: A Naval Epic of the American Revolution* (Baton Rouge: Louisiana State University Press, 1956); Maclay, *A History of American Privateers* (1899, reprint ed., New York: Books for Libraries, 1967).

14. Since this paper was presented another book on a state navy has been published. See John W. Jackson, *The Pennsylvania Navy 1775-1781: The Defense of the Delaware* (New Brunswick: Rutgers University Press, 1974).

15. Cooper, *The History of the Navy of the United States of America* (Philadelphia: Lea & Blanchard, 1839), 1:99.

AWFUL EXPLOSION OF THE *"PEACE-MAKER"* ON BOARD THE U.S. STEAM FRIGATE, *PRINCETON,* ON WEDNESDAY, 28ᵗᴴ FEBʸ: 1844.

The Navy in
an Age of Manifest Destiny:
Some Suggestions
for Sources and Research

Although I signed on this cruise to prepare a paper on the sources and research potentials of the Mexican War I will shape a slightly different course. The Mexican War does offer a number of interesting research topics as I will point out later, but it is a very narrow subject, except for the activities in California. Therefore, I am going to interpret my objective somewhat broadly and deal with both the war and some general topics that apply to the navy throughout the whole period of Manifest Destiny, which for the purposes of this paper can be assumed to be the quarter century preceding the attack on Fort Sumter.

Those twenty-five years were as revolutionary as any similar period in the history of navies and naval warfare. It saw the victory of steam over sail and that of explosive shell over the wooden walls of the old navy. These are developments which naval historians well understand and have long recognized. But there were no less revolutionary occurrences within the United States Navy at the same time which are less widely known. In 1842 specialization struck the navy with the establishment of the Engineer Corps. That year also saw the regularization of the Purser's Branch and the establishment of specialized bureaus to replace the line-manned Board of Navy Commissioners. This quarter century witnessed the departure of the native-born American seaman from the fleet in such numbers that by the end of the period he was a rare specimen. These changes, along with the varied and often colorful operational story, help

EXPLOSION OF THE "PEACEMAKER" (facing page). On the afternoon of February 28, 1844, the "Peacemaker," a large cannon invented by Capt. Robert F. Stockton, exploded on the deck of the U.S.S. Princeton during a cruise down the Potomac with a presidential party of 380. The explosion left four dead, including President Tyler's close friends Secretary of State Abel P. Upshur and Secretary of the Navy Thomas Gilmer. The ship docked at 4:10 P.M.; however, President Tyler remained aboard with the bodies of his friends until after eight o'clock that evening. (Photograph, courtesy of Franklin D. Roosevelt Library, Hyde Park, New York.)

explain the attention which these two and a half decades have attracted from historians.

The centerpiece for this period, both chronologically and dramatically, is the war with Mexico. Not only was that conflict the capstone of America's continental expansion but it was the most complex and demanding undertaking yet assigned to the United States Navy. It involved the conquest of California, the blockade of Mexico's two coasts, and the successful landing of over eighty-six hundred men across Collado Beach in less than five hours in America's first large amphibious operation. A more professional performance is hard to imagine. In its operations in the Gulf of Mexico, the navy for the first time confronted the realities of steampower in combat and, for the first time since the Barbary wars, conducted extended distant operations. In both instances, the problems the navy faced were logistic rather than operational. Nevertheless, the war did give the men who would lead the U.S. Navy and the Marine Corps during the Civil War extensive combat experience. For them, as for the army's leaders, the Mexican War served as a rehearsal for the fratricidal clash of 1861–65.

The primary sources for any study of the Mexican War are concentrated in the National Archives Building, nearly all of them in a single record group—the Naval Records Collection of the Office of Naval Records and Library (Record Group 45). That massive assortment houses the orders issued by the secretary of the navy to his commanders in the field[1] and their reports.[2] Record Group 45 also holds several important collections of personal papers, notably the letterbooks of Commodores David Conner and Matthew C. Perry and the journals of Capt. William Mervine, which illuminate the operations in California. Outside the National Archives there is only a handful of truly significant material bearing on the operational history of the war:

1. The Commodore David Conner Papers at the Library of Congress and the Franklin D. Roosevelt Library;

2. The Commodore Robert F. Stockton letterbook at Princeton University; and

3. The Commodore John D. Sloat Papers at the California Historical Society.

Operational history, however, does not hold a particularly high priority for study at the moment, but it is an area which most of us tend to overwork. Whether that is because the materials are easier to assemble or whether most feel safer dealing with operational or diplomatic topics is not certain. Unfortunately, very few have followed the lead of Harry Langley and Peter Karsten into social history, of Elting Morison into the history of technology, or of Vincent Davis and Gerry Wheeler into policy formation. We need more studies of the social history of the navy; the relationship of the navy to technology (especially the spread of technologies); and how the navy operated as a bureaucratic entity. These and

innumerable other areas offer equally fertile ground for the enterprising researcher. (See Appendix for additional suggested topics.)

One place for a researcher to start would be with the leaders of the navy in the
Mexican War. They have received less attention than they merit. Samuel Eliot
Morison's majestic study of "Old Bruin," Commodore Matthew Calbraith Perry,[3]
is the only modern study of any of the naval commanders. Neither David Conner,
Perry's predecessor as commander of the forces in the Gulf of Mexico; Robert F.
Stockton, the man who gained, lost, and regained most of California; nor the
able W. Branford Shubrick, who neutralized the Mexican west coast, have
received adequate treatment.[4] Yet all three are major figures in the navy between the War of 1812 and the Civil War, as well as some undoubtedly more
significant figures than Perry in American naval history.

Conner is a particularly strong candidate for a full-length biography. He
fought with distinction as a junior officer in the War of 1812; served a tour as
navy commissioner; headed the Bureau of Construction, Equipment, and Repair;
led the Home Squadron through the difficult times preceding the outbreak of
fighting along the Rio Grande; and commanded throughout the first year of
war. He established a blockade that denied Mexico desperately needed munitions and executed the landings on Collado Beach. Not only do we have his
official papers in the appropriate Navy Department files but many of his private
papers rest in an all too great obscurity at the Franklin D. Roosevelt Library in
Hyde Park. The latter include the very human and enlightening letters from
his wife, which recount her struggles to raise two sons in her husband's absence
and on his limited salary. They are, as far as I can determine, the only extensive
group of a naval officer's wife's letters in this period that have survived. They
deserve publication; Susan Physick Conner was quite a person.

Many individual aspects of Robert F. Stockton's career have been treated
separately.[5] Most naval historians remember him for his close connections with
John Ericsson and his role in having the U.S.S. *Princeton* constructed to demonstrate Ericsson's screw. While Stockton's connection with the ill-fated Peacemaker gun has been explored in depth by Lee Pearson, we know less than we
would like about his relationship with President John Tyler. We know something
about Stockton's role in the establishment of Liberia. Glenn Price has recently
studied his activities in Texas prior to annexation, and others have documented
his role in California. On the other hand, we know little about his political
activities or his participation in the 1861 Washington Peace Conference. Nor do
we know enough about Stockton's entrepreneurial activities involving the
Camden and Amboy Railroad and the Delaware and Raritan Canal.

The most fascinating of the three commodores is the Harvard-educated South
Carolinian, William Branford Shubrick. He came from a strongly navy-oriented
family (three of his brothers were naval officers) and was a life-long friend of

James Fenimore Cooper. Shubrick served on the *Hornet, Constellation,* and *Constitution* during the War of 1812. In 1838 he took command of the West Indies Squadron. Prior to relieving Stockton as commander of the Pacific Squadron, he served as chief of the Bureau of Supplies and Accounts. After the Mexican War he took charge of the Philadelphia Navy Yard and became the last line officer to head the Bureau of Construction, Equipment, and Repair. With time out to undertake two important naval-diplomatic missions, he served as chairman of the Lighthouse Board from 1853 until his retirement in 1861.

Shubrick's two special assignments included command of the special Eastern Squadron during the flare-up of the Northern Fisheries dispute in 1853 and leadership of the Paraguayan Expedition of 1858–59. In both instances, his diplomatic talents helped cool tempers and arrange settlements. A careful study of his career might bear out his contemporary reputation as the best naval diplomat of his time.

The three men had dissimilar backgrounds. Conner was the son of an Irish immigrant farmer, Stockton was the grandson of a signer of the Declaration of Independence, and Shubrick was the son of a revolutionary war veteran and plantation owner. If we add to this mix such contemporaries as Samuel Francis DuPont, from the new industrial aristocracy, and the land speculating, Jeffersonian Jew, Uriah P. Levy, we get a fascinating glimpse of antebellum diversity. But is this a reasonable cross-section of the officer corps? What would a study of that group in the generation before the "messmates of Mahan" disclose? My guess is that Conner or Sloat or Daniel Turner (all sons of farmers or artisans) would fit the resulting model better than Stockton or Shubrick. It seems reasonably clear from the available evidence that the navy attracted the upwardly mobile sons of artisans and farmers, despite its initial recruitment from the mercantile-based group which included Thomas Truxtun and Isaac Hull. If this pattern is true, does it parallel a similar development in the merchant marine? There seems to be some evidence that it does.

The study of the social history of the officer corps opens other interesting possibilities. What were the relations between these men of widely differing backgrounds? We get glimpses of the answers in the official record. They can be seen in the choosing up of sides in those sometimes extremely acrimonious squabbles which rent the service. They can be seen in requests by senior officers for the attachment to their commands of specific junior officers. Would a study of career patterns of Mexican War period officers give us some fresh insights? Possibly. It is an area in which a quantitative historian could have a field day. Was there a normal pattern of employment? Is there any pattern for the selection of officers for frequent active service as opposed to those of good health who saw only limited service? For instance, are we correct in assuming that Uriah P. Levy's thirty-three years of waiting for orders in a career of fifty years was so unusual as to reflect either intense antisemitism or the antagonisms developed by one of the more irascible personalities in the antebellum navy? Is it true, as we assume, that ship captains tended to select their own officers? The correspondence I have seen in this period is not conclusive. The raw material for the studies which could answer these questions is in the correspondence of the secretary of the navy in Record Group 45. As far as the career patterns of individual officers are concerned, the abstracts of service and statements of service are preserved in the Records of the Bureau of Naval Personnel (Record Group 24).

In addition to the better known names of the period, a few of the lesser officers also deserve study. Charles H. Haswell not only served as the first chief engineer of the navy but played a major role in shaping the Engineer Corps. After leaving the navy he became one of the great American mechanical engineers of the nineteenth century. By the end of the century, he was revered as the grand old man of the profession. As a second candidate, I would nominate Commodore Joseph Smith who followed a successful career as a line officer with a twenty-three year (1846–69) tour as chief of the Bureau of Yards and Docks. There are others who merit study, such as James M. Gilliss, the astronomer, and Commodore Charles Morris, who served two terms as a navy commissioner and headed both the Bureaus of Construction, Equipment, and Repair (1844–47) and Ordnance (1851–56). During the Mexican War he served as the chief uniformed adviser to the secretary and was considered by many contemporaries to be the most scientific of the older officers. I would also suggest a biography of John Lenthall, who was Benjamin Franklin Isherwood's counterpart at the Bureau of Construction, Equipment, and Repair.

I am surprised that some of the younger members of the profession, trained in quantitative and other methodologies of the social scientists, have not made more studies of the enlisted men of the U.S. Navy. Harry Langley's pioneering study, *Social Reform in the United States Navy, 1798–1862*,[6] gives a steady platform from which to launch such an investigation. The raw materials exist in great quantity in the muster rolls preserved in Record Group 45 and in the personnel records of the Bureau of Naval Personnel. Do these records bear out the assumption that native-born sailors were almost unknown in the fleet? How did the navy's problems compare with those in the merchant marine at the same time? Were the navy's recruiting problems comparable to the army's? We do not know the answers to those questions, although we do know that a shortage of trained men played a major role in the establishment of the naval apprentice system for young boys in the 1830s and that the navy could not recruit enough men during the Mexican War to reach its 10,000-man ceiling. The answers should give us interesting insights into the mind of the American of the late-Jacksonian period. By extension, such a study should help us to understand better the nature of military and naval services in the period and the social role of these services in antebellum America. It would also add to our knowledge of the dynamics of American civilization in the nineteenth century.

What were the conditions of service during the Mexican War? As we are only too aware, few enlisted men wrote memoirs, and most officers who did said little about conditions of life. Nevertheless, several good sources for information do exist for the researcher who is willing to dig. The logbooks in the Bureau of Naval Personnel records give insight into life afloat. Not only do they chronicle the activities in which the crew found itself engaged, but they record punishments, deaths, and the consumption of supplies.

A second source for researchers is the journals which all midshipmen were required to keep. These often record details left out of the official account, frequently in highly colorful language. Many of these journals are preserved among the Private Logs and Journals in Record Group 45. Others can be found in innumerable repositories from coast to coast. Unfortunately, logs and journals are not easy to use. They are voluminous and record vast quantities of worthless detail for each speck of usable information. Moreover, during the Mexican War period they were kept according to the nautical day, which ran from noon to noon. That ensured that half the events were recorded under the wrong date! The records of the courts martial and courts of inquiry are the third and potentially most important source for most researchers. Those records covering the mid-nineteenth century are lodged in Record Group 45 along with an indispensable index. The court proceedings preserve detailed accounts of events and copies of correspondence which exist nowhere else. Most historians ignore them except for a handful of famous cases. Yet by their very nature they deal primarily with social history. The court proceedings are admittedly very time consuming to use, and most historians often find it difficult to determine which ones are likely to be valuable to their study. Nevertheless, a little ingenuity and imagination will produce results well worth the effort.

I am surprised that no one has investigated the execution of Seaman Samuel Jackson in 1846 on board the *St. Mary's* off Veracruz. This has been suggested, quite erroneously I think, as a possible basis for Herman Melville's *Billy Budd*. The story has great possibilities. Jackson was convicted of assailing the officer-of-the-deck, both physically and verbally, after that august personage had kicked Jackson's shoes overboard upon finding them on deck following an inspection.[7] The severity of the sentence reflected the problems encountered by the blockaders off Mexico. They had little to occupy their time, only aimless cruising back and forth off ports and river mouths which seemed never to attract visitors.

Another interesting case for study would be that of Lt. Charles G. Hunter, who was dismissed from the Home Squadron by Commodore Perry for his premature seizure of the port of Alvarado in 1847.[8] The record is not clear as to how that banishment was accomplished, but it did not prevent Hunter's return to sea and later dismissal from the service for ignoring the orders of another superior. A study of the relief and exile of unwanted officers would make a good project for someone interested in personnel matters.

The entire area of medical attention needs study. Surgeon Jonathan M. Foltz wrote a treatise on the scurvy which troubled Conner's squadron during the summer of 1846,[9] but little or no systematic work has been done on yellow fever.[10] We know that the squadron off Mexico established temporary hospitals on some of the low islands near Veracruz but little else about them. We do not even have good figures on the number of men taken sick or even of those killed by the scourge. We have some accounts of the efforts to fumigate vessels in the fever zone, a number of which make good reading. On the steamer *Vixen*, for instance, they filled the spaces below deck with steam. It did wonders in eliminating rats and roaches but ruined the woodwork and gave only temporary relief from the mosquitos.

Anesthesia was just coming into use at the time of the Mexican War. Did naval surgeons make any use of it? I have seen no evidence that they did but it should be checked into. We do know that an army surgeon used it in Veracruz in early 1847. Indeed, how was specialized knowledge spread among naval surgeons at this time? We know that some of the senior surgeons such as William P. C. Barton were among the most highly regarded in the nation, but how good were the bulk of the members of the Medical Corps?

There is room for a study of military government in the Mexican ports under navy control. The records are elusive but some exist in the Home Squadron Letters and others might be found scattered among the reports in the various Letters Received section of Record Group 45. There is also a volume of ledger entries recording the duties collected at the ports under naval administration.

As far as operations on the west coast are concerned, very little has been done on the governments set up by Commodores Sloat and Stockton in California. This is unfortunate since Stockton's plans envisioned a popularly elected assembly and full local self-government, even during wartime. Although it is less significant, we lack any study of the government imposed by Shubrick on Mazatlán. Unfortunately, Shubrick's reports have been lost except for some copies in the Area File of Record Group 45 and those printed in the contemporary annual reports of the secretary of the navy. To a degree that lack can be offset by the Elie A. F. La Vallette Papers at Yale, since La Vallette was the occupation governor. Another area is that of the relations of Shubrick with the Mexican leaders in Baja California. He convinced many of them that the United States would annex the peninsula, only to discover that such a provision had been dropped from the Treaty of Guadalupe Hidalgo. Some three hundred of the

Baja Californians concluded that their personal safety required them to leave
with the occupation forces.

Much has been written about the clash of Stockton and John C. Frémont with
Gen. Stephen W. Kearny over control of the military government in California,
but little has been said about the relations between the two services in eastern
Mexico. They were generally good but there was one classic incident involving
Comdr. David G. Farragut. He was the ranking naval officer at Veracruz in
August 1847 when a British mail steamer discharged a passenger who turned out
to be the intensely anti-American ex-Mexican President Gen. Mariano Paredes y
Arrillaga. Neither Farragut nor the army authorities at the port boarded the
steamer until after Paredes escaped. Each service vehemently blamed the other,
and Commodore Perry issued a strong directive to his officers to board every
vessel entering an occupied port.

Despite my comments earlier about overattention to diplomatic areas, there
are some topics which should be covered. As far as the Mexican War is concerned, these are relatively few. One exception is the complex relations of
Commodores Conner and Perry with the insurrectionary authorities in Yucátan;
some portions of this topic were covered in a dissertation by Francis Manno. [11]
Although the materials for the study are diplomatic rather than naval, a
study of the diplomatic campaign to prevent the outfitting of Mexican privateers in foreign ports is long overdue.

The question of containing privateers opens the larger one—the role of the
navy in policing the seas, especially the Caribbean. We know something about
the role of the navy during the Latin American and Texas revolutions but
very little about the activities of the vessels that tested the blockades proclaimed
during local insurrections and looked after the safety of Americans ashore.
Did American naval commanders normally act alone or in concert with
others? Are there precedents for Duncan Ingraham's extreme extension of
the protection of American citizenship in the Koszta Affair? I suspect that
a student who went through the reports of the Home Squadron might well
find some. Indeed, if I am correct in my reading of the state of our knowledge
of naval-diplomatic history during the second quarter of the nineteenth
century, we know very little about how the system worked. We know about
the foreign office chief-of-government–ambassador level diplomacy, but we
have not yet thoroughly studied foreign relations at the working level. We
need to know more about how the local consul worked, whether or not he co-
operated with the visiting naval commander, and how the naval commander
viewed his responsibilities when lacking local policy guidance.

One good starting place for such a study would be the Home Squadron.
What was it doing in the days before the outbreak of fighting about areas
away from the Mexican coast. We know, for instance, that Commodore
Conner had instructions to send a vessel to investigate conditions in Haiti.

The Home Squadron is not along in its need of a history. We have yet to produce a good study of the African Squadron, despite the current interest in Afro-American relations. Nor do we know much about the activities of the navy in the Rio de la Plata during the Rosas period. What support did it give the local American diplomats? Most of them seem to have complained about it, yet we know that some of the earliest uses of naval landing parties occurred there. Unfortunately, aside from the listing in Ellsworth's *One Hundred Eighty Landings of U.S. Marines*, [12] most of us know nothing about them. This whole area of landing parties deserves a thorough study. How frequently were they tested? Under what conditions were they employed? Whom did they protect? Although the motivation seems to have been humanitarian in most instances, it would be desirable, in today's climate of skepticism about motives, to revisit those operations. The information is in the squadron letters and, in some instances, in reports filed by the senior marine officer with the commandant.

I have mentioned the Paraguayan Expedition in connection with Commodore Shubrick. It is time that it received a full study. Not only is it a good example of naval diplomacy but the preparations for it reveal a good check on the success of the navy in putting into practice the lessons learned in the Mexican War. Among other matters, the expedition required outfitting the navy for a river war for which it was not then equipped. The preparations included the purchase by the navy of the first group of steam colliers built in the United States. Although this leads away from the consideration of naval records, the tale of the diplomacy that prevented the incident from becoming a full-fledged war is a fascinating one.

The Mexican War involved considerable river fighting, most of it by a small squadron of light draft vessels called, with great lack of originality, the mosquito flotilla. The acquisition and outfitting of that flotilla is an interesting but largely untold story. Among other craft, the group included a pair of steamers and three schooners, which were being built in New York for the Mexican Navy, and a trio of coastal freighters converted into bomb vessels, in case it became necessary to attack the massive fortress of San Juan de Ulua off Veracruz. The sources exist in the secretary's correspondence with the naval agents and the officers involved, notably Commodores Perry and Lawrence Kearny. The material I have seen is not entirely clear on how the decisions for the purchase of the vessels were made. Apparently, the secretary of the navy, on the advice of the bureau chiefs involved, ordered the purchase of one or more vessels but gave authority for the selection either to the supervising naval officer or to the local naval agent—or in some cases both. That arrangement looks rather slipshod on paper, but was it in practice?

As mentioned earlier, the Mexican War was the United States Navy's initial experience with an overseas steam war. The logistics problems of the war were horrendous, and if the nearly universal complaints of the participants are accurate, those problems were not always overcome. Very clearly, the United States Navy—like the United States Army—was ill-prepared to fight an overseas war. Nor was it prepared to handle the demands of distant steam-powered operations. But neither did any other navy have significant experience in planning and executing such activities. There is much material in the reports of the naval agents in the major ports, Records of the Bureau of Ships (Record Group 19), and in the printed annual reports of the war period that document the steps taken to provide fleets with coal and other necessities. The Home Squadron Letters, the log books, and the Conner Papers at Hyde Park give the other side of the story: the details of the receipt, storage, and use of supplies as well as the shortages which were not filled. The Home Squadron reports and the Conner Papers record the steps taken by Commodore Connor on his own initiative to secure fresh food and water for his vessels.

Another aspect of the steam navy that deserves greater attention is the area of steam engineering. Someone should write a history of the development of steam engineering in the navy based upon broader sources than Frank Bennett's classic study. [13] From Ted Sloan's work, [14] a great deal is known about Benjamin Franklin Isherwood and the developments during and after the Civil War, but little work has been done on the earlier period. In addition to Charles H. Haswell, mentioned earlier, many other early navy engineers were particularly concerned about boiler design and experimented widely in the period before the Civil War, but nobody has studied that work in detail. This is unfortunate because it represents some of the earliest efforts directed at federal support for technical research. Clark Reynolds and others have given insight into another early example of naval support of technological experimentation—Lt. William W. Hunter's horizontal paddle wheels. [15] No one, however, has made a similar study of the contemporary comparisons of the Loper and Ericsson screw designs. It would be an interesting study. Incidentally, vessels using Hunter wheels as well as Loper and Ericsson screws fought in the Mexican War.

Howard Chapelle has studied the development of sailing-ship designs both within and without the navy [16] but no one has attempted a similar study of steamers. The same plan series which Chapelle exploited so successfully, the Dash-Plan files in the Bureau of Ships, contains the hull plans of the navy's steamers. It also holds the raw materials for a study of the development of specialized small craft. While we know something about ships' boats and about the surfboats of the Mexican War, we have no studies of yard craft.

Where did the navy get its timbers for the wooden fleet? To a very large degree, they came from the timber preserves in the South. We need some studies of those timberlands and of the activities of the naval patrol which attempted to protect the supply of live oak against poachers. Record Group 45 contains correspondence of the timber agents and of the officers who commanded the timber patrol. This would be an excellent area for someone with conservationist interests. The protection of the southern white- and live-oak reserves was the earliest conservation program undertaken by the federal government. An estimate of the success of the program would make an interesting comparison with that of the royal mast surveyors in northern New England before the Revolution.

It is well known that the administrative aspects of the navy for the second quarter of the nineteenth century are among the best documented naval records. This is certainly true of the Mexican War and simply proves that a bureaucracy, not surprisingly, preserves its own records best. Despite this, we are very short of studies of naval bureaucracy and administration, especially for the period under consideration. Charles Oscar Paullin's pioneering work some sixty years ago [17] pointed out the way but did not exhaust the materials; Leonard D. White, [18] in more recent times, placed essentially the same material in a broader prospective. I hope that when the long gestating "American Secretaries of the Navy" finally sees the light of publication in the near future we will see the problem even more clearly. Nevertheless, there are innumerable subjects available for monographic treatment. An outstanding one would be a history of the Naval Asylum. Another would be the tentative steps towards academic training of midshipmen before the establishment of the U.S. Naval Academy. Contrary to what many of us have been led to believe, the idea did not spring full grown from the mind of George Bancroft.

In a slightly different field, an interesting topic, possibly worth a doctoral dissertation, would be a study of the nineteenth-century commissions and individual officers who were sent to Europe to study technical and professional developments. What role did they play in the transfer of technology between the two sides of the Atlantic? Such a study should give some idea of how original the United States Navy was in its application of technology to the problems which it faced. Did we fall behind Britain in this respect as many of us think? For instance, standardization of ordnance did not come to the United States until 1845, six years after it did in the Royal Navy. Such a study would also complement Stan Falk's discussion of the efforts in the army to achieve a similar standardization. [19] For that matter, the whole question of exchange of technical information between the services needs exploring. Glimpses of it can be found in the Executive Letterbooks of the secretary's office in Record Group 45 and more appears in the bureau records.

I suggested earlier that too little attention has been devoted to the support of technology and applied sciences by the services during this period. In the area of ordnance, we need a study of the development of explosive shells in the United States, especially the Bordentown and Sandy Hook experiments. There is a good article by Philip K. Lundeberg on Samuel Colt's mine experiments. [20] Further research might disclose Colt's method of determining when a vessel was within range of a mine. Studies should also be undertaken on the development of drydocks — particularly, floating ones — diving bells, and those "patent India rubber camels" which Perry took along on the second expedition to Tabasco.

In the area of operational history of the Mexican War, except for a few studies of the expeditions against Tabasco, Tuxpan, and Tampico, there has been very little coverage of riverine operations, despite the revival of interest in such activities during the Vietnam War. Areas of possible interest would be, for example, studies of the expeditions up the Coatzacoalcos River; the Alvarado River; or those by Lt. Samuel Lockwood and Capt. W. A. Howard, of the Revenue Marine, in the waterways around Frontera. How successful, in fact, was the American blockade in the Mexican War? I think it worked well, but Robert Scheina, [21] working from Mexican customs figures, suggests that it did not. A careful search of the blockaders' logs would probably show that the figures Scheina discovered were as misleading as those that Marcus Price derived for the Confederate blockade runners in the Civil War.

For those interested in exploring a more controversial issue, but one that does not quite fall within the span of these discussions, I suggest trying to find out just what did happen to the marines on the causeway leading to Mexico City's Belén Gateway during Gen. Winfield Scott's assault on the Mexican capital. Were they really skulking in the ditches?

In conclusion, I hope that this discussion has given some idea of the wealth and variety of information buried in the records of the National Archives and some hint of those whose discovery would enhance our knowledge of the history of the United States Navy and the nation which it serves.

NOTES

1. There are two pertinent series: Letters to Officers and Record of Confidential Letters.
2. Most Mexican War reports appear in either the Home Squadron or Pacific Squadron Letters series of Record Group 45. A few missing items, notably some of the reports of Commodore W. Branford Shubrick, are in the Area File. Occasional reports by junior officers submitted directly to the secretary of the navy turn up in the appropriate Letters Received series.
3. Samuel Eliot Morison, *"Old Bruin," Commodore Matthew C. Perry* (Boston: Little, Brown, 1967).
4. Beyond their biographies in the *Dictionary of American Biography* the only studies

of these three men are Philip Syng Physick Conner, *The Home Squadron under Commodore Conner* (Philadelphia: N.p., 1896); [Samuel J. Bayard], *A Sketch of the Life of Com. Robert F. Stockton* (New York: Derby & Jackson, 1856); Susan F. Cooper, "Rear Admiral William Branford Shubrick," *Harper's*, August 1878, pp. 400-407; and Andrew P. Butler, *Commodore Shubrick* (Washington, D.C.: Globe, 1856).

5. For modern accounts of aspects of Stockton's career see: Lee M. Pearson, "The *Princeton* and the Peacemaker: A Study of 19th Century Naval Research and Development Procedures," *Technology and Culture* 7 (1966): 163-83; Robert Seager II, *And Tyler Too* (New York: McGraw-Hill, 1963); Glenn W. Price, *Origins of the War with Mexico: The Polk-Stockton Intrigue* (Austin: University of Texas Press, 1967); and K. Jack Bauer, *Surfboats and Horse Marines* (Annapolis: U.S. Naval Institute, 1969).

6. Harold P. Langley, *Social Reform in the United States Navy, 1798-1862* (Urbana: University of Illinois Press, 1967).

7. The incident is described in considerable detail in Fitch W. Taylor, *The Broad Pennant* (New York: Leavitt, Trow & Co., 1848), pp. 262-83.

8. Hunter's tempestuous career is sketched in Caspar F. Goodrich, "Alvarado Hunter: A Biographical Sketch," *U.S. Naval Institute Proceedings* 49 (March 1918): 495-514.

9. Jonathan M. Foltz, *Report on Scorbutus* (Philadelphia: T. K. & P. G. Collins, 1848).

10. Lucius W. Johnson, "Yellow Jack: Master of Strategy," *U.S. Naval Institute Proceedings*, 76 (July 1950): 1074-83 touches upon the problem.

11. Francis J. Manno, "History of United States Naval Operations, 1846-1848" (Ph.D. diss., Georgetown University, 1954).

12. Harry A. Ellsworth, *One Hundred Eighty Landings of United States Marines, 1800-1934* (1934, reprint ed., Washington, D.C.: U.S. Marine Corps, 1974).

13. Frank M. Bennett, *The Steam Navy of the United States* (Pittsburgh: W. T. Nicholson, 1896).

14. Edward William Sloan III, *Benjamin Franklin Isherwood, Naval Engineer* (Annapolis: U.S. Naval Institute, 1965).

15. Clark G. Reynolds, "The Great Experiment: Hunter's Horizontal Wheel," *American Neptune* 24 (January 1964): 5-24.

16. Howard I. Chapelle, *History of the American Sailing Navy* (New York: W. W. Norton, 1949); *The History of American Sailing Ships* (New York: Bonanza Books, 1935); and *The Search for Speed under Sail, 1700-1855* (New York: Bonanza Books, 1962).

17. Charles Oscar Paullin, *Paullin's History of Naval Administration, 1775-1911* (Annapolis: U.S. Naval Institute, 1968).

18. Leonard D. White, *The Jacksonians: A Study in Administrative History, 1829-1861* (New York: Macmillan Co., 1954).

19. Stanley L. Falk, "Artillery for a Land Service: Development of a System," *Military Affairs* 28 (Fall 1964): 103-9.

20. Philip K. Lundeberg, *Samuel Colt's Submarine Battery: The Secret and the Enigma* (Washington, D.C.: Smithsonian Institution Press, 1974).

21. Robert L. Scheina, "Seapower Misused: Mexico at War, 1846-8," *Mariner's Mirror* 57 (July 1971): 203-4.

Appendix

LIST OF SUGGESTED RESEARCH TOPICS

1. Biographies—individual or collective—for example, Commodores David Conner, W. Branford Shubrick, Robert F. Stockton, John D. Sloat, Charles Morris, Joseph Smith, Capt. James M. Gilliss, Chief Engineer Charles H. Haswell, and Naval Constructor John Lenthall

2. Sources of manpower for the navy

3. Conditions of service in the United States Navy

4. Punishments in the antebellum navy

5. Execution of Seaman Samuel Jackson

6. Naval basis for Herman Melville's tales

7. Career patterns of antebellum officers

8. Social origins of the naval officer corps

9. Naval Apprentice Program

10. Relief of officers on distant stations

11. The Naval Asylum

12. Establishment of the bureau system

13. Development of naval steamships before 1860

14. The navy and experimentation in boiler design

15. The Loper propeller

16. Development of yard craft

17. History of the Ordnance Board

18. Standardization of ordnance

19. Development of shell guns

20. Samuel Colt's mine experiments

21. Development of drydocks

22. Development of diving bells

23. Utilization of officers and commissions to study foreign technical developments

24. Interservice exchange of technical information

25. The live oak plantations

26. Standard of medical care in the antebellum navy

27. Introduction and spread of medical knowledge in the navy

28. Scurvy in the United States Navy

29. Yellow fever and U.S. naval operations

30. Efforts at academic training of midshipmen before the establishment of the Naval Academy

31. Relations of naval officers and consuls

32. The U.S. Navy and Latin American insurrections

33. Naval landing parties

34. The U.S. Navy and the suppression of the slave trade

35. History of the Home, African, East Indian, or Brazil Squadrons

36. The Paraguay Expedition

37. Logistics in the Mexican War

38. The navy and military government

39. Stockton's plans for the California government

40. Shubrick and Baja California

41. Army-navy relations in Mexico

42. American experience with riverine warfare before the Civil War

43. The acquisition and outfitting of the mosquito flotilla

44. Blockade in the Mexican War

45. Development of amphibious doctrine before the Civil War

46. The Marine Battalion in the Mexico City campaign

DAVID F. TRASK

Research Opportunities in
the Spanish-Cuban-American War
and World War I

S pecialists in naval history recognize that their field is now experiencing a certain rebirth, but at the same time they do not rate it among the more highly developed areas of historical study in this country. What is to be done about this circumstance? Perhaps the best strategy for naval historians is simply to write more histories. Surely the conditions which could stimulate a great leap forward in both quantity and quality are present. If the past is any guide, innovation in any field of historical study springs principally from the impact of one or more of three circumstances. These include the availability of new methods, access to hitherto unexploited materials, and, possibly most important, alteration in perspective. All these circumstances are now present, and they ought to facilitate a considerable body of creative scholarship in naval history during the next few years.

circumstances are now present, and they ought to facilitate a considerable body of creative scholarship in naval history during the next few years.

In arguing this view I specifically do not disparage prior work in naval history. I urge, instead, that new departures proceed from the solid achievement of the past. As one who came recently to the study of naval history from other fields, I consider that writers such as Samuel Eliot Morison, and Elting E. Morison ranked with the best of their generation, and I feel similarly about writers of more recent vintage, such as William Braisted, Arthur Marder, and Peter Karsten.

Nevertheless, the law of life is change, and clearly one task ahead is to reconsider the overall periodization of American naval history. In the past naval historians concentrated on eras of warfare, a natural tendency, since naval activity commonly declined precipitately after a martial interlude. This emphasis accorded with the national proclivity to view warfare as an exceptional phenomenon rather than a frequent and expectable event. Present perspective, however, draws attention increasingly to interwar periods and to the realization that warfare has been a fundamental component of the national experience.

In this connection, therefore, it seems useful, when dealing with the naval history of the Spanish-Cuban-American War and World War I, not to treat these conflicts simply in terms of 1898 or 1917–18, isolating them as disparate processes, but to view them as aspects of a larger developmental process that occurred within the period 1883–1922. I have in mind the evolution of the "new navy," the navy of Mahan, Luce, Tracy, Sampson, Dewey, Sims, Benson, and many others over approximately forty years, from the beginnings of the steel navy until the great international naval conference in Washington during 1921–22. If someone projected a multivolume history of the United States Navy, it might well include a study devoted particularly to these years. Historians in other fields, especially those interested in politics such as Sam Hays and Robert Wiebe, provide a clear precedent, as do some naval historians. Among them are Elting Morison, in his biography of Adm. William S. Sims, and William Braisted, in his extraordinary two-volume study of the navy in Pacific waters.

All this is simply to point out that these comments relate to research opportunities and materials for the period 1883–1922, bearing in mind, of course, that this time span includes two wars of special significance, along with some lesser military episodes that ought not to be ignored, e.g., the Philippine Insurrection, the China Relief Expedition, and operations in various parts of the Caribbean such as those associated with the Mexican Revolution. Scholars who undertake specialized studies of given historical processes within the time span 1883–1922 might well consider their topics in the context of the larger historical phenomenon to which I have referred, i.e., the development of the new steel navy, which itself is an aspect of an even broader process—the nation's acquisition of great-power status and capabilities.

In preparing this presentation I asked assistance of a fairly sizable and representative group of scholars who have in the past examined aspects of naval history during the years from 1883 to 1922 (see Appendix A). Most of what follows derives from this survey. Although a broad spectrum of viewpoints appeared during this exercise, I seem to detect among practitioners certain broadly shared attitudes which exert considerable influence. Of these general attitudes the following seem most important:

1. No general consensus exists which defines the shapes and limits of naval history as a specialized object of inquiry. Predictably, most scholars emphasize those aspects of the field to which they have given attention. Yet one senses a general yearning to achieve larger comprehension—an interpretive matrix within which further investigations might develop profitably.

2. Many scholars seem greatly attracted to comparative history. They hope to encourage research which plays the American experience against that of other naval powers, particularly Britain, Germany, and Japan. This desire

may reflect their wish to move beyond a national and nationalistic version of American naval history in order to eliminate vestiges of xenophobia still affecting present scholarship.

3. Quite frequently specialists refer to the possibility of utilizing novel methods to probe certain subjects more systematically than in the past. An example would be the application of the great body of new theory developing within the social sciences to the study of naval questions. These specialists would also make use of computer techniques.

4. Two broad political concerns also seem to interest practically everyone. How did the navy relate to the general phenomenon of overseas expansion? More generally, how did the navy contribute to the nation's acquisition of great-power capability and status during the years from 1883 to 1922?

5. Finally, a surprising number of scholars sense a need for additional reference materials—particularly bibliographies and guides to manuscript collections—which would expedite the search for appropriate sources and authorities.

If my panel of experts is indeed representative, then it cannot be argued that naval historians lie outside the general parameters of the historical profession in this country at the moment, because much of this list might well have resulted from a survey of a number of other fields.

In considering these general attitudes, I sense also two areas of animus. One is a strong tendency to reject what is often called "drum and trumpet" history— studies of heroic tactical exploits which teach the lessons of patriotism. The second is a feeling that naval historians do not have at their disposal an appropriate amount of support, especially financial, to allow them to pursue their studies efficiently. Some believe that the army has been more helpful to military historians than the navy.

I mention these broad considerations because they influence proposals of topics worthy of research in the period 1883-1922. In this connection, following are certain suggested potential research areas that appear to require particular attention.

No area attracts more mention than the history of naval science and technology. There is widespread conviction that scholars must devote special energies to the study of material—its capabilities and its limits. In this regard, of course, the history of ships afloat comes to the fore. The development of hull design, armor, armament, munitions, methods of propulsion, gunnery, crew organization, navigation, and communications all require additional investigation. During the earlier twentieth century two new forms of naval combat began to develop, undersea warfare and naval air warfare, the origins of which remain unclear. Many historians interested particularly in naval-political history now realize the extent to which the sheer technological advances of the period 1883–1922 affected naval developments, and they would like others to provide them with knowledge of the technological considerations which influenced policy determination.

Another area of special concern is administrative history. How did the navy plan and conduct its everyday business in times of peace as well as in times of war? Scholars believe that the Navy Department requires examination in minute detail. They urge investigation of bureaus, offices, and units at sea. The Office of Naval Intelligence and the activities of naval attaches in particularly sensitive posts, e.g., London, Tokyo, and Berlin, stimulate curiosity. Like the State and War Departments, the Navy Department expanded greatly during the period 1883–1922 and also proliferated its connections with other components of government as well as nongovernment entities. This fact suggests the need for studies of administrative relationships which some speculate might constitute a "naval-industrial complex."

Scholars also feel drawn to the general area of social history, which they perceive as a particularly underdeveloped aspect of naval history. Much mention is made of the enlisted man. How were seamen recruited? What personnel policies and educational opportunities were provided to meet the needs of the new naval establishment? As one might expect, interest abounds in the nature of race relations within the navy and also in the question of the degree to which the navy reflected the general characteristics of the "progressive era," particularly its role as an instrument of social uplift and mobility.

The fourth area which scholars believe demands study concerns certain aspects of operational activity, although not particularly for either the Spanish-Cuban-American War or World War I. The history of squadron activities in various parts of the world—especially in Latin America, East Asia, and the Mediterranean—attracts frequent mention. Certain specific events such as the naval role in the Philippine Insurrection, the China Relief Expedition, and sundry interventions in the Caribbean also interest the specialists. In this connection mention should be made of a related service—the United States Marine Corps—which played an important role as the enforcer of the Theodore Roosevelt corollary to the Monroe Doctrine.

Although few scholars now seem preoccupied with tactical questions, another area of widespread interest is the development of strategic doctrine. Many suspect that the ideas of Captain Mahan and his school may be overstressed in the extant literature and that actual practice might depart considerably from the theoretical doctrines of those who contributed articles to the *United States Naval Institute Proceedings*.

The sixth and most regularly discussed area of research remains naval-political history. This emphasis may reflect the extensive influx of historians into the field of naval history who have worked earlier in the history of foreign relations. At the core of most topics proposed for investigation in naval-political history is the puzzle of the relations between force and diplomacy during the period 1883–1922. How was seapower to be organized and exerted in connection with both general and particular aspects of foreign policy? We need studies of the role of naval officers as diplomats, continuing the work of Paullin and others. How did naval officers conduct themselves as governors of various insular possessions, for example, Guam? To what extent did the navy support the aims of dollar diplomacy? How did the navy relate to the House and Senate committees dealing with naval affairs? What role did the navy play in developing the building programs of 1916 and 1919? How did the navy monitor and react to naval innovation by competing naval powers as advances elsewhere impinged upon the nation's foreign policy? Although some of these topics and others that readily suggest themselves have been studied in recent years, scholars seem generally dissatisfied with the extant work, and they frequently advert to ongoing investigations of their own which fit into this category.

Finally, many scholars urge continuing biographical investigations, stressing particularly those figures who have not been written about or for whom inadequate biographies or memoirs exist. Significant naval officers such as Henry C. Taylor, Bradley Fiske, and Hugh Rodman receive mention as do second-echelon civilian figures, for example, George von Lengerke Meyer. Some also believe that collective biography, such as that pioneered by Peter Karsten, will yield fruitful insights, particularly in regard to the history of enlisted personnel.

In addition to the above-mentioned topics, Appendix B contains a list of further potential research areas that merit investigation.

If even a small part of this scholarship should be completed during the next ten or twenty years, it would indeed contribute greatly to a larger synthesis of naval history for the period 1883–1922, and it would also help significantly to achieve a better understanding of the overall American experience during these critical years of the national past.

Very few of the research areas described here can be dealt with entirely by visiting the collections of materials relevant to American naval history held by the National Archives; those who wish to make truly useful contributions must accept the burdens of multiarchival research. By the same token, however, most investigations of the period 1883–1922 must rest on the solid foundation of record groups deposited in the National Archives. Fortunately, no great obstacles block the way to the appropriate naval records or naval-related records. Very few materials are still withheld from investigators because of classification. Moreover, a most helpful, although not entirely complete, set of finding aids prepared by staff members of the National Archives since

1940 may be consulted. Of course, researchers must move beyond the prepared finding aids in many cases. When this necessity arises, scholars may draw upon the expertise of archivists located in the various administrative units which house the several collections—most importantly, of course, those who staff the Navy and Old Army Branch and the Modern Military Branch of the National Archives. As it happens, the chronological division between these two branches falls within the years 1883–1922, so that many investigators must search collections in both of these administrative units in order to exhaust available materials.

The record groups in the National Archives containing materials of the Navy Department to which investigators may wish to direct attention fall into several general classes. These are (1) certain record groups of general importance which will have to be considered in connection with most topics; (2) a second set of record groups dealing with specific administrative bureaus, offices, and units that existed within the naval establishment during the years at issue; and (3) a third set of record groups relating to naval or maritime affairs, which are held in branches of the Archives other than the Navy and Old Army and Modern Military branches but which may be of great importance for certain investigations.

Three record groups come under the first category—materials of broad general interest:

1. Record Group 38, the Records of the Office of the Chief of Naval Operations. This collection includes many types of information, ranging from those pertaining to the Office of Island Governments to those associated with special missions.

2. Record Group 45, the Naval Records Collection of the Office of Naval Records and Library. Here are located many varieties of critical information—ship logs, secretarial correspondence, personnel records, and the like.

3. Record Group 80, the General Records of the Department of Navy, 1798–1947. Here are found the files of the secretary of the Navy Department, his principal civilian assistants, and the chief of Naval Operations.

The second category of naval records includes the record groups of specific administrative entities below the level of the secretaries and chiefs of naval operations. No less than ten record groups fall within this category, as follows:

Record Group 19, Records of the Bureau of Ships.

Record Group 24, Records of the Bureau of Naval Personnel.

Record Group 37, Records of the Hydrographic Office.

Record Group 52, Records of the Bureau of Medicine and Surgery.

Record Group 71, Records of the Bureau of Yards and Docks.

Record Group 72, Records of the Bureau of Aeronautics.

Record Group 74, Records of the Bureau of Ordnance.

Record Group 78, Records of the Naval Observatory.

Record Group 125, Records of the Office of the Judge Advocate General (Navy).

Record Group 143, Records of the Bureau of Supplies and Accounts (Navy).

Included in the third category are five record groups of a miscellaneous character, all of which are of great importance:

Record Group 127, Records of the U.S. Marine Corps.

Record Group 181, Records of Naval Districts and Shore Establishments.

Record Group 225, Records of Joint Army and Navy Boards and Committees.

Record Group 313, Records of Naval Operating Forces.

Record Group 405, Records of the U.S. Naval Academy.

Thus, no less than eighteen prime record groups in the National Archives include Navy Department materials, which may provide extensive documentation for topics dealing with the period 1883–1922. All of these collections are located in the Navy and Old Army and Modern Military Branches.

But this listing does not exhaust the holdings of materials of direct or indirect interest to students of certain topics. Several other branches of the National Archives control another twenty record groups to which naval historians might well direct attention in connection with certain topics. Following are some examples of these collections.

Record Group 23, Records of the Coast and Geodetic Survey, located in the Industrial and Social Branch.

Record Group 26, Records of the U.S. Coast Guard, located in the Legislative, Judicial, and Fiscal Branch.

Record Group 126, Records of the Office of Territories, located in the Natural Resources Branch.

Record Group 185, Records of the Panama Canal, located in the General Archives Division.

Record Group 350, Records of the Bureau of Insular Affairs, located in the Natural Resources Branch.

There are, of course, many other such collections.[1] In addition, a significant amount of collateral material is located in other record groups which contain State Department and War Department materials. For an excellent summary of all the various resources for naval history located in the Washington area, including those of the National Archives, one should consult the excellent guide prepared by Dean C. Allard and Betty Bern of the Naval History Division entitled *U.S. Naval History Sources in the Washington Area and Suggested Research Topics* [3d ed. (Washington, D.C.: Department of the Navy, 1970)].

It is, of course, as impossible to give any real indication of the extraordinary riches of the material to be found in the National Archives relating to naval history for the period 1883–1922 as it is to cover all the possible topics that might fruitfully attract scholarly attention to coming years. It is perhaps appropriate to conclude with a plea that efforts to stimulate use of the National Archives collections should be increased. Every time I go to the Archives, I cannot help but marvel at the surprisingly small number of serious scholars who take advantage of them. If and when these sources are properly exploited, we will assuredly possess more of that illusive "new naval history" about which we hear so much and which indeed is attainable in our time.

NOTE

1. Others are Record Group 27, Records of the National Weather Bureau (Natural Resources Branch); Record Group 32, Records of the U.S. Shipping Board (Industrial and Social Branch); Record Group 36, Records of the U.S. Customs Service (Legislative, Judicial, and Fiscal Branch); Record Group 41, Records of the Bureau of Marine Inspection and Navigation (Industrial and Social Branch); Record Group 55, Records of the Government of the Virgin Islands (Natural Resources Branch); Record Group 139, Records of the Dominican Customs Receivership (Natural Resources Branch); Record Group 140, Records of the Military Government of Cuba (Natural Resources Branch); Record Group 151, Records of the Bureau of Foreign and Domestic Commerce and Successor Agencies (Industrial and Social Branch); Record Group 178, Records of the U.S. Maritime Commission (Industrial and Social Branch); Record Group 199, Records of the Provisional Government of Cuba (Natural Resources Branch); Record Group 217, Records of the U.S. General Accounting Office (Legislative, Judicial, and Fiscal Branch); Record Group 284, Records of the Government of American Samoa (Federal Records Center, San Francisco); Record Group 301, Records of the Hawaiian Territorial Government (Office of Federal Records Centers); Record Group 348, Records of the Alaskan Territorial Government (Federal Records Center, Seattle); Record Group 401, National Archives Gift Collection of Records Relating to Polar Regions (Center for Polar Archives).

Appendix A

SCHOLARS OF NAVAL HISTORY

This is a list of scholars of naval history for the period from 1883 to 1922 who were surveyed for this study.

Bailey, Thomas A.
Stanford University

Braisted, William R.
University of Texas

Challener, Richard
Princeton University

Coffman, Edward M.
University of Wisconsin

Cooling, B. Franklin
U.S. Army Military History
Research Collection

Crowl, Philip A.
Naval War College

Evans, Lawrence
SUNY at Binghamton

Fowler, Wilton B.
Naval War College

Gelfand, Lawrence E.
University of Iowa

Gwinn, Paul
SUNY at Buffalo

Hagan, Kenneth J.
United States Naval Academy

Karsten, Peter
University of Pittsburgh

LaFeber, Walter
Cornell University

Leopold, Richard W.
Northwestern University

Lundeberg, Philip K.
Smithsonian Institution

May, Ernest R.
Harvard University

Merli, Frank
Queens College, CUNY

Morison, Elting E.
Peterborough, N.H.

O'Connor, Raymond F.
University of Miami

Reynolds, Clark
University of Maine, Orono

Ropp, Theodore
Duke University

Ryan, Captain Paul B.
U.S.N., Ret.

Smith, Myron J., Jr.
Huntington (Ind.) Public Library

Turk, Richard W.
Allegheny College

Weigley, Russell F.
Temple University

Appendix B

POSSIBLE TOPICS FOR STUDIES
OF NAVAL HISTORY, 1883-1922

This list includes topics for investigation suggested in various ways by scholars who have studied aspects of American naval history during the period 1883–1922. Purely illustrative and suggestive, it is by no means exhaustive. No attempt is made to distinguish between more important and less important topics. Some topics might require book-length treatment while others might be manageable as articles or essays. Certain topics may well be under investigation, while others may have been previously studied. The list should be particularly useful to advisers of theses and dissertations. Some topics may be pursued more extensively than others in records held by the National Archives. In any event, although most of the topics require multiarchival investigation, few of them could be thoroughly researched without consulting the National Archives record groups relating to naval history.

Personnel

A History of Naval Recruitment and Its Results

The Navy as an Instrument of Social Uplift and Mobility: Education and Training in the Trades and Crafts, 1890–1920

A History of Naval Personnel Policies

A Social History of the American Seaman

Struggles for Position and Status within the Naval Officer Corps

A History of Race Relations in the United States Navy

The Navy "Career Pattern": Characteristics and Consequences

The Activity of Retired Naval Officers

A History of Naval Education and Training

A History of the Psychological and Social Consequences of Life Afloat

A History of the Politics of Naval Personnel

Strategy and Planning

Mobilization Planning in the Navy

The Navy and Demobilization

Contingency Planning: Realism or Fantasy?

War Games and War Gaming in the Navy

The Impact of the Royal Navy on American Strategy

Contingency Planning against Potential Enemies

Technological Limitations on Strategic Options

A History of the Naval War Board, 1898

Operations

"Showing the Flag": A Study of Naval Visits

The Navy and Continental Shore Defense

The Evolution of Submarine Warfare and Its Implications

"Foiling the U-Boats": An Analysis of the Convoy System, 1917–1918

The Naval Air Arm during World War I: Campaigns against Submarines and Submarine Bases

The Naval Contribution to the Pacification of the Philippines

Naval Operations in Russia and Siberia, 1918–1920

The Navy, Marine Corps, and Amphibious Warfare

Naval Operations in the Mediterranean Sea

Operations of the Marine Corps in the Caribbean Area

The Navy and the China Relief Expedition of 1900

Naval Science and Technology

A History of the Introduction of New Types of Vessels, 1883–1922

A History of Naval Weaponry: Development and Employment

A History of Naval Communications

A History of Private Industrial Contributions to Naval Development

The Influence of Naval Technology upon International Law

The Scientific and Technological Lessons of the Spanish-Cuban-American War

The Navy and the Iron and Steel Industry

Naval Administration

The Development of the Office of the Secretary of the Navy

The Development of the Office of Chief of Naval Operations

A History of Fleet and Squadron Organization

A Comparison of the Activities of the American Joint Board and the British Committee of Imperial Defense

The Navy and "Crisis Management"

The Navy's Participation in Interdepartmental Consultation and Coordination

The Growth of the Naval Bureaucracy and Its Consequences

Studies in Bureau Organization and Management [Bureau of Naval Personnel, Bureau of Ships, Bureau of Ordnance, among others]

The Role of the Assistant Secretaries of the Navy

Naval-Political History

The Navy and the Consular Service

Military Government in the Caribbean Sea and the Pacific Ocean [e.g., Guam and Samoa]

The Navy and the London Conference of 1909

Perceptions of Germany and Japan as Enemies

Naval Officers as Diplomats

Naval Officers in Their Relations to Imperialism

The Navy and Dollar Diplomacy

The Navy and Isthmian Policy

The Role of the Office of Naval Intelligence

The Work of Naval Attaches

The Navy and Neutrality, 1914–1917

The Navy and the Enforcement of the Monroe Doctrine

Projects for Base Development in the Caribbean and Pacific Regions

Naval Questions at the Paris Peace Conference

Biography

A Collective Biography of Naval Flag Officers

Francis M. Ramsey

John G. Walker

Henry C. Taylor

Bradley A. Fiske

Winfield S. Schley

William T. Sampson

Washington Irving Chambers

Charles O'Neil

Eugene Hale

Nathan Sargent

Albert Gleaves

Stanley C. Hooper

Montgomery Sicard

William Benson

Hugh Rodman

George von Lengerke Meyer

The Navy and Domestic Politics

The History of Naval Appropriations

Naval Base Development and Sectional Interest

The Navy's Relations with the Congressional Committees on Naval Affairs

The Public Reaction to Naval Building Programs

The Political Attitudes of Naval Personnel

Miscellaneous Topics

A Comparison of European and American Navalism

Naval Interest in the Merchant Marine

Foreign Naval Thought and Practice as They Influenced American Behavior

The Philosophy of Sea Power: A History

The Navy and the Economy during World War I

The Relationship between Naval Administration and Naval Technology:
A Study of Bureau Practice

The Navy and the Doctrine of the Freedom of the Seas

Big-Navy Propagandists and Their Influence

The Development of Anti-Naval Thought

A Comparison of the "Naval Mind" and the "Civilian Mind": A Study in
Socialization

A History of Naval Shore Establishments

Commentary

The presentations in this session make it abundantly clear that, regarding the history of the United States Navy prior to 1923, the research potential of extant sources is rich indeed for those laboring in this congenial sector of maritime studies. As Drs. Morgan, Trask, and Bauer have amply demonstrated, naval biography continues to afford a particularly attractive avenue of approach, enhanced increasingly now by an evident deepening commitment to serious consideration of the impact of technological and social environment upon the select figures concerned. The range of naval types suggested by these authors as available for fruitful investigation is an ever-widening one, beginning obviously with operational leaders—some long overlooked and others requiring deeper insight, proceeding to no less embattled administrators and reformers, and extending to a variety of significant contributors to naval science and technology. Judging by the recent monograph on blacks in the United States Marine Corps,[1] whose prime era of consideration unhappily lies beyond this session's time span, the range must now extend to the careers of notable, or simply observant and communicative, men from the ranks of our naval services, on whose individual witness in journal and sketchbook, as well as emerging quantitative analyses of muster rolls, prisoner-of-war lists, and court martial proceedings, we are reliant for shaping an accurate social history of our sea services.

We have certainly neglected important operational leaders, as both Dr. Morgan and Dr. Bauer have indicated. Considering the length and rich variety of service evident in the careers of such figures as Commodores Connor and Shubrick, Professor Trask's call for careful reconsideration of the periodization of American naval history is particularly pertinent, especially in dealing with their years of peacetime service and also more glamorous wartime endeavors. One grasps the validity of such broader frames of reference in examining that notable multivolume achievement to which I have often previously alluded, the monumental *Svenska Flottans Historia,*[2] that challenging demonstration of collaborative scholarship that must ultimately find an American response. Many more solid building blocks are needed, however, notably in the area of naval technology, before we can undertake such a comprehensive and multi-faceted synthesis.

Looking at the history of American naval technology, one finds still challenging us at the dawn of the federal navy that British-trained naval architect Josiah Fox, seen against the background of his Old Country apprenticeship as well as of his American associates and rivals. Rich as the resources are of the Peabody Museum and the National Archives regarding Fox's career, his story clearly suggests one variation on the importance of a considerable research investment in European archives, museums, and specialized libraries.

The elements of paradox and irony emerge in the perspective of more lengthy naval careers. These become evident when one examines John Dahlgren's notably fruitful contributions to mid-nineteenth-century ordnance development and then considers the irony of his indirect and unwonted success in providing the Confederate navy with large quantities of excellent ordnance at the outset of the Civil War. They emerge also when one examines the consequences of what may be described as a classic example of technological nonfruition. I refer to that colorful embodiment of a reverse career pattern, of failure and success, represented in the Yankee inventor and entrepreneur Samuel Colt.[3] Long frustrated in his efforts to provide advanced firearms and mine warfare systems to our armed services, Colt had his opportunity in repeating arms with the onset of the Mexican War. Late in his tragically shortened career, the Hartford magnate enjoyed the spectacle of Matthew Fontaine Maury's efforts in 1861, starting from evident theoretical scratch, to develop and integrate mine warfare systems with emerging Confederate coastal and riverine defenses.

One gains an even more compelling sense of periodization in the process of internationalizing the scope of technological investigations. No account of Colt's secretive submarine battery venture, characterized by his deliberate and successful efforts to avoid close surveillance, much less assistance, from professional military and naval engineers and ordnance specialists, could be placed in adequate perspective without careful examination of notably successful contemporary developments by British military engineers in the field of galvanic salvage operations, reported throughout the professional world in connection with the salvage of the wreck of the *Royal George* from 1839 to 1844. In this regard, it is important to emphasize the high relevance of contemporary professional journals for tracing the international flow of technological development. From the *Royal George* operation, one may detect significant spinoff effects in galvanic mine warfare not only in the United States but Russia as well. Thus I should like to suggest, particularly in the area of the history of technology, the relevance of our own resources in archives, museums, and libraries in the United States and, in addition, the surprisingly rich sources of insight lying in wait for use in Ottawa, Paris, London, Madrid, Stockholm, Copenhagen, and Freiburg. A notable example is Col. Howard I. Chapelle's remarkable discovery in Copenhagen of detailed plans for Robert Fulton's steam battery, providing one of those solid building blocks which he designedly contributed to the emergent history of naval technology.

Surrounded by the intimidating resources of our National Archives, as well as of our naval and maritime museums and specialized libraries, we may indeed be tempted to neglect the international perspective in pursuing our missions as historians. Yet as Professor Trask's allusion to comparative military history reminds us, we can no longer remain in our nationalistic box. We will all derive much encouragement in following the lead taken at least two decades ago by our colleagues in the field of literary history in breaking out of nationally oriented envisagements in their fields of specialization. In this connection we need to pay close attention to the themes proposed by several of the international commissions for the meeting of the International Congress of Historical Sciences in San Francisco in August 1975. I would note in particular the broad theme of "La Technique Militaire," adopted by the International Commission of Military History, and secondly, pertaining to Dr. Morgan's call for new investigation on privateering, the theme chosen by the International Commission of Maritime History, "Piracy and Privateering." The economic as well as political and military overtones in this theme are apparent.

In concluding my brief commentary on these papers that promise to be of permanent reference value, I should like to return to Dr. Morgan's apt characterization of our naval documentary resources on the American Revolution as "a scattered but fruitful seedbed." We at the Smithsonian Institution have reason to add our hearty confirmation to this judgment in connection with the ongoing documentation of the Continental gondola *Philadelphia.* That venerable veteran of Benedict Arnold's northern campaign of 1776 has been viewed by perhaps fifty million Americans and foreign visitors during the last half decade, yet she has been possessed of a hauntingly enigmatic character, despite the wealth of documentation regarding her construction and brief service north of Ticonderoga, owing to the fact that the identity of her captain and indeed the size and background of her crew have remained obscure. To the National Archives we are deeply indebted for generous assistance in dispelling these uncertainties and in opening up the gunboat's full human dimension. In early spring, 1973, the National Archives Center for the Documentary Study of the American Revolution, then engaged in canvassing libraries, archives, museums, and historical societies throughout the land for documents related to the Continental Congress and other Bicentennial themes, received a letter from the Fort Concho Museum at San Angelo, Texas, a frontier post restoration seemingly quite remote from the context of our 1976 preoccupation. Included in that museum's manuscript holdings, as reported to the Archives, was nothing less than the original payroll of the gondola *Philadelphia*, an item of somewhat peripheral interest to the center's own project but of surprising significance to the denizens of our Museum of History and Technology. Nothing might have happened. But happily, Kenneth E. Harris, of the center, made an immediate mental connection with our exhibit of this national treasure and, as quickly, alerted the Smithsonian Division of Naval History. The result, evident in our Hall of Armed Forces History, was the donation of a document that not only opens up the whole human dimension of this remarkable time capsule but entirely clarifies, in conjunction with her captain's pension application (also among National Archives holdings), the long debated identity of the *Philadelphia*. Here indeed is a classic example of enlightened professional courtesy.

NOTES

1. Henry I. Shaw, Jr., and Ralph W. Donnelly, *Blacks in the Marine Corps* (Washington, D.C.: History and Museums Div., Headquarters, U.S. Marine Corps, 1975).
2. S. Artur Svensson et al., *Svenska Flottans Historia*, 4 vols. (Malmo: Allhems förlag, 1942–45).
3. Philip K. Lundeberg, *Samuel Colt's Submarine Battery* (Washington, D.C.: Smithsonian Institution, 1974).

V

SOME NAVAL ASPECTS
OF THE SECOND WORLD WAR

Buildup and Activities of German Defensive Offshore Forces in World War II

Hardly anything has been published about the defensive offshore forces and their activities in World War II. Yet approximately one hundred thousand men of the German navy in 3,000 vessels were busy all along the coasts minesweeping, escorting, patrolling, and submarine hunting. Of course, there were considerable forces of this type in service during World War I, mainly for minesweeping purposes. However, after clearing the minefields in the areas allotted to Germany, they were paid off. Only two minesweepers were left on active duty, with a small unit which had been responsible for the minesweeping gear during the clearance work.

From 1920 to 1921 I was captain of one of these minesweepers. Thirty of these coalburning M-boats (500 tons) were laid up. The German navy was allowed to keep them because they were too insignificant even for the Treaty of Versailles. The first German postwar naval periodical, *The Weyer* (now also in English), did not mention them at all.

In 1924 a squadron of four of these minesweepers was commissioned. The unit responsible for the minesweeping gear now was officially charged with the task of developing new mines and minesweeping gear as well as antisubmarine warfare (ASW) weapons. It was called the "Sperrversuchskommando" (SVK). I served in this unit from 1920 to 1923 as an assistant for several developments, in addition to being captain of a minesweeper. Following this, after a year ashore, I studied for two years at a technical university, and in the following two years was captain of a minesweeper in the active squadron.

From 1928 to 1932 I was in charge of mine development in the SVK and served as senior officer of the Minesweeping Squadron (MSw) for the succeeding two years. After another spell ashore, I was made commander of minesweepers in the spring of 1937. Of course, I kept in close contact with the SVK at all times. It corresponded to the British H.M.S. *Vernon*, but received only about 10 percent as much funding. Nevertheless, as we found out after the war, we were always a bit ahead of the British until deep into the war. The reasons for this were able commanding officers; excellent cooperation among scientists, engineers, naval officers, mechanics, and others; close cooperation between the SVK and MSw squadrons and a thorough evaluation of the World War I experience. (This evaluation was made by several officers who had been in the MSw.) Early in the war, the Russian mines and methods were also considerably better than the British. During the second half of the war, though, the British caught up, but they had the additional advantage of their geographical situation.

From spring 1917 on, the German navy was fully occupied keeping channels open for getting submarines out to sea and back. The big U.S. minefield laid in 1918 between the Shetlands and Norway could not be reached by minesweepers. However, it did less damage than would be expected, because of defects in the mines.

The German MSw gear was of two types, "light" and "heavy." The light gear consisted of thin wires kept down by paravanes. It could be used as exploratory sweep by up to five vessels in line, abreast, and in this way cover 1,500 meters (almost a land mile). It was very accurate, although not as accurate as was believed at the time. It could also be used for sweeping mines with the help of explosive grapnels, one between two boats. This method was time consuming because for each mine the gear had to be reeved again. The great drawback was that it forced the sweepers to cross the minefield too often. The heavy gear was unwieldy and inaccurate but good for fields of straight lines which were marked with the help of the light gear. Altogether it was found that the German gear had been fairly good, but that sweeping consumed too much time and losses were too high.

At first, not much was known about British methods and gear, especially their single-ship sweep (with paravanes). But somebody had kindly left a British admiralty manual in an old destroyer to be broken up at Kiel (where SVK was stationed). It dealt with mines, minesweeping gear, and ASW and made most interesting reading, besides being of considerable help. I had the job of translating the manual. We kept our old gear but developed single-ship gear, too, with paravanes for fast ships like destroyers and torpedoboats and with shearing otter boards for the normal comparatively slow sweeps. In this way, we were well prepared to deal with anchored mines.

In 1918 the British had begun laying ground mines with magnetic ignitions off the coast of Flanders. They were touched off by the magnetic field of a passing ship. These mines could be used in shallow water only but there they proved very dangerous, and no gear existed for sweeping them. The German navy at once started developing a similar mine and took the work up again in 1920. At the same time, the defense against this type of mine was developed. A method was found to reduce the magnetic field by horizontal cable coils around the whole vessel. Then a simple magnetic sweep was built by putting large magnets into hulls of fishing cutters, which were towed in pairs by small wooden tugs. As a third measure "barrage breakers" (Sperrbrechers) were tried out. These were steamers with several thousand meters of cable wound horizontally around them forward of the bridge. This method gave a very strong field, and it was kept most secret.

As to minesweepers, there were, besides the M-boats, a few motorboats originally built as sub-chasers. Both types were improved—the M-boat somewhat enlarged and equipped with oil fuel. (Incidentally, during the war, a new class was built with coal again.) A series of motorboats of about fifty tons proved too small, not seaworthy enough. However, during the war they could pass the French canals and served on the North African Coast. An improved class of 100 tons followed and was excellent. They were called "R-Boote," i.e., Raumboote, and used for sweeping shallow mines, which were dangerous for the larger minesweepers.

In about 1935 a fast minesweeping and escorting vessel was designed, the so-called F-boat, i.e., "Flottenbegleiter" (fleet escorts). Ten were ready before the war but too much had been attempted with them. Their boilers broke down over and over again, and after a few months, their fast sweeping had to be done by torpedoboats. These were all equipped with paravane gear, but this kind of work was disliked and thus was not done very well.

Trawlers and drifters were earmarked as auxiliary minesweepers. They had done service of this kind in the First World War. They were very seaworthy, but not very maneuverable and had too much draft. Nevertheless, they were a great help during the war, particularly for routine sweeps.

The shallow waters along the German coasts made good minesweeping imperative. In 1933 a minesweeping force was created under Fleet Command. At that time it consisted of two squadrons of M-boats and two of R-boats. At the outbreak of the war, there were two squadrons of modern M-boats and three of new R-boats, in addition to one of the fleet escorts. A number of methods were tried out to sweep mines quickly and with the least danger to the sweepers. Exercises were arranged to resemble war conditions as closely as possible. In spring exercises, all the squadrons worked together by day and by night. It was quite a feat to have thirty to forty sweepers, completely darkened, cooperating to break a gap through a minefield. Twice a year our Experimental Unit (SVK) laid a deep barrage. These mines had very small explosive charges of about two pounds.

There were a number of accidents—mainly from carelessness—but we learned how to handle dangerous gadgets, and the Experimental Unit gained practical knowledge on some of its new inventions. Only when a boat full of sight-seeing admirals struck one of the mines was there general regret among junior officers that the charges had not been a bit stronger. However, even if this had been the case, for most of them it would not have changed promotion very much. For the Bureau of Personnel, the minesweepers were generally last on the list, particularly after 1933 when the fleet started growing rapidly. Because of this growth, the fleet received more than its share of officers who were promoted from the ranks. Most of them were good, but they had to get additional training. Sociologists generally overlook the difficulties in finding qualified people for the higher positions in a rapidly expanding organization like our navy. The only other organization we could turn to was the Merchant Marine, and we got a small number of very good officers from that source. But we had to pay more attention to training and education than previously. Training went on throughout the year, with the exception of a few short breaks for boiler cleaning and about two months for the annual overhaul. During this time most petty officers and older enlisted ratings went to school for general education and preparation for civilian life (vocational training). In the fall, all squadrons came together at one of our bases for a week. Then all officers and chief petty officers were informed of the general situation, current problems of training, plans for the year, new gear, and so forth. Particular care was given to all problems of leadership, but the overall training went further. Each senior officer of a squadron had to give a talk on a subject of his choice not connected with the naval service. Our slogan was "The local paper and a glass of beer are not sufficient for improving education."

All this may seem unimportant compared with the great events of the war. However, I think that history is composed of an immense number of seemingly insignificant details which nevertheless form the greater events and influence the general course history will take. In our case, without this careful peacetime training it would hardly have been possible to build up the large defensive organization all along the occupied coasts and to get it into working order.

THE POLISH CAMPAIGN

The Polish campaign was a kind of dress rehearsal for the minesweepers. After the declaration of war by Great Britain and France, all the real warships went to the North Sea, and the minesweepers had to serve as maids of all work in the Baltic during the Polish campaign. They had to not only sweep mines but also to blockade the Polish ports, to hunt submarines, and to fight light guns ashore. Minesweeping gear and procedures proved satisfactory; the Polish minefields (French horned mines) were no great obstacle. We always had our swept channels behind the Polish lines on land. The first mines that were

swept were towed ashore and examined—this had not been done in the first
war. It was determined that the Polish had laid dummy mines to give the
appearance of minefields and yet to be able to pass that area freely. The boats
in the blockade positions always had their MSw gear out. This gave them a
good chance of detecting mines without hitting them. There were no losses
until after the armistice had been concluded. Then an M-boat struck a mine
and sank with great loss of life. Because hostilities were over, her captain had
taken a short cut outside the swept channel, but the mines did not acknowledge
the armistice.

Another experience did not cost any lives but was rather humiliating. The
Poles had five submarines. The German navy submarines, destroyers, and
minesweepers sank *seven* of them "with absolute certainty." Nevertheless, all
five managed to reach neutral or Allied ports, although in a more or less
damaged condition, and their crews talked freely to reporters. Evidently, our
sonar and our depth charges were quite good. What was lacking was tenacity.
This evaluation soon paid dividends in the North Sea.

THE NORTH SEA, 1939-40

At the beginning of the war, geographical conditions in the North Sea had
been altered by a large system of minefields reaching from outside Dutch
territorial waters about one hundred fifty miles to the north, to a latitude of
the Skagerrak. This "West Wall," as it was called, protected the eastern part
of the North Sea from raids by surface ships. Moreover, in the eastern part
of the North Sea and through the West Wall, there was a system of swept
channels—"roads," as we called them—which had to be controlled with minesweeping gear at short intervals. For this work, there were eleven squadrons,
each with eight to twelve boats. Four were composed of trawlers or drifters;
three of M-boats, old and new; two of R-boats; and one each of escort vessels
and barrage breakers. Headquarters were at Cuxhaven at the mouth of the
Elbe. There were also several squadrons of patrol boats and sub-chasers under
"senior officer patrols." Together with a group of minelayers, all of these
forces were under a rear admiral "commanding the protective forces."

On an average, four squadrons were at sea occupied with sweeping. In the
daytime the courses of the sweepers crossed and recrossed the "roads" in order
to give the enemy air reconnaissance a wrong picture. One of these routine
sweeps detected the first British mines in the channel just south of the West
Wall along Dutch waters. They were quickly cleared without any losses.

Until the spring of 1940 mines remained a negligible factor, contrary to
expectations. Our own mines caused more worry. The sinker of our anti-

submarine mine turned out to be too light, and in a heavy swell the mines started wandering. They had been laid in great numbers, so deep that surface ships could pass over them, but their migrations brought them into shallower water. Eventually, they all had to be swept, which was quite a lot of work.

Planes were also rather harmless at first. Their code was broken early, and a squadron of minesweepers was very proud when it was reported as "six destroyers proceeding at 30 knots."

Submarines, however, were more dangerous. In December 1939 they damaged two light cruisers. When these were brought in, one of our escort vessels was torpedoed and sank with great loss of life. But in January and February, minesweepers sank three British submarines, taking two complete crews as prisoners. Tenacity paid dividends. One minesweeper had damaged a submarine which waited on the bottom of the sea until late into the night. When it surfaced to escape, it did so exactly between two lighted buoys, which the minesweeper had laid to fix the place of the submarine. The crew surrendered at once. From that time on the German bight was free from submarines. These comparatively quiet times were fully utilized to train the reserve squadrons. Part of their crews had never seen any military service. It was particularly important to utilize these men according to their capabilities and experience.

THE CAMPAIGNS OF 1940

The Norwegian Campaign

During the Norwegian campaign, in April 1940, North Sea minesweepers occupied Ports of Esbjerg and Thyboron on the West Coast of Jutland. Work increased because there were more "roads" to sweep and fewer workers, since several squadrons had been sent to the Baltic entrances and to Norway.

The British began to drop a few magnetic mines into the North Sea estuaries, but our barrage breakers and minesweepers, with newly introduced magnetic gear, removed them quickly.

The French Campaign

On the morning of May 10, 1940, the radio gave the news of the German attack in the West. The minesweepers had not been told and did not get any orders. So we started sweeping a channel to the West along the Dutch islands without orders. We also sent some officers by car to the Dutch and Belgian ports to find out about the situation there. They found that both sides had done quite a bit of mining, and that our own air force was somewhat uncertain about the places where it had dropped mines from the air.

Clearing ports and channels along the coast was urgent. In the second half of May, channels were swept along the Dutch coast into Belgian waters and the entrances to several ports were cleared. In June the second phase of the German operations brought the area of the French coast to the Spanish frontier into our possession. This improved the position for conducting naval warfare considerably, but it also made it necessary to find protective forces for sweeping and patrolling channels along approximately twelve hundred miles of coast with twenty-five ports, which were mined for the most part.

In April we tried to convince the powers above that additional squadrons of minesweeping cutters would come in handy, but with little success. In May we began to form squadrons from small vessels we found in Holland. Now, more energetic steps had to be taken to procure ships, men, and weapons. I made a rapid survey of the ports on the Bay of Biscay, north of the Loire (Brest, Lorient, and Saint-Nazaire), because they had to be made available to our submarines as quickly as possible. Therefore, our only modern unit (all the others were still in Norway)—second squadron R-boats—made an exploratory sweep all along the north coast of France and arrived in Brest the end of June 1940. Early in July it conducted the first submarines in safely. Then a squadron of modern minesweepers was released and also sent to the Bay of Biscay. Two more and two R-boat squadrons were to follow, but the North Sea could not be entirely depleted, and some squadrons had to remain in Norway. The preparations for Operation Sea Lion (landing in England) had to be made, so we had to find other ways and means.

Increasing the minesweeping forces.   The general idea was to create local flotillas of several "stationary" squadrons which would remain in the same stretch of coast all the time. This would make the modern squadrons available for special tasks, such as protecting valuable ships and quick concentrations. There were many vessels in the western ports which we could use, from trawlers and drifters down to lobster boats. There were also shipyards available to convert them into minesweepers. What we needed were arms and men. We had built up a good reserve of trained personnel at Cuxhaven, but it was not enough for the approximately two hundred vessels we appropriated for use as minesweepers. And all this had to be done quickly; there was no time for training and exercises. Therefore, each new squadron was given a "godfather" squadron. This was a dubious honor, for it had to give half its crew to the new squadron and to assist it in every way. The two senior officers would divide the crews and then draw lots to decide who would get which half. In this way, the division was made as equal as possible, and the new squadron had a sufficient number of experienced men to start work at once. All of these units were filled with recruits, with infantrymen released by the army, and finally with 500 naval cadets. They stayed on board the minesweepers for six months. Later, the Naval Academy complained about their habits and manners. We answered that this was the job of NA, and did anybody find fault with their practical seamanship and general war experience? Nobody did, for a great deal had been done for their practical training.

Equipment and mine clearing.   There was enough minesweeping gear in the depots at home, and boats of the new squadrons swept live mines as early as July 4. The greatest difficulty was in procuring antiaircraft armament. In store there was only a very primitive 75 mm gun, which generally was called the "people's gun." The output of the factories was limited, and the mine-sweepers were low down on the priority list. However, in the first weeks after the French campaign, considerable numbers of weapons were left lying around, and we helped ourselves. Up to open theft, anything could be covered up. This was more difficult when our men began to filch 20 mm and machine guns from insufficiently guarded airfields. Wrecks in the ports yielded more guns. We even found consignments of arms with unusual calibers, an indication they had been sold to neutral countries. In this manner, our boats received a somewhat mixed but quite powerful armament.

Minesweeping went on continuously. Its main object was not to sweep as many mines as possible but to keep the traffic lanes open at all times with minimal losses. We did not encounter any British barrages with many rows of different types, as we trained for in our exercises. Therefore, it was the rule to carry on when mines were encountered, until clear of the field, waiting until later to find a way around the field.

Clearing the mines was left to the shallow-draft R-boats, if possible. Looking into the mines proved a great help because the British laid many fields with a device which disarmed them after a fixed time. We went around them until the time expired, after which time we could use the old channel again. The British were somewhat surprised when we told them this after the war.

EVENTS IN 1940-41

Losses were kept very low with the methods we employed. On the Atlantic Coast, a French squadron assisted in removing the French minefields. When they finished this work, they were allowed to sail for the Mediterranean, after a farewell dinner. Magnetic mines were mainly swept by the barrage breakers with their strong magnetic field, particularly in the entrances of ports. The danger from the air was still insignificant. During the battle of England, mine-sweepers picked up around fifty German pilots who had bailed out over the sea. Therefore, our flotillas could always get a combat air patrol when it was necessary.

In the summer of 1940 a lot of work had to be put into the preparations for Operation Sea Lion. The staffs had to move to Trouville, not far from Le Havre. In view of the vast distances, I subdivided my minesweeping command by putting the most experienced senior officers in charge—one off the coast of Holland, one off northern France, and one off the Bay of Biscay. My colleague commander of the patrols put his squadrons in the Netherlands and in the Bay of Biscay under the same officers. His trawlers were now equipped with simple minesweeping gear, which they used when on patrol. All this was arranged in an entirely friendly manner. We did not know the theories of some sociologists; therefore, there was no "conflict for this innovation." It was all arranged unofficially, because it was sensible and economical. In February 1941 the system was adopted officially. Five divisions were organized—all having minesweepers and patrol vessels—one each in Holland, Brittany, the North Sea, the southern Bay of Biscay, and north of France. The staff had to be in Paris near Navy Group West. I was put in charge of these divisions, with the exception of the one in the North Sea.

In the spring of 1941 the greater part of our air force went to Russia. The number of air attacks on our vessels increased, along with losses. In October a squadron of R-boats lost 40 percent of its men in a few minutes. Movements in the narrow part of the Channel were no longer possible by day, in spite of the now good armament. Light armor around the bridges and shields for the guns were needed to fight aircraft for any hope of success; the squadrons designed and put them on. Because armor plates were in short supply, only the first shields were made from normal steel. They protected only against splinters, but they gave a feeling of security which improved aiming. During 1941-42 an average of one attacking plane was shot down for every two of our men killed.

Magnetic and Acoustic Mines

Britain's main effort against our traffic channels and submarines leaving and entering port was groundmines dropped from the air. These caused us a lot of trouble, but they were not as successful as the British imagined.

The British first used only magnetic mines, later adding acoustic mines; and they made sweeping difficult by a number of brilliant ideas. It would be too lengthy to describe these in detail here, for they used at least sixty-eight different combinations of fuses, time devices, and grades of bluntness, among other mechanisms. "Blunt" mines were directed against the barrage breakers, whose strong field detonated normal mines far ahead of it. These had to be replaced in shallow water by towed floats with magnetic coils and in entrance ways by double cables with fluctuating magnetic fields.

Officers and Recruits

The longer the war lasted, the more it became necessary to keep up the spirit and discipline of our men. Justice, firmness, and good personal relations were the best means. The staffs were kept small; their members, including the senior officers, went regularly to the bases and took part in operations of all kinds. When the squadrons were in port, the crews had living quarters outside the harbor areas, and only small groups for fighting fires and leaks remained on board. For the midshipmen and younger petty officers, special courses were arranged to teach them the fundamentals of leadership. This was combined with close combat training in anticipation of attempts to board at sea and raids against our ports on land. Since many officers had little actual practice of the law, a legal officer went from squadron to squadron to lecture on military law and justice and to discuss related problems. An experienced supply officer with a group of cooking experts and accounting specialists went from ship to ship to aid in these matters. Food was rationed, but its quality and quantity were good. Strict supervision saw to it that each man, from senior officer to youngest recruit, received the same amount of food, prepared in the same way.

We set up our own signal and minesweeping schools and antiaircraft courses. In addition, we had courses in arts and crafts and singing — separate, initially, and later combined because many a woodcarver had a good voice and singers efficiently wielded the glue pot.

Most of the married men had moved their families to coastal towns in Germany, but very early in the war these towns came under heavy air attack. Therefore spending one's leave at home could not give much recreation. Consequently, we set up our own recreation home in the wooded hills near Wiesbaden, which was easy to reach from France or northern Germany. It was open to all married officers and ratings with their families. Everyone was accommodated and treated in the same way; they wore civilian clothes and had their meals at small "family tables" with white cloths. Food served was the same for everyone. The children were looked after by trained nurses in a separate building. Their parents could take them for walks, but often their offspring preferred to play with their new friends.

Overall, there were hardly any disciplinary difficulties throughout the war. Even now there is much contact among the old minesweepers, and we have a reunion at Cuxhaven every five years.

Convoys and Escorts

In 1941 about twelve million gross registered tonnage moved along the coasts of the Western Defense Area, approximately half of it between German and Dutch ports. At first a great number of ships passed the narrow part of the English Channel in both directions. There were raiders and their supply ships, steamers that had been repaired tankers, colliers, and coastal ships. As the war progressed, getting them through the Channel became more and more difficult. The British attacked with light watercraft and sometimes destroyers. Their radar and the shooting of their coastal batteries was improving. From the end of 1943 on it was practically impossible to bring larger ships through the narrow part of the Channel.

There were many battles during attempts to get through the Channel at this time. The major event occurred while the battleships *Scharnhorst* and *Gneisenau* were being taken from Brest to the North Sea. These large ships could no longer be protected in France against air attack. The attempt to go north around England seemed hopeless in view of the air situation and lack of training. Therefore it was decided to take them through the Channel. The British reasoned the same way and laid a great number of minefields to catch them. However, of the sixteen fields west of the Dover Strait, we avoided fourteen by selecting a course as far north as possible. The fifteenth was detected by a trawler squadron east of Cherbourg one day before the operation, and a gap was swept, with the loss of one trawler. No shallow draft squadron was available; forces were stretched very thin because promised reinforcements did not arrive. The sixteenth field was found by a squadron of new M-boats four hours before the ships passed, and a gap was swept just in time. The battleships left Brest after dusk and passed Dover at noon. They were discovered so late that the British batteries were not ready and the distance had already increased when they opened fire. In spite of attacks by motor torpedoboats and planes, the ships did not receive a single hit while they were in the Western Defense Area. Shortly after leaving it, the *Scharnhorst* was damaged by a groundmine but soon could proceed. Later each ship took another groundmine without much damage.

Another event during this time was the British raid against Saint-Nazaire six weeks later. The leading ship, the ex-American destroyer *Buchanan,* now the *Campbelltown,* reached her objective, the outer gate of the largest lock. She put commandos ashore and later blew up. The accompanying motor torpedoboats suffered heavily from the fire of antiaircraft guns, some minesweepers, and a small barrage breaker. They could not reach the smaller lock, which was actually more important, because our submarines used it. Nor could the commandos reach it. They were beaten back by men of a minesweeping squadron. Boats of that squadron efficiently protected the submarine pens. The small groups of men who had stayed on board acted on their own initiative. In one of the boats the senior of the three stokers was only nineteen years old. Close combat training and foster initiative provided good results. This was also the case when the British tried to raid Dieppe in August 1942.

One of our convoys, five motorbarges protected by three trawlers, ran into the eastern wing of the 25-vessel landing fleet. A fierce fight followed, the German boats firing with all guns and ramming where they could. Only one of the trawlers and one of the barges were sunk. All the others succeeded in extricating themselves and reaching the small port of Treport.

A final example of these events occurred in July 1943 when five M-boats, sweeping from Cherbourg to Brest, were attacked by the same number of Allied destroyers. In a night action lasting one and a half hours, the M-boats defended themselves so well that the destroyers finally hauled off. One M-boat had to be towed in and sank in shallow water; the others were damaged but continued to Brest.

Protecting the submarines was not so spectacular but was at least as important. Between the summer of 1940 and the invasion in 1944, a U-boat entered or left one of the Biscay ports nearly four thousand times. Of these, two or three may have struck anchored mines, which the British sometimes laid on the edge of the continental shelf. This was too far out for sweeping, due to danger from the air. There could be only exploratory night sweeps with new M-boats and old destroyers. If mines were found, another route had to be taken. Of the 3,600 U-boats that crossed the shallow water protected by minesweepers, only one was sunk by a mine and one was damaged. In 1944 a third vessel was sunk from the air, despite antiaircraft protection. The losses were tolerable. The barrage breakers suffered the most, but with little loss of life.

During the Invasion of Normandy, a great many vessels were destroyed, mostly in port by bombs. The squadrons on the Bay of Biscay soon had to be laid up; the greater part of their crews marched home with the army, and the rest helped defend the fortified places there. The vessels still intact in the ports on the Channel fought their way back and did good service, particularly when they enabled our Fifteenth Army to cross the Schelde River and later in the Baltic, where in the first months of 1945 over two million people were evacuated by sea to escape the Russians.

Of course, there were large German minesweeping and patrol forces in all other theaters of the war. I have limited myself to their organization and activities mainly in the western theater of the war because there they were confronted with the newest inventions and the most determined efforts of the other side; therefore, it was the area where the most important experience was gained. Great pains were taken to pass this on to the relevant authorities at home and to the other theaters. There were always exchanges among officers and petty officers, and our experimental unit at Kiel held conferences every six months or so. At the same time morale was kept up, in spite of the growing superiority of the Allies and the certainty of defeat.

The main reasons for the comparative success of the defensive offshore forces would seem to be (1) good evaluation of the lessons of World War I; (2) drawing on the practical consequences of training, tactics, and development; (3) good cooperation among scientists, technicians, and sailors, as well as between frontline units and development authorities; (4) a flexible organization in war; and (5) hardly any interference from above (they accepted our slogan: "Act and inform").

The Allies made excellent use of technical novelties and tactical changes, but they preferred to lay their mines rather closely inshore, where the Germans could utilize all sorts of small craft otherwise hardly fit for warlike operations. In the second half of the war, the direct attack from the air was by far the greatest danger.

The Germans had to put a very great effort into keeping the waters along the coasts navigable. It is difficult to say how much this influenced the general war effort.

Repair work of the torpedoed destroyer U.S.S. Kearney, *lying alongside U.S.S.* Vulcan *in Iceland. While work was going on, the first air raid alarm for the area was sounded. Gunners manned their stations, but the repair work continued. (RG 80, No. 80-G-425654.)*

The Neutrality Patrol
and Other Belligerencies

Perhaps the most misleading, yet politically astute, statement made by any statesman during World War II was that of Winston Churchill on February 9, 1941, when he appealed to President Roosevelt: "Give us the tools, and we will finish the job!"

By that time there could have been no doubt in the mind of any responsible military or political leader in either the United Kingdom or the United States that there was any way that Britain alone could "finish the job." Germany controlled Europe from North Cape to the Pyrenees, from Brest to the Russian border. Italy, to be sure, had been checked in Greece. In North Africa, Maj. Gen. Richard O'Connor, the forgotten man of the Desert Campaigns, had driven the Italians 500 miles west and had captured 130,000 men.[1] Nevertheless everyone knew that this was a peripheral effort. And O'Connor's triumph was soon to be thrown away as his troops were sent to Greece in a vain effort to stop the Germans from coming to the aid of the frustrated Italians.

"Give us the tools . . . " was nonsense, and everyone knew it. But the statement was powerful propaganda for the passage of the Lend-Lease measure about to come before the U.S. Senate. It had passed the House of Representatives the previous day.

The period between the outbreak of war in September 1939 and December 7, 1941, was a time of delusions on the part of the American people, many of these delusions skillfully exploited by Roosevelt in his long-range goal of ensuring victory for the free peoples of the world and the destruction of tyranny.

The first of these delusions was that of neutrality. In the fall of 1939, and, indeed, during the whole of the "phoney" war period, the illusion of neutrality was not hard to maintain. The sudden attack of Germany on hapless Poland aroused profound sympathy on the part of the American people. But they also had a sense that there was nothing much they could do. President Roosevelt made the first unneutral move by ordering that the German liner *Bremen* be delayed in New York, on any convenient pretext, for forty-eight hours in order to give the British time to intercept and capture the valuable ship. But the *Bremen* made it home anyway. The same technicalities delayed the sailing of the *Normandie* as well. As a result, the French government decided to leave her in New York, where she remained until that tragic day in February 1942 when she burned and capsized at her pier in North River.[2]

In this paper I do not propose to review the many steps by which the United States passed from formal neutrality to pro-British neutrality to nonbelligerency to unabashed, undeclared war in the Atlantic. This, of course, is familiar ground, having been done definitively by William L. Langer and S. Everett Gleason in their two volumes, *The Challenge to Isolation* and *The Undeclared War*. My purpose is not to rehash the familiar, but to suggest areas which need investigation, particularly in the ways that the United States Navy was called upon to implement political decisions.

In a "fireside chat," a few hours after Britain and France had declared war on Germany and the American people had just learned of the sinking of the passenger liner *Athenia* by a U-boat, with the consequent loss of American lives, President Roosevelt left no doubt as to his own feelings:

> It is easy for you and me, to shrug our shoulders and to say that conflicts taking place thousands of miles from the whole American Hemisphere do not seriously affect the Americas—and that all the United States has to do is to ignore them and go about its own business. Passionately though we may desire detachment, we are forced to realize that every word that comes through the air, every ship that sails the sea, every battle that is fought, does affect the American future.
>
> Let no man or woman thoughtlessly or falsely talk of America sending its armies to European fields. . . .
>
> This nation will remain a neutral nation, but I cannot ask that every American remain neutral in thought as well. Even a neutral cannot be asked to close his mind or his conscience.[3]

Thus, at the very beginning, Roosevelt laid out his program: aid the Allies and keep America out of the war. It was all there for anyone astute enough to follow a concept to its conclusions. Many Americans, however, were not that astute.

A few days later, the president proclaimed a state of limited national emergency and formal neutrality in the conflict. Believing that the safety of the United States was inextricably interwoven with the safety of the other American states, he was instrumental in convening a conference with Latin American nations in Panama, to open on September 23. The resulting Declaration of Panama marked a clear effort on the part of the American powers to keep the war at a distance. Two key provisions should be kept in mind.

First, there was the recognition that parts of Latin America and certain islands in the Caribbean belonged to belligerent powers, and any idea of their

transfer to Germany in the event of a French or British defeat was most un-
welcome. Hence, the conference adopted the resolution:

That in case any geographic region of America subject to the jurisdiction
of any non-American state should be obliged to change its sovereignty and
there should result therefrom a danger to the security of the American Continent, a consulative meeting such as the one now being held will be con-
voked with the urgency that the case may require.[4]

The other, more positive, and of more significance to the American navy,
was Resolution XIV:

As a measure of continental self-protection, the American Republics, so
long as they maintain their neutrality, are of inherent right entitled to have
those waters adjacent to the American Continent, which they regard as of
primary concern and direct utility in their relations, free from the commission of any hostile act by any non-American belligerent nation, whether
such hostile act be attempted or made from land, sea, or air.[5]

The consequence of this resolution was that a zone extending out approximately
three hundred miles from the Western Hemisphere was established in which
no belligerent activities were to be permitted. Each nation in the Western
Hemisphere was expected to carry out its part of the patrol necessary to enforce
the Declaration of Panama, but, as usual, the United States had to assume the
principal part of the job.

Even before the resolution was signed, the belligerents protested, Britain
claiming her age-old doctrine of freedom of the seas. Roosevelt, however,
desirous of keeping the war as distant as possible from American shores, turned
a deaf ear and ordered the Navy Department to commission eighty destroyers
laid up after the last war and send them out to enforce the neutrality zone.

The president's order caused consternation in the navy, for the areas were
vast and the ships few in number. Since it would take months for the re-
commissioned four-pipers to become operative, even supposing crews could be
found for them, the burden fell on a handful of ships constituting the Neutrality
Patrol under Rear Adm. A. C. Pickens in the cruiser *San Francisco*.

The missing parts of this story have yet to be told. How did the navy build
up for this effort? What administrative, logistic, operational, doctrinal, and
strategic decisions were involved at all levels? What were the instructions given
and how were they interpreted? If a belligerent warship were encountered,
what action was to be taken in the event the intruder declined to remove himself from the proclaimed neutrality zone? An operational and administrative
history of the Neutrality Patrol will cast considerable light on the buildup of
the U.S. Navy in preparation for more responsible assignments in the months
and years ahead.

As it happened, the Neutrality Patrol was not tested for some time. U-boats generally kept to the eastern Atlantic. German surface raiders posed little problem until mid-December, when the pocket battleship *Graf Spee* was brought to bay by a British cruiser force under Commodore Sir Henry Harwood off the mouth of the River Plate. Although the action took place outside the area of United States responsibility, the fact that a sea battle took place at all, and clearly within the Pan-American Neutrality Zone, at that, made it plain to everyone that the belligerents had no intention of respecting it. The American nations had to make a stand or the Declaration of Panama would go into limbo by default. Although some South American nations favored action only in cases where belligerent actions in the Neutrality Zone interfered with the rights of neutrals freely to use the seas, President Roosevelt would have no part of half measures. Formal protests were sent in the name of all signatories to the Declaration of Panama to both Britain and Germany. In one of his first "former naval person" messages, Churchill, as first lord of the admiralty, expostulated that while the British were keeping their submarines out of the Neutrality Zone, he could not promise to leave untouched any Germans that might be found therein. With this Roosevelt was well content. He had made his protest without hampering the British. The Germans were quite another situation.

The repeal of the arms embargo in the fall of 1939, after a bitter fight in the Congress, meant, of course, that the Neutrality Zone would leak like a sieve. The "cash and carry" policy that was substituted for the arms embargo resulted in British and other Allied ships regularly sailing into American harbors to carry the war materials for which the cash was paid. Since American ships were forbidden in the war zones, belligerent ships had perforce to take on that task. At that time, there was no question of escorts coming in, for the Royal Navy had neither the escorts nor the weapons to afford more than minimal convoy protection for only a limited distance out from the British Isles. But if U-boats began sinking Allied ships in the Neutrality Zone, the British would be sure, in time, to do something to defend them. Or, would the United States take action, as a part of the prohibition against belligerent ships in American waters?

Contingency plans for this period need study in order to determine the possibilities had events been otherwise. We know what happened. But what were the possibilities? Was the United States prepared to take drastic action in the event of open challenge to its Neutrality Patrol?

The German spring offensives of 1940 posed a very direct challenge to the American nations, and most especially to the United States. What was to become of the New World possessions of the countries defeated by the Nazis? Since the Dutch maintained a government in exile, their colonies could be defended by any American power on the invitation of the displaced Dutch government. But Denmark and France posed more of a problem. At any time, as a part of his surrender of occupation demands, Hitler could require the French or Danish government to cede to Germany any or all of their New World possessions. What then? Such cession was clearly in violation of the Declaration of Panama, but would American counteraction be viewed in Latin America as hemispheric defense or as Yankee imperialism? In order to settle this question, the United States instigated a conference in Havana, even as events seemed to be moving to force her into unilateral action before the conference could convene.

The basic problem was the question of the French fleet. Neither the United States nor Great Britain could view with equanimity the prospect of the fine French ships falling into the hands of the Germans. Even though the armistice between France and Germany provided that the units of the French navy would remain French and be immobilized in French ports, neither Roosevelt nor Churchill trusted Hitler's word nor the ability or will of the Vichy government to resist his demands.

The story of the British actions against the French units at Mers el Kebir, the naval port of Oran, has been told in considerable detail in a number of books, including one of my own,[6] but no one so far has presented the details of the problem at Martinique.

Here was another case of what might have happened. At the time of the armistice, there were in Martinique's harbor of Fort de France the aircraft carrier *Bearn*, which had on board 106 American-built aircraft purchased by France; the cruiser *Émile Bertin*; the gunboat *Barfleur*; and six new tankers. In addition, there was the training cruiser *Jeanne d'Arc* at Guadaloupe. Also at Martinique were a few merchant vessels, recently arrived from France, laden with huge quantities of gold, the monetary reserves of France sent thither to keep them from German hands. While Roosevelt, preserving American "neutrality," could not permit these ships to fall into German control, he had no objections to their joining de Gaulle's Free French or even the British.

Commanding this naval miscellany was Rear Adm. Georges Robert, who, in 1939, had been appointed high commissioner of the French Antilles. He was a particularly difficult man to deal with. At first, the British governor of Trinidad paid him a call to persuade him to throw his lot in with the British or with de Gaulle. With hauteur born of injured national pride, Admiral Robert totally rejected either idea. When the news came of the attack on the French fleet at Mers el Kebir by British Force H on July 3, he felt he had every reason to fear such an ultimatum himself and prepared to meet the British with force.

But the British contented themselves with establishing a blockade of Martinique. This action, while better than an ultimatum, merely stiffened Admiral Robert's resolve.

The British blockade presented Washington with a dilemma. It was a clear violation of the Declaration of Panama and could not be countenanced. Yet if the British had not imposed a blockade, the U.S. Navy would have had to do it. Already the United States had looked the other way when British ships operating from Caribbean bases had intercepted and captured German surface raiders, but a blockade was an entirely different matter. It was too public, too dangerous, and it was being done too close to home. It could not be ignored. As a consequence, on July 6, an American force of a cruiser and six destroyers was sent to Martinique, and there ensued the ridiculous situation of valuable British ships standing off Fort de France watching the French, while farther out valuable American ships kept tabs on the British.

The conferees in Havana, fortunately, came up with some pretty strong language on belligerent activities in American waters, which forbade the transfer of any Western Hemisphere real estate from one European power to another. This action gave the United States the pretext by which she might take over Martinique in order to settle the problem of the French ships once and for all. In fact, a marine detachment was alerted for a possible landing at Fort de France. Since this was clearly the least desirable solution, diplomatic means were tried first. Admiral Robert being unwilling to join the Free French, Secretary of State Hull approached the French and British ambassadors with the suggestion that the British buy the aircraft on the *Béarn* and that the French ships be sailed to American ports for internment. At first this solution seemed possible, but the Germans got wind of the scheme and let Vichy know that grave consequences would ensue if the French transferred their aircraft or their ships to the British, or to any other power. At the same time, Secretary Hull let the British know that any attempt on their part to occupy Martinique or to seize the French ships would lead to "real trouble" between the United States and Great Britain.

To attempt to find a way out of this situation, each day growing more seriously ridiculous, the United States sent Rear Adm. John W. Greenslade to talk to Admiral Robert, sailor to sailor. It was a fruitless visit, for while Admiral Greenslade talked like a sailor and diplomat, Admiral Robert talked like a French aristo being badgered by a particularly impertinent member of the peasantry. He listened haughtily and promised nothing.

The situation remained unsatisfactory at best. Following the attack on the French fleet, the Vichy government had broken diplomatic relations with Great Britain, and there was a very real chance that she might heed the intriguing voice of Pierre Laval and declare war on her former ally.

There was no reason for the United States to break relations with the government at Vichy, which was, after all, technically a legitimate one, maintaining its sovereignty over its possessions in the New World. And, so far, Pétain had kept the fleet from the Germans and Italians and had prevented any change in the ownership of French overseas territories. Martinique remained a problem, but diplomatic efforts continued.

The impasse was broken in October when Admiral Greenslade paid another call on Admiral Robert. Hitler and Pétain had just met at Montoire, and this meeting aroused deep suspicions in London and Washington. Was France about to ally herself with Germany? If so, the situation at Martinique had better be cleared up and speedily. Therefore, Admiral Greenslade was authorized to use some pretty salty language. He told the French commissioner that he was prepared to patrol off Martinique with an aircraft carrier and other ships and that any French ships attempting to sortie would be sunk. This was language Admiral Robert understood, and he entered upon a "gentleman's agreement" that he would give four days' notice of any movements of French ships, that he would permit an American naval observer to be quartered at Fort de France, and that American ships and planes would be permitted in Martinique's territorial waters. In return, the United States promised to keep the island supplied with food. It was not always possible to keep this American commitment because of the shortage of ships, but Admiral Robert was as good as his word. The *Béarn* and the other ships remained at Fort de France until after the Germans denounced the armistice in November 1942 and occupied all of France following the North African landings. The *Béarn* then sailed to New Orleans and was converted into an aircraft transport, serving as such until the end of the war. Other ships were refitted in other American ports.

In this brief outline is a miniature of the American dilemma in the summer of 1940: how to observe the strict neutrality she claimed and at the same time give all aid possible to Britain. A thorough study of the Martinique affair would reveal a great deal about American plans and American strategic thinking in that period.

While the Martinique matter was being played to its somewhat unsatisfactory conclusion, the principal advisers to President Roosevelt were spending many anxious hours wondering how and what and how much, if any, war materials should be given to Great Britain. The "Arsenal of Democracy," as President Roosevelt was to proclaim it in December, resembled Mother Hubbard's cupboard more than an arsenal. The few factories which had converted to war production had their hands full dealing with British orders. The tiny American army had no equipment to spare, and what it had was largely of World War I vintage.

The request of the British for escort vessels, which ultimately led to the destroyers-for-bases deal, caused much agonizing thought by American government officials. Even if the ships could be found, would the British be able to withstand the German onslaught? The blitz was at its height, and the British armed services and the un-uniformed Home Guard members were braced for the expected German invasion of the British Isles. In view of the desperate situation, did the American leaders have any right to send ships, guns, and planes across the sea where they might be seized by the Germans and used against us? Ambassador Joseph Kennedy in London was little help. He had small faith in the ability of the British to hold out, and his gloom tended to darken counsel. Eventually, as is well known, the destroyers-for-bases deal was arranged and the faith in Britain justified, but it took bold action and a lot of faith for Roosevelt and his advisors to act.

Roosevelt's Republican opponents were disappointed that Wendell Willkie would not oppose the president on foreign policy, and the isolationists grew more strident. Despite their dark prophecies, Hitler did not declare war over the destroyers deal. He considered breaking diplomatic relations, and Admiral Raeder urged that U-boats be sent into American waters, but Hitler decided against both measures. As a result of his failure to act then or to act later after the passage of the lend-lease legislation, it became clear that Hitler was refusing to be goaded into war with the United States. When he was ready, he would act. Until then, within limits, the United States could do pretty much what it liked in the Atlantic. The question was where were those limits?

Once the Lend-Lease Act was passed, the obvious question was how far the United States would go in protecting the ships carrying lend-lease materials. By one line of thinking, since lend-lease goods technically remained American property, the United States had every right to protect its own possessions on the high seas, but this idea was never advanced in justification of U.S. protection. If American warships were to protect British merchant vessels when they were carrying lend-lease goods, they might as well protect them at all times. This was going a little far, even though, in accordance with the ABC-1 Staff Agreement of March 27, 1941, the U.S. Navy was committed to taking over escort of convoy operations on the North Atlantic route.

Since the transatlantic convoy escort of belligerent merchant ships by American warships might well lead to hostilities with Germany, naval planners cast covetous eyes on the Atlantic islands farther out than those already available. Specifically, these were the Azores, Cape Verde, Madeira, and the Canaries. Since these were all Portuguese or Spanish possessions, and Spain and Portugal were neutral, the problem of their acquisition was diplomatic rather than military. But the military made plans—just in case. One of the things that the British feared most was an advance of Germany through the Iberian peninsula with the consent of Spain, in order to take Gibraltar from the rear. Churchill was, therefore, anxious for a show of American naval power to stiffen the will of dictators Franco and Salazar. Roosevelt sought an invitation for units of the Atlantic Fleet to visit the Azores and Lisbon, but Salazar refused, lest the action bring about the very action on the part of the Germans it was supposed to avert. Here was a proposed "neutral" use of the U.S. Navy to assist the British and to foil the Germans. It came to nothing, but it might have worked.

Since even a show-the-flag visit was ruled out, it was obviously unprofitable to pursue the idea of American bases in the Atlantic islands and the idea was allowed to drop.

Before long, ideas of transatlantic convoy operations were put aside, and the decision was made to take a much less risky action. The United States Navy would take over the stretch from Argentia, Newfoundland, to Iceland. This was a natural decision, since American forces were soon to relieve the British in Iceland, and a strong case could be made that the United States had every right to protect its own ships bound to supply its own forces. Since Iceland, however, was not in the Neutrality Zone proclaimed by the Declaration of Panama, Hitler declared it in the war zone where any ships might be sunk on sight.

Escort of convoy operations being obviously more dangerous than patrol, Roosevelt decided first to try the alternative of extending the Neutrality Zone in which peaceful patrols would operate rather than the quasi-belligerent convoy escorts. Accordingly a line was drawn down the twenty-six meridian, roughly half way between the western bulge of Africa and the eastern bulge of Brazil. At the top, the line curved eastward to include Iceland. This area was declared to be the Western Hemisphere, thereby settling a question that had stumped geographers for years.

In the official statement defining the zone, the warning was given: "Entrance into the Western Hemisphere by naval ships or aircraft of belligerents other than those powers having sovereignty over territory in the Western Hemisphere is to be viewed as possibly actuated by an unfriendly interest toward shipping or territory in the Western Hemisphere."[7]

It is small wonder that Admiral King, on whom this patrol responsibility fell, remarked that he was being given a big slice of bread with damn little butter. Shortly thereafter the battleships *Idaho, Mississippi,* and *New Mexico,* the carrier *Yorktown,* four light cruisers, and two destroyer squadrons were transferred from the Pacific to the Atlantic. The president then asked King how he liked the butter he was getting. He replied: "The butter's fine, but you keep giving me more bread."[8]

King's additional "bread" included not only preparations for convoys to Iceland, but, following the breakout of the *Bismarck* in May 1941, the need for keeping an eye on likely places in Greenland where anything from German weather stations to U-boat havens might be hidden. Accordingly, he organized Task Force 11, under Comdr. Edward H. Smith, U.S. Coast Guard, with a mixed lot of Coast Guard and naval ships to do whatever was necessary to keep the Germans out of Greenland. Commander Smith, quickly yclept "Iceberg Smith," found all manner of things to do, from carving out airstrips and setting up weather stations to establishing a northeast Greenland Patrol. This patrol soon intercepted a Norwegian schooner, which included in its crew a

Occupation at Reykjavik, Iceland (1941). Among the ships in the harbor is the Canadian destroyer Saint Croix, formerly the U.S. destroyer McCook. (U.S. Navy photograph.)

member of the Gestapo. The ship was taken to Boston and the Gestapo man interned, the first capture to my knowledge of a German officer by American forces in the war.

Although the German government protested and put pressure on the Danish king, Roosevelt considered the matter settled by replying that the United States was obliged to "take steps which are tantamount to holding Greenland in trust for Denmark until such time as the Royal Danish Government ceases to be subject to duress on the part of an occupying nation and full Danish control over Greenland may be restored."[9]

The airstrips in Greenland proved extremely useful later in ferrying aircraft across the Atlantic. The "Bluies," as they were known, became part of the folklore of the European war.

The occupation of Iceland by American troops in relief of the British in July 1941 led, of course, to incidents that brought the United States into un-declared war in the Atlantic. As had been done with Greenland, U.S. officials ignored the Danish government in Copenhagen and dealt directly with Ice-landic premier Hermann Jonasson in Reykjavik. It took considerable pressure on the part of Churchill to persuade Jonasson to "invite" American troops, but finally he did, just as the convoy bearing those same troops was rounding the point at Kflavik and steaming into Reykjavik harbor.

Thus invitation, acceptance, and execution were practically simultaneous. This was all according to plan in order to present the Germans with a fait accompli and avert serious reaction.

President Roosevelt's declaration of unlimited national emergency at the end of May 1941 had conditioned the American people to expect more activity in the Atlantic, and, to most, the presence of American troops in Iceland seemed a prudent precaution.

Naturally, if American troops were stationed in Iceland, it was necessary to keep them supplied. Equally naturally, it was necessary to protect the supplies en route—so convoys were established after all. It was soon understood that any ship of any nationality was welcome to join those convoys. As Churchill put it, in the House of Commons:

> The position of the United States forces in Iceland will, of course, require their being sustained or reinforced by sea from time to time. These consign-ments of American supplies for American forces on duty overseas for the purposes of the United States will, of course, have to traverse very danger-ous waters and, as we have a very large traffic constantly passing through these waters, I daresay it may be found in practice mutually advantageous for the two navies involved to assist each other, so far as is convenient, in that part of the business.[10]

The Germans viewed the American occupation of Iceland most seriously, and Admiral Raeder even inquired whether Hitler looked on it as an act of war. Hitler, however, fully expecting a victory over Russian forces in the fall of 1941, instructed his naval commander in chief to accept the situation. Raeder vainly argued that "the whole situation in the Atlantic has become more unfavorable for all our forces because of the occupation of Iceland and the increasing effect of United States support of Britain." But Hitler, unwilling to divert aircraft from the Eastern Front, refused to consider a change, explaining that he intended to avoid war with the United States for "another one or two months." By that time he expected to have beaten Russia. [11]

The existence of convoys in the waters between Argentia and Iceland inevitably led to brushes with U-boats. Since the United States was still technically at peace, even though it was conducting operations usually considered belligerent, Admiral King's directives had to be very carefully worded to avoid the suggestion that the country was at war. They were so carefully worded that commanding officers had a real problem deciding what they should do if they met up with a German surface raider, aircraft, or submarine. Should they shoot first or should they wait for the other side to open fire? They were instructed to report the presence of German ships or planes by radio, and undoubtedly the British would listen to the radio and move to intercept if they could.

The answer was given, of course, by the famous *Greer* incident of September 4, 1941. Although the events are well known, they may well be summarized here because of the consequences which followed.

The four-piper *Greer* was steaming alone en route to Iceland from the United States carrying passengers and mail. When she was about one hundred seventy-five miles from her destination, she was informed by a British patrol plane that there was a submerged U-boat about ten miles ahead of her position. *Greer* soon picked up contact with *U-652* on her sonar and harassed it for several hours. The patrol plane inquired whether the *Greer* intended to attack and, being informed in the negative, dropped a stick of depth charges in the general direction of the U-boat. In response, *U-652* fired a torpedo at the *Greer*. It missed. The *Greer* dropped depth charges. They missed. The German fired another topedo. It missed. The *Greer* replied with more depth charges. They missed. Then the *Greer* lost contact and, after searching for awhile, gave up and headed for Iceland. *U-652* went about her business. No harm was done to either side except to reveal a gross lack of accuracy in the use of depth charges and torpedoes.

This incident, however, was just what Roosevelt had been waiting for. The neutrality laws, which forbade the arming of American merchant ships and their entry into the war zones, kept America from doing much that she might to aid Britain and Russia. Seizing on the *Greer* incident, the president found a pretext to bring about the repeal of the neutrality laws. On the evening of September 11, he broadcast to the world:

> No act of violence or intimidation will keep us from maintaining intact two bulwarks of defense: first, our line of supply of materiel to the enemies of Hitler, and second, the freedom of our shipping on the high seas.
>
> No matter what it takes, no matter what it costs, we will keep open the line of legitimate commerce in these defensive waters. . . .
>
> If submarines or raiders attack in distant waters, they can attack equally well within sight of our own shores. Their very presence in any waters which America deems vital to its defense constitutes an attack.
>
> In the waters which we deem necessary for our defense, American naval vessels and American planes will no longer wait until Axis submarines lurking under water, or Axis raiders on the surface of the sea, strike their deadly blow—first.
>
> Upon our naval and air patrol now operating in large number over a vast expanse of the Atlantic Ocean—falls the duty of maintaining the American policy of freedom of the seas—now. That means, very simply and clearly, that our patrolling vessels and planes will protect all merchant ships—not only American ships but ships of any flag—engaged in commerce in our defensive waters.

The speech concluded with the famous "shoot on sight" warning intended for Hitler's ears.

> But let this warning be clear. From now on, if German or Italian vessels of war enter the waters the protection of which is necessary for American defense, they do so at their own peril. [12]

Although Roosevelt's opponents in Congress and elsewhere charged that the president had committed the United States to war in the Atlantic, as indeed he had, Hitler refused to be baited. He once again denied Raeder permission to lift all restrictions on U-boat operations in the Atlantic and to attack American ships where they might be found. Instead Hitler ordered that precautions be taken "to avoid any incidents in the war on merchant shipping before about the middle of October." [13]

But if Hitler held off, his U-boats did not. The torpedoing of the *Kearny* and the sinking of the *Reuben James* meant that America would have to pay for her activities in the Atlantic. The price was cheap compared to what it cost later when the United States was fully in the war. But the payment had begun.

These incidents, which I have selected from many others in the history of the Atlantic between September 1939 and December 1941 are pivotal, and each of them would merit a full-length study. For the most part, we have the operational histories, or they can easily be obtained. What is needed is the full story of each, told with all the delicate interplay of government leaders, acting in what they believed to be the best interests of the United States. The full story is not to be found in the files of the Department of the Navy nor in the files of the State Department. I doubt that President Roosevelt's own files would give us what we need. Actions followed decisions, and decisions produced other actions, which produced more decisions. Many of them began at the White House, but the effects of those decisions ran through the entire government and the entire defense establishment. It is perhaps a pity that Roosevelt did not tape record his conferences. Transcripts of those tapes would make better reading than some more recent ones.

This paper began by presenting a delusion—that Britain could defeat Germany—"Give us the tools. . . ." This delusion enabled the president and the American people to do some of the things necessary for Britain's survival. But the greatest delusion of all was that America could keep out of the war. Whether Japan attacked Pearl Harbor or not, the day would surely come when the United States would have to face up to the realization that she was in the war against Germany, for the nation would not have accepted a British defeat, nor a German victory—not, at any rate, on Hitler's terms.

The ironic final note is that even if the United States had declared war on Germany at the end of 1940 instead of at the end of 1941, things would not have been a great deal different as far as the long-range picture was concerned. Different operational events, of course, would have taken place, but during 1941, the U.S. Navy was already doing just about all that it could do in the Atlantic. Admiral King had all the bread he could handle. There was no more butter.

NOTES

1. Corelli Barnett, *The Desert Generals* (New York: Viking Press, 1961), pp. 49-63.
2. William L. Langer and S. Everett Gleason, *The Challenge to Isolation* (New York: Harper & Brothers, 1952), p. 202.
3. Ibid., p. 204
4. Ibid., p. 211.
5. Ibid., p. 212.
6. Henry H. Adams, *Years of Deadly Peril*: *The Coming of the War* (New York: David McKay Co., 1969), *passim*.
7. William L. Langer and S. Everett Gleason, *The Undeclared War* (New York: Harper & Brothers, 1953), p. 427 ff.
8. Ernest J. King and Walter Muir Whitehill, *Fleet Admiral King*: *A Naval Record* (New York: W. W. Norton, 1952), pp. 339-40.
9. Langer and Gleason, *The Undeclared War*, p. 430.
10. Ibid., p. 578.

11. "Führer Conferences on Naval Affairs" in *Brassey's Naval Annual, 1948*, ed. H. G. Thursfield (London: William Clowes & Sons, 1948), p. 221.
12. Langer and Gleason, *The Undeclared War*, pp. 745-46.
13. *Führer Conferences*, pp. 232-33.

Fleet Adm. Chester W. Nimitz shown during press conference on March 11, 1945.
(RG 80, No. 80-G-308852.)

Nimitz as CINCPAC:
The First Six Months

When someone asked Fleet Adm. Chester W. Nimitz at what point in our war against Japan he felt the deepest anxiety, he replied, "The whole first six months." Nimitz was too well aware of America's latent strength to doubt the ultimate outcome. Yet during these crucial months, victory seemed ever receding, as the United States and its allies paid in blood and treasure the price of unpreparedness.

Admiral Nimitz took command of the Pacific Fleet the last day of 1941, standing on the deck of the submarine *Grayling* at the submarine base in Pearl Harbor. It was not a happy scene. There hung over the harbor a miasma of black oil, charred wood, blistered paint, and burned and rotting bodies.

Not far away, poking above the surface, were the masts of the battleship *Arizona*, one mast leaning crazily askew. During the recent Japanese raid, the *Arizona* had been blown to pieces in a terrible explosion. More than a thousand of her ship's company had lost their lives. Three years before, when Nimitz had been commander, Battleship Division One, the *Arizona* had been his flagship. Her commanding officer then had been Nimitz's old friend Capt. Isaac Kidd. At the time of the Pearl Harbor attack, Kidd, promoted to rear admiral, had succeeded to command of Battleship Division One, and his flagship had been the *Arizona*. He had been aboard when the attack came, and he was among the missing.

Present at the simple assumption-of-command ceremony was Adm. Husband E. Kimmel, who had been commander in chief. He was wearing two stars instead of the four he had rated as Commander in Chief of the Pacific Fleet (CINCPAC). A portly man of imperious presence, he now looked a little stooped, somehow deflated. Present, too, was Vice Adm. William S. Pye, formerly commander of the sunk and damaged battleships. When Kimmel

This essay is based upon research for the author's recent book *Nimitz* (Annapolis: Naval Institute Press, 1976). Copyright 1976 by E. B. Potter.

was relieved of his command on December 17, Pye had been ordered to assume temporary command pending the arrival of Nimitz, the choice of President Roosevelt and Secretary of the Navy Frank Knox.

The Japanese raid had aroused the fighting spirit of the personnel at Pearl Harbor. They were determined to save Wake Island, under siege by the Japanese. Admiral Kimmel, as his last official act, had sent out a Wake relief expedition comprising carrier forces built around the *Saratoga,* the *Enterprise,* and the *Lexington.* Pye recalled the expedition and Wake surrendered to the enemy, whereupon gloom settled over the base like an invisible pall.

When Nimitz arrived, on Christmas day, he warmly pressed the hand of his old friend Kimmel. "You have my sympathy," he said. "The same thing could have happened to anybody." Both men were conscious of the irony of the moment. A year earlier, Nimitz had been offered the CINCPAC command and had begged off for lack of seniority, earnestly recommending Kimmel, the alternate choice. From Nimitz's personal point of view, that may have been the luckiest decision of his career. Still junior, but with a towering reputation, Nimitz had again been ordered to Pearl Harbor. With his country at war, he did not now question the order.

To the surprise of nearly everyone, Nimitz made up his new staff from key members of the staffs of Kimmel and of officers who had lost their commands through damage to the fleet. He said that he had complete and unqualified confidence in every one of them and that he certainly did not blame them for what had happened. Moreover, he continued, as recent chief of the Bureau of Navigation he knew that they had been chosen for their competence. Now he wanted them to stay with him to provide continuity through familiarity with their duties. In that simple, short speech, Admiral Nimitz began to lift the incubus off the spirits at Pearl Harbor.

Nimitz plunged with his usual vigor into the task of learning his new job. In this he was loyally assisted by Pye and other admirals who had been much senior to him until he had assumed his four stars as CINCPAC. Admiral Kimmel made himself available to Nimitz whenever possible, but Kimmel had to spend several hours each day before the Roberts Commission, appointed by the president to investigate the Pearl Harbor disaster.

At Nimitz's insistence, Pye and Kimmel took their evening meals with him. For lesser men the association could have been trying, for over them like a shadow hung the embarrassing matter of the relief and also of the failure to rescue Wake. But nothing that had happened in any way marred the friendship of the three admirals then or later.

Nimitz was well aware that such advice and guidance as he could get from Kimmel was temporary, for it was not in the books that that unhappy officer should remain at Pearl Harbor after he had finished testifying before the Roberts

Commission. Nimitz did, however, secure permission for Pye to remain for a while as his unofficial adviser.

Nimitz's immediate objectives on taking command were to restore morale; to hold the line against further Japanese expansion in the Pacific; to assure the safety of United States communications to Hawaii, Midway, and Australia; and to divert Japanese strength away from the East Indies. He judged he could best achieve all these objectives by using the Pacific Fleet offensively. He favored beginning promptly with a carrier raid on the enemy-held Gilbert and Marshall islands.

Most of the CINCPAC officers opposed such raids, seeing little chance of taking the Japanese by surprise, since their own success at Pearl Harbor would have alerted them to the threat of a carrier attack. The enemy was bound to realize that if the U.S. Pacific Fleet intended to counterattack it would have to be with carriers. The obvious targets were the Japanese bases nearest Pearl Harbor — the Gilberts, the Marshalls, and Wake.

The officer most vocal in opposing the raids was Rear Adm. Claude Bloch, commandant of the Fourteenth Naval District, which included Pearl Harbor. In another ironic twist, when Nimitz three years earlier had commanded Battleship Division One, Bloch had been his senior, wearing four stars as commander in chief, U.S. Fleet. Now Nimitz, with four stars, was senior to Bloch, who had reverted to two stars.

Psychologically, Bloch, of the Naval Academy class of 1899, could not altogether accept the seniority of Nimitz, of the class of 1905. Bloch had seen another junior admiral, Kimmel, raised over senior heads to CINCPAC and then lose the Pacific Fleet battleships. He was damned if he was going to sit back now and see Nimitz lose the Pacific Fleet carriers. They were the nation's last mobile line of defense. With those gone, the Japanese could go where they pleased in the Pacific and take what they wanted.

Bloch pressed his views on Nimitz both in conference and in private. In effect, he put an avuncular arm around Nimitz's shoulders and proceeded to tell him how to run the war. Nimitz considered himself fully competent to do the job without such tutelage, but he was at a disadvantage because most of the air officers agreed with Bloch, and Nimitz was not an aviator and had never commanded carriers.

On Wednesday, January 7, the *Enterprise* force returned to Pearl from patrol, and its commander, crusty warrior Vice Adm. William F. Halsey, came ashore. We lack eyewitness records of what happened next, but we know that Halsey barged into the CINCPAC conference that day or the next and cleared the air by sounding off loudly, and no doubt profanely, against the defeatism he found. He then and there permanently endeared himself to his commander in chief by backing him and the raiding plan to the hilt, offering to lead the attack on the Gilberts and Marshalls himself. Because Halsey was a vice admiral and commander, Aircraft Battle Force, and was liked and respected by all, his words carried decisive weight. The raids would be executed as planned.

Early on January 11 Halsey, with the *Enterprise* force, departed Pearl Harbor and shaped course for Samoa, where he would pick up the *Yorktown* force, newly arrived from the Atlantic. The two carrier groups, under Halsey's command, would then advance on the Gilberts and Marshalls from the southeast. Officers in the know, ashore and afloat, had cause for apprehension. Left guarding the Hawaiian Islands were only the *Saratoga* and *Lexington* forces, with the latter scheduled to attack Wake. Radio intelligence indicated that the six-carrier striking force that raided Pearl Harbor had departed Japan on January 6. It could be headed for Midway, Pearl Harbor, the Marshalls, or Samoa.

Late on January 11 came the shocking news that the *Saratoga*, patrolling 450 miles southwest of Oahu, had been struck by a submarine torpedo. On the thirteenth she came limping into Pearl Harbor, where an examination in drydock revealed that she would have to go to the West Coast for major repairs and rebuilding that would keep her out of the war for several months.

From Adm. Ernest J. King, commander in chief, U.S. Fleet, in Washington, came a dispatch insisting that the attack on Wake be executed. Though Nimitz was reluctant to tie up all his carriers at once, he radioed Vice Adm. Wilson Brown, then cruising with the *Lexington* some five hundred miles southwest of Pearl, to advance and take Wake under attack. He sent out the *Neches,* his only available oiler, to refuel Brown's vessels, but on the twenty-third the *Neches* was sunk by a submarine, so Nimitz canceled the Wake raid and ordered the *Lexington* to return to Pearl Harbor.

In the midst of this period of anxiety, Admiral Nimitz was startled to learn that on the Palmyra and Johnston island airbases all work had been stopped. The stoppage, it appeared, was by order of Admiral Bloch, who was convinced that those outlying islands could not be held and saw no point in building facilities for use by a conquering enemy. Similarly, Bloch had failed to spur and cooperate with the army teams assigned to fortify Christmas and Canton islands. Nimitz peremptorily called a conference to settle these matters and to look into slack handling of supplies by the Fourteenth Naval District. He neither shouted nor thumped the table, but he made clear what he expected and intended to have done. Bloch got the message. Though sometimes bull-headed and mischievous, he was a loyal and disciplined officer. He accepted his instructions from the younger, but now senior, Nimitz with a respectful "Aye, aye, sir."

Officers observing Nimitz during these tense weeks afterward recalled his patience and apparent serenity and his unfailing optimistic bearing. From his letters to Mrs. Nimitz, however, we know that at last he felt the loneliness of high command, for nobody in the Pacific theater could share his appalling responsibility. "I lie awake long hours," he wrote her but could not tell her what was troubling him.

In late January, as the *Enterprise* and *Yorktown* forces were heading toward their targets, Nimitz was relieved to be able to radio Halsey that the Japanese carrier force was down south supporting a landing at Rabaul. Thus it could not possibly interfere with Halsey's forthcoming raid. On the other hand, Japanese at Rabaul were a threat to the Australian base at Port Moresby, New Guinea, and, ultimately, to the United States-Australia communication line, which Nimitz had been ordered to guard.

Halsey made good his raid, at least to the extent of bombing and bombarding installations on some of the enemy islands and getting away with the loss of thirteen planes and bomb damage to a heavy cruiser. The attack achieved only moderate destruction, but newsmen, long starved for good news, shamelessly puffed up the claims of the raiders. Stateside editors added their bit, producing such absurd headlines as "PEARL HARBOR REVENGED!"

Nimitz, however, was both disappointed and disillusioned. The Gilberts-Marshalls raid had no discernible effect on enemy operations elsewhere. In the Philippines the Japanese continued to press the American and Filipino troops into the tip of Bataan Peninsula and nearby Corregidor Island. Their drives on Rangoon and Singapore and into the Dutch East Indies showed no signs of slowing.

Admiral King, alarmed at the growing threat to U.S.-Australia communications, ordered Admiral Nimitz to rush to the South Pacific planes and ships, including the *Lexington* force. King directed Nimitz also to stage more and heavier diversionary raids, using all available forces, not omitting the half dozen old battleships now based on the West Coast.

Nimitz had concluded that such raids were useless. The proposal to raid with battleships he regarded as nonsense. The old battlewagons, none faster than twenty-one knots, were too slow to operate with the thirty-four-knot carriers, and there were not enough cruisers and destroyers available to form separate screens for the battleships and the carriers.

When Nimitz's radioed objections elicited from King only sharp and caustic replies, Nimitz sent Admiral Pye by plane to Washington to explain the situation in the Central Pacific. As an emissary to Admiral King, Pye was an inspired choice. He was a highly respected strategist and an experienced commander of large forces. Somewhat cautious by nature, he could be counted on to council prudence. Since until lately he had been commander, Battle Force Pacific, his advice against attempting to use the old battleships would carry weight. By no means least important, he was King's Naval Academy classmate and one of his few intimate friends.

In addition to information and counsel on strategy, Nimitz sent to King, via Pye, a small personal request. It appeared that Admiral Bloch still could not refrain from advising Nimitz on how to run the war. The latter was anxious not to injure Bloch's service reputation, but he would be most grateful to have King remove him to a command where his advice was needed.

Nimitz decided to send Halsey with the *Enterprise* force to raid Wake and Marcus islands. Such raids, if nothing more, would give the men experience and lift American morale, and he hoped they would satisfy King. As for the battleships, he refused to send them out with the inadequate screens he could provide them and have them sunk by enemy submarines or aircraft.

On February 14 Halsey left Pearl Harbor. The following day a conciliatory dispatch came from Washington, apparently reflecting the good offices of Pye. King would be satisfied, it now appeared, with occasional raids by Pacific Fleet forces on the Japanese Central Pacific island bases.

Down in the South Pacific, Wilson Brown's *Lexington* force on February 20 attempted a raid on the new Japanese base at Rabaul, but Brown backed off when his force was discovered and attacked by enemy planes. He insisted that if he had an additional carrier, he would go back and finish the job. So Nimitz sent down the *Yorktown* force under Rear Adm. Frank Jack Fletcher. Instead of returning to attack Rabaul, however, Brown, with his two-carrier force, raided shipping at a pair of tiny Japanese footholds, Lae and Salamaua, on the New Guinea north coast.

That same day Halsey's *Enterprise* force came steaming into Pearl Harbor. The force had raided Wake and Marcus, but even the optimistic Halsey could not claim much success—a few buildings and possibly a fuel storage tank set afire and one small patrol craft sunk. In the opinion of one officer who had participated in the raids, "The Japs don't mind them any more than a dog minds a flea."

The Japanese advance in the East Indies area had not been slowed down in the slightest. Singapore had surrendered on February 15. The defensive Allied striking force had been shattered in the Battle of the Java Sea, and the U.S. cruiser *Houston* was sunk while trying to escape. Rangoon fell on March 8; Java, the following day. The Japanese carrier force then headed into the Indian Ocean to take a few cracks at the British Eastern Fleet and at the bases on Ceylon.

Admiral Nimitz, as always, radiated confidence, but in his private moments he could not throw off the depression that ever more burdened him. He felt frustrated that he could do so little to turn the tide of war, and he suspected that he had disappointed his early sponsors. To Mrs. Nimitz he wrote, "Ever so many people were enthusiastic for me at the start, but when things do not move fast enough they sour on me. I will be lucky to last six months. The public may demand action and results faster than I can produce."

At the CINCPAC morning conference of April 9, the fleet intelligence officer, Lt. Comdr. Edwin T. Layton, presented a briefing that contained little but bad news. Corregidor remained in American hands, but Bataan had just fallen to the enemy. The Japanese carrier force was still operating in the Indian Ocean. After raiding the base at Colombo on Ceylon, it had sunk two British cruisers at sea. Signs pointed to an early Japanese offensive against eastern New Guinea.

That last announcement Nimitz found particularly disturbing. He knew that it was obtained through radio intelligence, which he had come to trust. Radio intelligence was based on traffic analysis, radio direction finding and tracking, and code breaking. For Pearl Harbor it was evaluated and interpreted at the local Combat Intelligence Unit, which was headed by the cryptanalytic expert Lt. Comdr. Joseph Rochefort and housed in a well-guarded basement under the Fourteenth Naval District headquarters. The specialty of the local unit was cryptanalysis of the Japanese naval operational code. Before the raid on Pearl Harbor, the Japanese had cautiously refrained from sending messages by radio concerning their proposed attack, but since the attack they had become steadily less discreet in disseminating information by radio in the code that Rochefort and his assistants were reading.

The warning about the impending new Japanese offensive must have disturbed Admiral King too, for he took the unprecedented step of communicating directly with Commander Rochefort. The Japanese carrier force had now raided Trincomalee, another base in Ceylon, and had sunk a British carrier, the *Hermes*. What, King wanted to know, did radio intercepts indicate about Japan's immediate and long-range plans?

Rochefort, after reviewing his sources of information and consulting with his staff, replied with a four-part estimate, which he sent to both King and Nimitz: (1) The Japanese had concluded operations in the Indian Ocean, and their fleet was withdrawing to Japan; (2) they had no plans to attack Australia; (3) they would soon launch an operation to seize the eastern end of New Guinea; and (4) they would follow this move with a much bigger operation in the Pacific, an operation involving most of the Combined Fleet.

Admiral Nimitz and his staff concluded that the coming enemy campaign in New Guinea could only mean an assault on the Australian base at Port Moresby on the Coral Sea, an obvious preliminary to an advance to New Caledonia to cut U.S.-Australia communications. As for the ensuing Pacific Ocean operations, Nimitz and his planners estimated that the Japanese would attack the Aleutians, Pearl Harbor, or Midway. Whatever their ultimate objective, it seemed unlikely they would bypass Midway, the westernmost fortified U.S. outpost in the Central Pacific. Nimitz recognized as a cardinal rule that he must not risk such losses in defending Port Moresby that would render him helpless to counter the later Pacific Ocean offensive.

By mid-April a radio intelligence unit in Australia was able to predict that in early May a group of Japanese transports would enter the Coral Sea escorted by the light carrier *Shoho* and supported by a striking force including two big carriers, veterans of the Pearl Harbor raid—probably the *Shokaku* and the *Zuikaku*. When the Japanese began to refer to their coming attack as Operation MO, Nimitz was strengthened in his assumption that their main objective was Port Moresby.

Admiral Nimitz and General MacArthur, commander in chief, Southwest Pacific Area, agreed that the enemy must be stopped. The means were slim. MacArthur had a couple hundred army planes, but the pilots were not trained for over-water operations or ship recognition. If the Japanese were to be thrust back, it would have to be by means of carrier planes. Unfortunately, Halsey, the Pacific Fleet's most skilled and experienced carrier commander, was off with the *Enterprise* and *Hornet* forces raiding Tokyo—a dangerous and militarily useless mission dreamed up in Washington. Even if Halsey and his two carriers escaped destruction, they could not get to the Coral Sea before the second week in May. Recognizing this, Nimitz ordered Fletcher's *Yorktown* force, then operating in the Coral Sea, to retire to Tongatabu for hurried upkeep and replenishment and to return to the Coral Sea ready for action before the end of April. He ordered the *Lexington* force, at Pearl Harbor, to head south and report to Fletcher on May 1.

On April 25 Admiral Halsey with the *Enterprise-Hornet* force steamed jubilantly into Pearl Harbor, his Tokyo mission accomplished, his ships intact. Instead of the period of rest and relaxation he and his men had anticipated, he was allowed just five days' upkeep for his force, after which he was to hasten with it to the Coral Sea. It was unlikely that he could complete the 3500-mile voyage in time to participate in the coming battle, but there was a chance the enemy might be behind schedule. In that event, Halsey was to join Fletcher and assume overall tactical command.

As it turned out, the Japanese were on schedule. On May 7, while planes from the *Shokaku* and *Zuikaku* were striking at an American oiler and accompanying destroyer under the impression that they were attacking the American carrier force, Fletcher's aircraft located and sank the light carrier *Shoho*, whereupon the ships of the Port Moresby expeditionary group reversed course, the first time in World War II that a Japanese attack had been turned back.

The next morning the main action of the battle of the Coral Sea opened as planes from the big American and Japanese carriers struck at opposing forces,

U.S.S. Enterprise *steaming into Pearl Harbor under the command of Vice Adm.*
William F. Halsey in April 1942. Instead of the hoped for rest period following raids
on the Japanese coast, the Enterprise-Hornet *force was immediately dispatched to do*
battle in the Coral Sea, and from there on to Midway. (RG 80, No. 80-G-20285.)

then about 175 miles apart. The *Yorktown,* the *Lexington,* and the *Shokaku*
suffered bomb damage, and the *Lexington* was struck by two torpedoes. These
broke aircraft fuel lines that set off fires and explosions so severe that the
Lexington had to be scuttled.

At Pearl Harbor the triumph of May 7 turned into something like despair
on the eighth. Said Nimitz grimly, "The *Lexington* could have been saved."
Then, reverting to his usual optimistic tone, he added, "Remember this, we
don't know anything about the enemy—how badly he's hurt. You can bet
your boots he's hurt, too. His situation is no bed of roses either."

Admiral Nimitz could waste no time pining. He now had to turn his attention to dealing with the coming enemy attack in the Pacific. Rochefort and
his assistants at the Combat Intelligence Unit had concluded that the new

Japanese objective was indeed Midway. Radio traffic analysis disclosed that Japanese ships were assembling in great numbers in home waters and in the Marianas. Cryptanalysis revealed that the Japanese were calling their forthcoming attack Operation MI. Nimitz, even before the battle of the Coral Sea, had been so convinced that the enemy would not bypass Midway that he flew the 1100 miles out to the lonely atoll to check on its defenses and see what else was needed.

Not everybody agreed with Rochefort's findings. The Army Air Force, for example, was expecting a raid on San Francisco and for that reason would not release to Admiral Nimitz all the bombers he felt he needed. The British were arguing, contrary to all evidence, that Japan's next move would again be into the Indian Ocean. General MacArthur was of the opinion that the Japanese would resume their drive into the New Guinea-Solomons area. Maj. Gen. Delos Emmons, army commander of the Hawaiian Department, objected to sending bombers out to Midway because he considered that the Japanese were likely to attack Pearl Harbor again.

Nimitz had no intention of diffusing his efforts and scattering his limited forces in an attempt to meet every sort of attack of which the Japanese were capable. His situation was desperate and he knew it. The Japanese *Shokaku* was undergoing repair from her bomb damage, and the *Zuikaku* could not obtain replacements for trained aviators lost in the battle of the Coral Sea. That much Nimitz suspected, but he also knew that the Japanese still had eight carriers available, while the Americans could be sure of only two, the *Enterprise* and the *Hornet*. The *Yorktown* had made it to Tongatabu, but experts there reported that it would take ninety days of repairs to make her battleworthy again. The *Saratoga* was now repaired and en route to San Diego to form a task force, but it was unlikely she could reach the mid-Pacific in time. The *Wasp*, Pacific-bound, was still on the far side of the Atlantic. Much nearer were three British carriers operating in the Indian Ocean. Nimitz requested the loan of one of these, but the Admiralty, still bemused with the notion that the next Japanese drive would be into these waters, replied that none could be spared. As for other major types, the Japanese had twenty-three cruisers; Nimitz had eight. They had eleven fast battleships; Nimitz had none fast enough to operate with the carriers.

Admiral Nimitz lost no time in assembling and deploying such forces as he could collect. He ordered Admiral Halsey with the *Enterprise-Hornet* force and Fletcher with his *Yorktown* force to head for Pearl Harbor on the double. He would himself have a look at the *Yorktown*'s damages. Learning that the enemy probably expected to make landings in the western Aleutians, he felt obliged to send thither a cruiser-destroyer force. It would be hard to find positions of less strategic value, but the fact remained that they were U.S. territory.

Should he let them go by default, he would face public condemnation out of all proportion to their worth.

Admiral Nimitz now decided it was time he and his associates had a personal interview with Rochefort. Accordingly, he ordered the cryptanalyst to report to headquarters on the morning of May 25. At the appointed hour the admiral and members of his staff were assembled, but Rochefort failed to make his appearance. The officers present exchanged glances. One did not customarily ignore appointments with the commander in chief.

At last, half an hour late, Rochefort, looking a bit rumpled, was admitted. Nimitz eyed him icily. Rochefort apologized, explaining that he and his associates had been up all night trying to break a date-time cipher concealed within the Japanese operational code. They had succeeded to the extent that he could now predict that a two-carrier force would attack the Aleutians on June 3, that a four-carrier force would strike Midway on June 4, and that the actual invasion of Midway was scheduled for June 6. There was little chance of more information becoming available through cryptanalysis before the attack, he explained, because the Japanese had routinely changed their code. Weeks might pass before enough traffic built up in the revised code for the repetitions to occur on which cryptanalysts rely.

The purported exposure of Admiral Yamamoto's operation plan, together with precise dates, merely deepened the suspicions of the doubters. Why, they asked, should practically the whole Combined Fleet be assigned to the capture of one tiny atoll? Might not the messages be fakes, deliberately planted to mislead the Americans? Such top secret information is usually not transmitted by radio, even in the securest codes, for all the world to record, scrutinize, and perhaps cryptanalyze.

Admiral Nimitz, for want of more definite intelligence, decided to base his plans on the assumption that the intelligence estimates were correct. The Japanese could be operating at full strength in order to meet an unexpectedly formidable opposition. Their main objective might even be to draw out the inferior U.S. Pacific Fleet for destruction. The transmission of the plan by radio could mean that they were operating on so tight a schedule that they could get it distributed in time by no other means.

Commander Layton, on orders from Nimitz, minutely studied the decoded plan and compared it with data from his other sources of information. Seeking absolute certainty, he reviewed the intelligence findings of the past three weeks, brooded over charts, and studied Pacific Ocean winds, weather, and currents. He thus took a little too much time for Nimitz's patience. The admiral sent for him and demanded something definite and detailed.

"All right then, Admiral," said Layton. "I've previously given you intelligence that the carriers will probably attack Midway on the morning of the 4th of

June, so we'll pick the 4th of June for the day. They'll come in from the northwest on bearing 325 degrees and they will be sighted at about 175 miles from
Midway, and the time will be about 0600 Midway time."

This was a good deal more precision than Nimitz had counted on, but he
knew that Layton would not have gone into such detail unless he had very
good reason to support each fact and figure that he reported. The admiral
thanked him and ordered the information promptly passed on to Midway
and also to the plotting officers in Operations Plot.

The arrival of the U.S. carrier forces from the South presented Nimitz with
more problems. Again he was deprived of the services of Halsey, for the latter
had become so afflicted with an allergic dermatitis that he had to be hospitalized.
This meant that Frank Jack Fletcher would have the tactical command in any
forthcoming battle. Nimitz named Rear Adm. Raymond Spruance, Halsey's
cruiser commander, to replace Halsey in command of the *Enterprise-Hornet*
force.

Admiral Nimitz personally inspected the *Yorktown* in drydock and concluded that her hull could be patched and her internal damage adequately
shored up in three days. Within an hour welding equipment and steel plates
and other materials were being assembled at the dock and the repairs were
begun which would continue around the clock until the job was finished.

On the evening of May 27, the CINCPAC and task force staffs held a joint
conference to hammer out battle plans. They recognized that the wide dispersal of the segments of the Combined Fleet presented a rare opportunity
to defeat it in detail, and that if the Americans could disable the four-carrier
force approaching Midway, the rest of the Combined Fleet would have to retire
for lack of air cover. Accordingly, it had already been decided that the American carriers would be stationed northeast of Midway, on the flank of the oncoming four-carrier force. It was essential that the Americans get the jump
on the Japanese. With good timing and luck they would catch the Japanese
carriers with half their planes away attacking Midway. With better timing and
better luck, they might catch the enemy carriers with planes positioned forward while recovering the Midway attack group. That the Americans might
catch the Japanese carriers in the highly vulnerable state of rearming and
refueling the recovered planes was almost too much to hope for.

By May 29 both U.S. carrier forces had left Pearl, headed for a rendezvous
point 350 miles northeast of Midway—a position hopefully designated Point
Luck. There followed days of nervous waiting, with some officers at CINCPAC
headquarters still convinced that Nimitz was the victim of an elaborate Japanese hoax, that the messages decrypted by the Combat Intelligence Unit had
been planted specifically to lure the American carriers away from Pearl
Harbor.

An urgent message came from Midway on the morning of June 3. A Catalina search plane 700 miles to the west had sighted and reported the oncoming Japanese invasion force. Comdr. Maurice Curts, the CINCPAC communication officer, rushed the contact report to Nimitz's office, where the admiral was consulting with Commander Layton. Nimitz glanced at the dispatch, then sat suddenly erect.

"Layton," he said excitedly, "have you seen this?"

"What is it, sir?"

"The sighting of the Japanese forces!"

Nimitz was smiling. That in itself was nothing unusual, for he smiled often, and his smiles seemed somehow to involve his whole countenance: his ruddy complexion; his straight, white teeth; his light blue eyes, crinkling at the corners; even his sandy hair, just turning white. His expression now, however, was nothing less than radiant, what Layton called "that brilliant white smile."

"It just lights up," said Layton, as though "somebody let in the sun by raising a window shade. His smile and his blue eyes would go right through you." Nimitz had successfully concealed his anxiety but now he made not the slightest attempt to hide his relief. He handed the dispatch to Layton.

"This ought to make your heart warm," he said, chuckling. "This will clear up all the doubters now. They just have to see this to know that what I told them is correct."

Before sunset on the third, Admiral Nimitz knew that Dutch Harbor had been bombed that morning and that four Japanese carrier planes had been shot down over the Aleutians. To Midway and to his task force commanders he sent a special message: "The situation is developing as expected. Carriers, our most important objective, should soon be located. Tomorrow may be the day you can give them the works."

At dawn on June 4, all the CINCPAC staff were at their stations. They knew that when daybreak came to Midway, the Catalinas would be out to the northwest. They were aware also that the report they were awaiting might well be the most pivotal communication of the war. Shortly after 6 A.M. it came in, an urgent message in plain language via the cable from Midway: "Plane reports two carriers and Main Body ships bearing 320°, course 135°, speed 25, distance 180."

Nimitz glanced at the date-time group on the dispatch. He then went out and pinpointed the enemy's position on the plot. To Layton he remarked, "Well, you were only 5 miles, 5 degrees, and 5 minutes off."

The rest of June 4 was a day of terrible uncertainty at Pearl Harbor. That a battle was being fought was clear from bits and pieces of radio messages picked up. But the action was being fought in an area of static so intense that mere fragments came through. The only really dependable information reaching

CINCPAC was that Midway had been raided by carrier planes, with heavy losses among Midway's defending fighter planes, and that the *Yorktown* had been bombed, torpedoed, and abandoned. With Fletcher's flagship out of action, Spruance had necessarily taken over the tactical command. In the circumstances, even the serene and self-controlled Nimitz could not altogether conceal his apprehension. Said one officer: "Admiral Nimitz was frantic; I mean, as frantic as I've ever seen him."

By the end of the day, Nimitz knew that American carrier planes had attacked three Japanese carriers in the morning and one in the late afternoon. The careful Spruance, however, did not make his report until all his aviators had returned from the final attack and were fully debriefed. By then the *Enterprise-Hornet* force (Task Force 16) was out of the area of static. Spruance's message came in clear and ungarbled: "At 5 to 6 P.M. air groups of Task Force 16 attacked enemy force consisting of 1 carrier, 2 battleships, 2 or more heavy cruisers, several destroyers. Carrier hit several times with 500- and 1000-pound bombs and when last seen, burning fiercely. . . . Three ships believed carriers previously attacked were observed to southeastward still burning."

When Nimitz had read that far, he looked up. His countenance was glowing with "that brilliant white smile." If the newly hit carrier was burning fiercely and those hit that morning were still burning, all four carriers were almost certainly beyond salvage. An American victory seemed assured unless Spruance were to blunder badly, and Nimitz believed that Spruance was no blunderer. Nimitz immediately released a prepared message to all his forces: "You who participated in the Battle of Midway today have written a glorious page in our history. I estimate that another day of all-out effort on your part will complete the defeat of the enemy."

The rest of the story is known to all the world. Before dawn Yamamoto had faced the facts. He abandoned the operation against Midway and ordered all his forces to retire. Spruance chased them for two days, sinking a heavy cruiser and heavily damaging another. The *Yorktown*, under tow, was hit by a submarine torpedo and went down. Nevertheless, the battle of Midway was an unqualified defeat for Japan. Moreover, it proved the turning point in the war. Japanese forces made no more advances, and the Allies soon shifted to the offensive.

In the first euphoria of victory, before the cost in lives had been toted up, Admiral Nimitz could not resist a pun in his famous communiqué of June 6: "Pearl Harbor has now been partially avenged. Vengeance will not be complete until Japanese sea power is reduced to impotence. We have made substantial progress in that direction. Perhaps we will be forgiven if we claim that we are about midway to that objective."

CLARK G. REYNOLDS

Commentary

Throughout all three of these interesting papers runs a common question: why do admirals do what they do? For example, Admiral Ruge gives us an autobiographical account of how he, devoid of knowledge or orders regarding the invasion of France in 1940, sent his command into action anyway, gathering information and sweeping probable areas of enemy activity. Professor Adams tells how Admiral Greenslade's effectiveness in naval diplomacy with French Admiral Robert at Martinique was directly proportional to the amount of naval muscle he was allowed to flex by his political superiors. And Professor Potter demonstrates the well-known administrative genius of Admiral Nimitz at work as CINCPAC, delicately removing the thorn of Admiral Bloch by a careful word to the higher-ups, even in the midst of the heavy demands of the shattered post-Pearl Harbor Pacific Fleet situation.

Just such examples illustrate one problem in the historical writing of World War II, namely, that men and not machines were the real actors in the drama—the machines being the mere props. People make war, or quasi war; people build and drive the machine-weapons; and people write the documents that eventually fill the National Archives repository. Technology looms larger in naval than in land warfare because of the complexity of warships and seaborne weapons systems. That technology may indeed make a slave of its mortal master in tactical thinking, but people are still the active agents of the historical process. With this in mind, three important avenues of historical research and thinking regarding World War II are suggested from these thought-provoking papers and from other recent developments in historiography.

First is the search for historical continuity. World War II fascinates students and scholars alike, but all too often its events are viewed in a time and space vacuum, with writers ignorant of the larger contexts within which the war and its momentous events occurred. A recent example is Richard Steele's *The First Offensive, 1942*—an excellent treatment of General Marshall's attempt to gain for the U.S. Army a predominant role over Allied Strategic planning in 1942 with an early cross-Channel attack. But the book ignores the important habits of American generals in leading American defensive policy up to that time and the tendency of the admirals to be less assertive.[1] The student of this and of all American naval wars should therefore read extensively in general history and naval theory in order to understand some of the major definitions and choices open to navies before plunging naked into the attempt to fathom the wartime period. One danger in this is of course forming preconceptions; nonetheless, honest historical analysis should destroy preconceptions and even possibly lead to new hypotheses.

Broadly, the naval historian should seek to discern any patterns in naval history, be they what Theodore Ropp has called "modern military paradigms"[2] or generational traits[3] or just habits of conduct by particular types of navies or specific navies themselves.[4] Admiral Ruge in this paper and his other writings has shown a remarkable continuity of German naval thought and practices relating to inshore warfare from World War I down to the present that reveal certain definite patterns.[5] Following the treatises of Professors Wheeler and Mallison on navies vis-à-vis diplomacy and international law, Professor Adams's call for studies of the American-German/Quasi war of 1941 must be understood in the total context of the American concept of international law and naval diplomacy, from the quasi-war with France in 1798 to the Cuban missile quarantine of 1962, in order to reveal very definite consistencies of policy.[6] Professor Potter's anxiously awaited biography of Admiral Nimitz reveals certain distinctive features of that generation of American naval officers. For example, many of the admiral's actions throughout World War II stemmed from his midshipman days in the era of Theodore Roosevelt.

Indeed, the historical continuity in American naval affairs reveals a much clearer picture of historical reality than the artificial "episodic" nature of the American military past as propounded by several recent Army-oriented historians.[7]

The second suggested area of historical analysis involves psychology in history, a relatively new field of inquiry for American historians but not for Germans schooled in the works of Herder, Dilthey, and Freud. Frank E. Manuel has said recently that "any contemporary use of psychology in history must postulate the existence of the unconscious, a belief that the unconscious of past epochs has left behind visible traces, and a conviction that these traces are decipherable."[8] Put another way, for our purposes, the naval historian must seek to know the motives for the behavior of admirals and ratings alike. The documents can only go so far by recounting specific actions, but underneath them are hints of deep-seated psychological factors that help to complete the historical picture of men in peace and war. For instance, American military and naval leaders make much of their "win psychology." Is its meaning self-evident, or is there more to it? What happens when a perennial winner loses — either a nation, an armed service, and/or a specific leader?

Admiral Ruge's wisdom in consciously dealing with the morale of his men is more than just good sense. He unconsciously may have been recalling the unhappy circumstances that had led to the German naval mutinies of World War I, which Daniel Horn has traced directly to short-sighted officers who were oblivious to the morale factors.[9] Ruge kept his officers and chief petty officers well educated and informed on matters of the world, which no doubt lessened their fears based upon ignorance. He also reveals that his men loved to sing, which he encouraged. This was not a German monopoly if we remember Austria's best U-boat commander of World War I, Baron von Trapp, and his "sound of music" family, which subsequently came to New England, or the Greeks, who sang as they rowed into battle at Salamis, or Saxie Dowell's U.S. Navy swing band that played while the crew of the stricken carrier *Franklin* fought to save her from flames off the Japanese coast in 1945. There is much psychology in the story by jazz trumpeter Max Kaminsky, of Artie Shaw's U.S. Navy band, playing from the lowered aircraft elevator over a jammed hangar deck on the carrier *Saratoga* at New Caledonia early in 1943. Feeling the men's homesickness, he recalls in his autobiography:

> I began to fill up so much that when I stood up to take my solo on the "St. Louis Blues," I blew like a madman. On hearing me let loose, Dave [Tough, the drummer] started to swing the beat, and when I picked up my plunger and started to growl, those three thousand men went stark, raving crazy. Even the fellows in the band were shaken. . . . I decided from then on I'd try to break it up for the men everywhere we went and try to play the way I knew they felt inside. . . . And the men seemed to feel what I meant. . . . Once, at a base hospital . . . when I started to growl something happened and those broken men came to life again and banged their crutches and beat the arms of their wheel chairs, or just yelled and shouted themselves hoarse if they were too smashed up or too weak to applaud.[10]

Chester Nimitz was no stranger to good American popular music. One evening at a party at which pianist Claude Thornhill led a quartet of navy jazz musicians, Nimitz, "a piano buff, got an earful of Claude playing things like *Rhapsody in Blue*, . . . dropped anchor next to the piano for the rest of the night," and thereafter had Thornhill "over to his house every chance he could." He later kept Thornhill in Hawaii to form his own navy band when the Shaw band went off to the South Pacific.[11]

Admiral Nimitz also almost seems to have utilized staff instinctively in a sagacious and careful way: prompting Layton and Rochefort to deliver the goods, keeping on Kimmel's dispirited advisers after December 7, handling Bloch firmly but politely, and finally bringing in the brilliant Spruance to head his staff after Midway. But was this talent instinctive, or was it the result of his own education and experience? Considering his fiery contemporaries, MacArthur and King, how can Nimitz's behavior be explained by the historian? Biography is perhaps the most useful approach to solving this kind of problem, and hopefully Professor Potter will be able to discover the psychological wellsprings of "that brilliant white smile."

But however historians are able to utilize the alien language of the psychologists, the total and perfect personality profile will never be complete, leaving the historian to infer the individual's behavioral patterns from the oral and documentary evidence.

The third area for historical analysis is military sociology, the point at which individual and group behavior intersect. One pioneer of this methodology, Morris Janowitz, has advocated the study of military organization "to analyze the functions of primary groups within the military system" and to discover the interrelationships between the military system and the larger society.[12] For navies, the implications of this line of investigation are immense. Naval documents can reveal career patterns within navies that suggest which groups have emerged within the military's society. The related field of prosopography suggests a quantitative approach to patterns of training and promotion for particular groups, such as Nimitz's classmates of 1905.[13] In turn, this allows for comparative analyses of military careers. We know about Nimitz, King, and Halsey, but what about the men who Professor Adams mentions, those who apparently did not survive the early days of World War II in high command, like A. C. Pickens, J. W. Greenslade, and Wilson Brown? Or, we know of Raeder, Doenitz, and Ruge, but what of their lesser contemporaries who did not succeed? We need to look beyond their fitness reports and battle records to bureaucratic conditions, career favoritism, and subspecialty influences — e.g., the "Gun Club," aviation, subs, or minesweepers.

As for the interrelationships between the military and the rest of American society, I have suggested in my book, and Adams has also suggested in his treatment of Roosevelt's quasi-war, that navies are not always understood or appreciated by the nation at large. This was certainly also true in Germany. Is it merely the case of "bad press"? Or can it be traced to cultural, geographic, political, social, and economic factors? Political scientists, like Vincent Davis, have approached this problem from their perspective, and even social historians with a political bias, such as Peter Karsten, have done the same.[14] Such immense questions are not outside the purview of naval history, but rather they should enlighten importantly the events of World War II and other wars.

Finally, while these papers suggest such broad questions for further inquiry, each speaks also to particular historical issues.

Admiral Ruge has shown how low-priority inshore weapons have been treated in a continental navy in relation to the bigger, more glamorous tools of war. Comparable studies are Anthony Preston and John Major's classic work *Send a Gunboat!* for the Royal Navy; Robert Bulkley's history of PT boats in the U.S. Navy; and Arnold Lott's history of mine warfare.[15] Such works are a beginning to the systematic study of the "small boys" of World War II and other eras, not only to fill important historical gaps but to impress upon naval leaders the importance and uniqueness of such types of vessels. In answer to those German Naval Academy critics who accused the minesweeper forces of corrupting their midshipmen, Admiral Ruge and the naval historian can answer that it is the group cohesion of a small crew that leads both to tenacity and to a spirit of individual initiative not possible in the larger shipboard bureaucracy of, say, a battleship. America's carriermen and nuclear specialists would do well to take note of what destroyer-escorts and smaller vessels can offer the navy beyond purely tactical missions; one can only have mixed feelings over the 825 inshore and riverine craft—most of the navy's inventory—turned over to the South Vietnamese Navy five years ago.

Professor Adams calls for more studies involving the several aspects of the American-German quasi-naval war of 1941, and we have taken a major step in this direction in Patrick Abbazia's recent book on the subject.[16]

Professor Potter's presentation raises two areas of possible investigation that could add light not only to Midway but to the entire war in the Pacific and, indeed, naval warfare throughout the twentieth century. One area is long-range, sea-based aerial reconnaissance. The PBY Catalina was a fine naval aircraft, but how often did multiengine land or seaplane patrol bombers and carrier planes fail to provide fleet commanders with adequate aerial intelligence? Why were the Japanese apparently more successful at this than the Americans? The other problem is closely related, and one to which Professor Potter refers, namely, radio static from atmospheric interference. Scientific research is only now beginning to trace the causes of such radio behavior and will no doubt provide an explanation from the diverse realms of plasma and solar physics, planetary magnetic fields, and cosmic galactic "noise." One can only guess at what Nimitz, Spruance, and a host of other World War II leaders would have done if they had had clear signals rather than the myriad "garbled" or incomprehensible radio transmissions. We would like to know what caused this static then and even what causes it today.

Professor Potter does only one thing which troubles me in his setting of the stage for Nimitz's great triumph at Midway. He states:

It was essential that the Americans get the jump on the Japanese. With good timing and luck they would catch the Japanese carriers with half their planes away attacking Midway. With better timing and better luck they might catch the enemy carriers with planes positioned forward while recovering the Midway attack group. That the Americans might catch the Japanese carriers in the highly vulnerable state of rearming and refueling the recovered planes was almost too much to hope for.

A possible inference here is that Nimitz and his staff considered all these possibilities *before* such events actually occurred in the battle and that such minute considerations actually influenced their decisions. If such thoughts indeed did happen, I would urge Professor Potter to document his evidence very carefully, and, additionally, to question the hindsight of his interviewees. I do not challenge Admiral Nimitz's wise decisions, but I do question that either he or any of his staff that early in the war understood the intricacies of shipboard plane-spotting procedures on carriers, even American flattops let alone Japanese ships. My own research has satisfied me that even one or two years later CINCPAC remained sufficiently ignorant or disinterested in such minutia, which helps to explain Admiral Towers's endless crusade to keep Nimitz advised of carrier doctrine.[17] My guess is that Admiral Nimitz's real virtue lay in providing his intelligence estimates and *general* battle plans to Fletcher and Spruance and then letting them deal with the details of execution. I also believe that the close timing for the U.S. carrier strikes at Midway was worked out by Admiral Halsey's staff, led by the irascible Miles Browning and in the temporary service of Spruance. I hope that Professor Potter can enlighten us on this key question, but I urge him to use extreme caution and thus avoid reading perhaps too much into Nimitz's actual contribution to the battle.

And how do we explain luck? I guess we will have to leave that to the astrologers, or perhaps to old King Neptune.

In conclusion, I would reiterate that these interesting papers suggest endless possibilities for further work in the National Archives, in naval archives, in oral interviews (with the ubiquitous tape recorder of the Age of Watergate), and in the new techniques related to psychology and sociology, with all the historical tools of the experienced researcher, not to mention the computer. But, of course, when all the available evidence is in, historians must use their informed intuition, subjective as it may be, to try to fill in the gaps by inferences and educated guesses. We must guard against the "big guess" of the conspiratorial view, such as the belief among new leftists that the United States is out to conquer the world. But neither must we lack the intellectual nerve to draw the conclusions to which our evidence obviously leads us. I am not of the "let-the-evidence-speak-for-itself" school. The questions of war and peace in the contemporary world are too important to be left hanging. They must be spelled out clearly by the experts for the layman, the military and government leader, and other historians. If the conclusions are antithetical—if, indeed, naval heros "are shot"—then a dialogue must be developed among all of us in order to reach satisfactory answers.

NOTES

1. Richard W. Steele, *The First Offensive, 1942: Roosevelt, Marshall, and the Making of American Strategy* (Bloomington: Indiana University Press, 1973).
2. Theodore Ropp, "The Historical Development of Contemporary Strategy," U.S. Air Force Academy Harmon Memorial Lecture Number Twelve (1970), pp. 5, 18. Ropp bases many of his conceptualizations upon Thomas S. Kuhn, *The Structure of Scientific Revolutions* (Chicago: University of Chicago Press, 1964).
3. See my *The Fast Carriers: The Forging of an Air Navy* (New York: McGraw-Hill, 1968) for one example of generations in the U.S. Navy and its own aviation, broadly differentiated by the age at which an officer earned his wings—either as a young man or as a "latecomer." Fritz Redlich has had much to say about generations as well as continuity in German history. See his "German Literary Expressionism and Its Publishers," *Harvard Library Bulletin* 18, no. 2 (April 1969): 143-68, and his "German Economic Planning for War and Peace," *Review of Politics* 4, no. 3 (July 1944): 315-35.
4. See the differentiation between "maritime" and "continental" navies and their doctrinal habits in my *Command of the Sea: The History and Strategy of Maritime Empires* (New York: Morrow, 1974), pp. 3-9.
5. Friedrich Ruge, "German Naval Strategy across Two Wars," *U.S. Naval Institute Proceedings* 81, no. 2 (February 1955): 152-66; idem, *Der Seekrieg: The German Navy's Story, 1939-1945* trans. M. G. Saunders (Annapolis: U.S. Naval Institute, 1957); idem, "The Reconstruction of the German Navy, 1956-1961," *U.S. Naval Institute Proceedings* 88, no. 7 (July 1962): 52-65. See, also, Patrick James Kelly, "The Naval Policy of Imperial Germany, 1900-1914," (Ph.D. diss., Georgetown University, 1970); Theodore Ropp, "German Seapower: A Study in Failure," in A. M. J. Hyatt, ed., *Dreadnought to Polaris: Maritime Strategy since Mahan* (Toronto: Copp Clark, 1973), pp. 12-18; Jost Dülffer, *Hitler und die Marine: Reichspolitik und Flottenbau, 1920-1939* (Düsseldorf, 1973).
6. At both ends of the American experience, see John J. Kelly, Jr., "The Struggle for American Seaborne Independence as Viewed by John Adams," (Ph.D. diss., University of Maine, 1973), and Carl Q. Christol and Charles R. Davis (and Quincy Wright), "Maritime Quarantine: The Naval Interdiction of Offensive Weapons . . . to Cuba, 1962," *American Journal of International Law* 57 (July 1963): 525-65.
7. For example, Russell F. Weigley, *The American Way of War* (New York: Macmillan Co., 1973), p. 477 and passim; also, John Shy, "The American Military Experience: History and Learning," *Journal of Interdisciplinary History* 1, no. 2 (Winter 1971): 207.
8. Frank E. Manuel, "The Use and Abuse of Psychology in History," in Felix Gilbert

and Stephen R. Graubard, eds., *Historical Studies Today* (New York: Norton & Company, 1972), p. 230 and passim.

9. Daniel Horn, *The German Naval Mutinies of World War I* (New Brunswick, N.J.: Rutgers University Press, 1969). Ruge's chief during the prewar and early wartime years, Adm. Erich Raeder, certainly deserves much of the credit for an awareness of morale in the *Reichsmarine*. His former command, the cruiser *Köln*, with its partner *Königsberg*, were "the last ships with disciplined crews" during the mutinies of 1918. Erich Raeder, *My Life*, trans. Henry W. Drexel (Annapolis: U.S. Naval Institute, 1960), p. 90. See, also, Holger H. Herwig, *The German Naval Officer Corps* (Oxford: Oxford University Press, 1973), and Wallace Leigh Lewis, "The Survival of the German Navy, 1917-1920: Officers, Sailors and Politics," (Ph.D. diss., University of Iowa, 1969).

10. Max Kaminsky, with V. E. Hughes, *My Life in Jazz* (New York: Harper & Row, 1963), pp. 143-44.

11. Ibid., p. 139. The morale-lifting effect of American popular music during World War II may be seen in Glenn Miller's Army Air Forces Orchestra in the European Theater of Operations.

12. Morris Janowitz, with Roger Little, *Sociology and Military Establishment*, rev. ed. (New York: Russell Sage, 1965), p. 8, but especially Janowitz's *The Professional Soldier: A Social and Political Portrait* (Glencoe: Free Press, 1960).

13. See Lawrence Stone, "Prosopography," in Gilbert and Graubard, *Historical Studies Today*, pp. 107-140.

14. Vincent Davis, *The Admiral's Lobby* (Chapel Hill: University of North Carolina Press, 1967); Peter Karsten, *The Naval Aristocracy: The Golden Age of Annapolis and the Emergence of Modern American Navalism* (Glencoe: Free Press, 1972).

15. Anthony Preston and John Major, *Send a Gunboat! A Study of the Gunboat and Its Role in British Policy, 1854-1904* (London: Longmans, Green, 1977); Robert J. Bulkley, Jr., *At Close Quarters: PT Boats in the United States Navy* (Washington, D.C.: Government Printing Office, 1962); Arnold S. Lott, *Most Dangerous Sea: A History of Mine Warfare ...* (Annapolis: U.S. Naval Institute, 1959).

16. Patrick Abbazia, *Mr. Roosevelt's Navy: The Private War of the U.S. Atlantic Fleet, 1939-1942* (Annapolis: Naval Institute Press, 1975).

17. One major theme of my *The Fast Carriers* (New York: McGraw-Hill, 1968).

Biographical Sketches

HENRY H. ADAMS is a graduate of the University of Michigan and earned his doctorate at Columbia University. Following active duty in the navy in World War II, he taught at Cornell University, American University, the Naval Academy, and Illinois State University. He is now retired and free-lance writing. His most recent books are *1942: The Year That Doomed the Axis* (1967); *Years of Deadly Peril* (1969); *Years to Victory* (1973); and *Years of Expectation: Guadalcanal to Normandy* (1973). These books constitute a four-volume military, social, and political history of World War II.

DEAN C. ALLARD has been a historian and archivist with the Naval Historical Center since 1958 and currently serves as the senior archivist and head of Operational Archives at the center. During this time he has also taught history courses at the University of Virginia and George Washington University. He holds a B.A. from Dartmouth College, an M.A. from Georgetown University, and a Ph.D. from George Washington University. He is coauthor of *U.S. Naval History Sources in the Washington Area and Suggested Research Subjects* (1970) and *The United States Navy and the Vietnam Conflict*, volume 1 (1976), and has authored a number of articles on naval history.

K. JACK BAUER is a graduate of Harvard University with a Ph.D. from Indiana University and is currently professor of history and archivist of Rensselaer Polytechnic Institute. He has served on the staff of the National Archives and in the historical sections of both the Marine Corps and U.S. Navy. From 1957 to 1961 he was assistant to Samuel Eliot Morison for *History of United States Naval Operations in World War II* (1947-62). During the 1977-78 academic year he will be John F. Morrison Professor of Military History at the Command and General Staff College, Fort Leavenworth, Kansas. He has published numerous books and articles, including *The Mexican War, 1846-1848 (1974)*; *Ships of the Navy, 1775-1969*, volume 1 (1970); and *Surfboats and Horse Marines* (1969).

PAOLO E. COLLETTA received his B.S., M.A., and Ph.D. from the University of Missouri. He is currently professor of history at the U.S. Naval Academy, where he is also a television lecturer and director of television cultural activities. Previously, he has taught courses in history and diplomacy at the Universities of Missouri, Maryland, and Nebraska at Omaha and George Washington University. He was Fulbright Lecturer in American History at the University of Genoa, Italy, in 1971. Following three war-time years with the navy, he spent thirty years in the Naval Reserve, retiring in 1973. His publications include *The Presidency of William Howard Taft* (1973), a three-volume, biography of William Jennings Bryan (1964–69), and he was contributing editor of a book of essays on the foreign policies of William McKinley (1970). Forth-coming are *The Modern American Navy and Bradley A. Fiske* and *The U.S. Navy and Defense Unification, 1947–1953.*

MABLE E. DEUTRICH received her B.S. from Wisconsin State College and her M.A. and Ph.D. from the American University of Washington, D.C. Almost all of her career has been with the federal government. She worked for the Department of the Army, first in the field of records management and later as a historian. Since 1950 she has been an archivist at the National Archives, serving as director of the Military Archives Division and currently as assistant archivist of the United States for the National Archives. She is the author of *Struggle for Supremacy: The Career of General Fred C. Ainsworth* (1962) and a number of articles.

FRANCIS DUNCAN graduated from Ohio Wesleyan University and received his M.A. and Ph.D. degrees from the University of Chicago. He is currently the associate historian in the Office of the Historian, Energy Research and Development Administration (successor of the Atomic Energy Commission). He has been with the Administration since 1957. He is coauthor of *Atomic Shield, 1947/1952*, volume 2 of a series titled History of the United States Atomic Energy Commission (1969) and *Nuclear Navy, 1946–1962* (1974). Forthcoming works are *A Study of the United States Navy, 1898–1917*, and *A Study of the Application of Nuclear Energy in the United States Navy, 1961–1972*. He has also published various articles on naval history.

EDWIN B. HOOPER retired from the U.S. Navy in 1970 with the rank of vice admiral. He was graduated from the U.S. Naval Academy and the National War College and received an M.S. degree from the Massachusetts Institute of Technology. He established the Naval Long-Range Studies Project and the Institute of Naval Studies, serving as director of both. Upon his retirement from the navy he was retained as director of Naval History and curator of the Navy Department. Among his important assignments in research and development were assistant chief, Bureau of Ordnance; director, Anti-submarine Warfare Research and Development Programs; and deputy chief, Naval Operations (Development). He is author of *Mobility, Support, Endurance: A Study of Naval Operational Logistics in the Vietnam War* (1972).

PHILIP K. LUNDEBERG is curator-in-charge in the Division of Naval History, National Museum of History and Technology, Smithsonian Institution. Prior to this position he taught history at the U.S. Naval Academy and at Saint Olaf College and served as assistant to the historian for U.S. Naval Operations in World War II in the Naval History Division of the Navy Department. He received his B.A. and M.A. from Duke University and his Ph.D. from Harvard University. He is author of *Samuel Colt's Submarine Battery* (1974) and coauthor of *Sea Power: A Naval History* (1960) and *The Great Sea War* (1962). In addition, he has lectured and published numerous articles in professional journals on the history of undersea warfare.

SALLY V. MALLISON is research associate in the International and Comparative Law Program at the George Washington University Law Center. She studied the behavioral sciences and international affairs at the University of Washington. She is the joint author with W. Thomas Mallison, Jr., of several international law publications. Dr. and Mrs. Mallison are presently engaged in a study of international humanitarian law, a portion of which has appeared in *Case Western Reserve University Journal of International Law*.

W. THOMAS MALLISON, JR., is professor of law and director of the International and Comparative Law Program at George Washington University Law Center, where he has taught since 1951. During this time he has also served a one-year appointment as chief, Asian-African Branch, U.S. Atomic Energy Commission; visiting professor of law at the Law Faculty Center of Advanced International Studies, University of Tehran; Charles H. Stockton Chair of International Law at the Naval War College; and as an international law consultant. He has a J.S.D. degree from Yale University. In addition to many articles published in legal periodicals, books he has authored include *Studies in the Law of Naval Warfare: Submarines in General and Limited Wars* (1966) and *Political Crimes in the International Law of War: Concepts and Consequences* (1972).

WILLIAM JAMES MORGAN is chief civilian historian and head of the Historical Research Branch, Naval Historical Center, at the Navy Department. He received his Ph.D. from the University of Southern California, his M.A. from Columbia University, and his B.S. from Fordham University. He is editor of the multivolume series *Naval Documents of the American Revolution* (1964--) and authors of *United States Naval Chronology, World War II* (1955); *Captains to the Northward: The New England Captains in the Continental Navy* (1959); and *Civil War Naval Chronology 1861-1965* (1971). Other publications include numerous naval history articles in professional journals and magazines.

JOHN G. NEWTON is currently director of the Monitor Research and Recovery Foundation in Beaufort, North Carolina. For twelve years prior to establishment of the foundation, he was marine superintendent of the Oceanographic Program at Duke University Marine Laboratory and was chief scientist aboard the university's research vessel *Eastward* on the expedition that discovered the wreck of the *Monitor*. Previously he served as a geological consultant, a marine technician at Scripps, a cartographer, and a planning engineer, making undersea environmental surveys. He received his bachelor's degree from San Diego State College. He coauthored *An Oceanographic Atlas of the*

Carolina Continental Margin (1971) and *A Marine Biological Atlas of North Carolina* (forthcoming). Also in press is a book about the discovery of the *Monitor*.

RAYMOND G. O'CONNOR received his M.A. from American University and his Ph.D. from Stanford University. Since 1969 he has been professor of history and chairman of the Department of History at the University of Miami. Prior to this position, he taught history at the University of California at Berkeley, Stanford University, Temple University, and was Ernest J. King Professor of History at the Naval War College. He retired from the navy in 1955 after serving twenty years. Among his publications are *Force and Diplomacy: Essays, Military and Diplomatic* (1972); *Diplomacy for Victory: FDR and Unconditional Surrender* (1971); *The Japanese Navy in World War II* (1969); and numerous articles on military and diplomatic history.

ELMER B. POTTER received his B.A. from the University of Richmond and his M.A. from the University of Chicago. He taught at the U.S. Naval Academy as a reserve officer and after World War II joined the faculty full time. For twenty years prior to his recent retirement from the academy, he was chairman of the Naval History Division and during this time presented a forty-five-lecture series on television on naval history. Among the books he has coauthored are *Sea Power: A Naval History* (1960), which has appeared in whole or in part in eight languages, and *The Great Sea War* (1961). He is author of *The Naval Academy Illustrated History of the United States Navy* (1971) and *The Battle of Midway*, to the published by Rizzoli Editore of Milan in its Le Grandi Battaglie (Great Battles) series. His most recent book is *Nimitz* (1976), published by the U.S. Naval Institute Press.

CLARK G. REYNOLDS is professor and head, Department of Humanities, U.S. Merchant Marine Academy. Prior to this position, he taught courses in history at the University of Maine at Orono. He has a B.A. from the University of California at Santa Barbara and an M.A. and a Ph.D. from Duke University. In addition to many articles on naval history, he has published *Command of the Sea: History and Strategy of Maritime Empires* (1974) and *The Fast Carriers: The Forging of an Air Navy* (1968).

FRIEDRICH OSKAR RUGE, a native of Leipzig, Germany, retired as Inspekteur (highest officer and chief) to the Bundesmarine (West German Federal Navy) in 1961. His lengthy career in the German navy (beginning in 1914) spans two world wars. His commands were principally in the fields of mine development and minesweeping. He has served as commander of minesweeping operations, commander of security, head of the German Naval Command, admiral on the staff of Field Marshal Rommel, and chief of Naval Construction. Following World War II and his retirement, he has lectured and taught courses on naval history and diplomacy at Tuebingen University and other colleges and universities in West Germany. He has published numerous pamphlets and articles, mostly on the subject of seafaring and naval warfare history but also on nonmilitary topics. Among his books, many of which have been translated into other languages, are *Decision in the Pacific* (1951); *The War at Sea, 1939-1945* (1954); *Rommel and the*

Invasion (1959), currently being translated into English; and *The Soviets as Opponents at Sea* (being published by the Naval Institute Press).

DAVID F. TRASK is currently the historian, Office of the Historian, in the Bureau of Public Affairs of the State Department. He received his B.A. from Wesleyan University and his A.M. and Ph.D. from Harvard University. He has taught political economy at Boston University and history at Wesleyan University and the University of Nebraska. Some of the numerous books he has published include, *Victory without Peace: American Foreign Relations in the Twentieth Century* (1968); *World War I at Home: Readings on American Life, 1914-1920* (1970); and *Captains & Cabinets: Anglo-American Naval Relations, 1917-1918* (1972).

GORDON P. WATTS, JR., received his B.A. and M.A. degrees from East Carolina University. Since 1972 he has been an underwater archeologist with the North Carolina Division of Archives and History. The emphasis of his work with the division has been directed at establishing cooperative programs to survey North Carolina's underwater archeological resources. He has published articles in this field in the *International Journal of Underwater Archaeology* and *Spiegal Historiael*.

GERALD E. WHEELER was educated at the University of California and received his doctorate there in 1954. He is currently professor of history and chairman, Department of History, at San Jose State University. He has also taught history at the U.S. Naval Academy, San Jose State University, University of the Philippines, and the Naval War College. He is author of several books including, *Admiral William Veazie Pratt, U.S. Navy* (1974); *Prelude to Pearl Harbor: U.S. Navy and the Far East, 1921-1931* (1963); and *Outline of World Naval History since the Sixteenth Century* (1957).

Selected Bibliography

NATIONAL ARCHIVES SOURCES ON NAVAL HISTORY

GUIDES

A Guide-Index to the Official Records of the Union and Confederate Armies, 1861–1865:
Main Eastern Theater of Operations. Military Operations of the Civil War, vol. 2.
Compiled by Dallas Irvine. First Fascicle, containing section L: "Tables of Key
Reports for Principal Military Operations" (1968), pp. 1–76; 2d Fascicle, containing
section M: "Comprehensive Index of Recognized Military Operations," 1st part (1969),
pp. 77–172; 3d Fascicle, containing section M: "Comprehensive Index of Recognized
Military Operations," 2d part (1970), pp. 173–252; 4th Fascicle, containing section
M: "Comprehensive Index of Recognized Military Operations," 3d part (1971), pp.
253–331; 5th Fascicle, containing section N: "Checklist of Recognized Military
Operations by State and Date" and Section O: "Checklist of Recognized Military
Operations by State, County, and Date" (1972), pp. 333–428.

Civil War Maps in the National Archives. 1964. 127 p.

Federal Records of World War II. Vol. 1: Civilian Agencies. 1950. 1,073 p.; ibid.
Vol. 2: Military Agencies. 1951. 1,061 p.

Guide to Federal Archives Relating to the Civil War. Compiled by Kenneth W. Munden
and Henry P. Beers. 1962. 721 p.

Guide to Materials on Latin America in the National Archives of the United States.
Compiled by George S. Ulibarri and John P. Harrison. 1974. 489 p.

Guide to the Archives of the Government of the Confederate States of America. Compiled
by Henry P. Beers. 1968. 536 p.

Guide to the National Archives of the United States. 1974. 884 p.

Handbook of Federal World Agencies and Their Records, 1917–21. 1943. 666 p.

National Archives and Records Service sources, unless otherwise indicated, are published by the Government Printing Office, Washington, D.C., 20402.

INVENTORIES, PRELIMINARY INVENTORIES, AND SPECIAL LISTS

RECORDS OF THE EXECUTIVE BRANCH—EXECUTIVE DEPARTMENTS

Department of Commerce

COAST AND GEODETIC SURVEY (RECORD GROUP 23)

Preliminary Inventory of Records of the Coast and Geodetic Survey. Compiled by Nathan Reingold. PI 105. 1958. 83 p.

Department of Defense

Department of the Navy

BUREAU OF AERONAUTICS (RECORD GROUP 72)

Preliminary Inventory of Records of the Bureau of Aeronautics. Compiled by William F. Shonkwiler. PI 26. 1951. 9 p.

BUREAU OF MEDICINE AND SURGERY (RECORD GROUP 52)

Preliminary Inventory of the Records of the Bureau of Medicine and Surgery. Compiled by Kenneth F. Bartlett. PI 6. 1948. 18 p.

BUREAU OF NAVAL PERSONNEL (RECORD GROUP 24)

Preliminary Inventory of Records of the Bureau of Naval Personnel. Compiled by Virgil E. Baugh. PI 123. 1960. 135 p.

BUREAU OF ORDNANCE (RECORD GROUP 74)

Preliminary Inventory of Records of the Bureau of Ordnance. Compiled by William F. Shonkwiler. PI 33. 1951. 33 p.

BUREAU OF SHIPS (RECORD GROUP 19)

Preliminary Inventory of Records of the Bureau of Ships. Compiled by Elizabeth Bethel, et al. PI 133. 1961. 241 p.

BUREAU OF YARDS AND DOCKS (RECORD GROUP 71)

Preliminary Inventory of the Records of the Bureau of Yards and Docks. Compiled by Richard G. Wood. PI 10. 1948. 28 p.

HYDROGRAPHIC OFFICE (RECORD GROUP 37)

Inventory of the Records of the Hydrographic Office. Compiled by Maizie Johnson and William J. Heynen. Inv. 4. 1971. 28 p.

NAVAL DISTRICTS AND SHORE ESTABLISHMENTS (RECORD GROUP 181)

Preliminary Inventory of the Records of Naval Establishments Created Overseas during World War II. Compiled by Richard G. Wood. PI 13. 1948. 8 p.

OFFICE OF THE CHIEF OF NAVAL OPERATIONS (RECORD GROUP 38)

Preliminary Inventory of Cartographic Records of the Office of the Chief of Naval Operations. Compiled by Charlotte M. Ashby. PI 85. 1955. 17 p.

UNITED STATES MARINE CORPS (RECORD GROUP 127)

Inventory of Records of the United States Marine Corps. Compiled by Maizie Johnson. Inv. 2. 1970. 90 p.

Preliminary Inventory of Cartographic Records of the United States Marine Corps. Compiled by Charlotte M. Ashby. PI 73. 1954. 17 p.

UNITED STATES NAVAL ACADEMY (RECORD GROUP 405)

Inventory of Records of the United States Naval Academy. Compiled by Geraldine N. Phillips and Aloha South. Inv. 11. 1975. 57 p.

Joint and Combined Military Agencies

INTERNATIONAL MILITARY AGENCIES (RECORD GROUP 333)

Preliminary Inventory of Records of the Headquarters, United Nations Command. Compiled by Paul Taborn and Andrew Putignano. PI 127. 1960. 7 p.

UNITED STATES STRATEGIC BOMBING SURVEY (RECORD GROUP 243)

Inventory of Records of the United States Strategic Bombing Survey. Compiled by Marilla B. Guptil and John Mendelsohn. Inv. 10. 1975. 62 p.

Department of State

GENERAL RECORDS OF THE DEPARTMENT OF STATE (RECORD GROUP 59)

Inspection Reports on Foreign Service Posts, 1906–1939. Compiled by George Brent and Kent Carter. SL 37. 1974. 83 p.

List of Documents Relating to Special Agents of the Department of State, 1789–1906. Compiled by Natalia Summers. SL 7. 1951. 229 p.

Preliminary Inventory of General Records of the Department of State. Compiled by Daniel T. Goggin and H. Stephen Helton. PI 157. 1963. 311 p.

FOREIGN SERVICE POSTS (RECORD GROUP 84)

List of Foreign Service Post Records in the National Archives. Rev. ed. By Mario Fenyo and John Highbarger. SL 9. 1967. 35 p.

Preliminary Inventory of Records of Selected Foreign Service Posts. Compiled by Alexander P. Marvo. PI 60. 1953. 51 p.

RECORDS OF THE LEGISLATIVE BRANCH

U.S. House of Representatives (Record Group 233)

Preliminary Inventory of Records of the Select Committee of the House of Representatives Investigating National Defense Migration, 1940–43. Compiled by George P. Perros. PI 71. 1954. 30 p.

Preliminary Inventory of Records of the Select Committee of the House of Representatives on Post-War Military Policy, 1944–46. Compiled by George P. Perros. PI 70. 1954. 6 p.

Preliminary Inventory of Records of the United States House of Representatives, 1789–1946. Compiled by Buford Rowland et al. 2 vols. PI 113. 1959. 587 p.

Printed Hearings of the House of Representatives Found among Its Committee Records in the National Archives of the United States, 1824–1958. Compiled by Buford Rowland, et al. SL 35. 1974. 197 p.

U.S. Senate (Record Group 46)

Hearings in the Records of the U.S. Senate and Joint Committees of Congress. Compiled by Charles E. South and James C. Brown. SL 32. 1972. 91 p.

Preliminary Inventory of Records of the Special Committee of the Senate to Investigate Petroleum Resources, 1944–46. Compiled by George P. Perros. PI 61. 1953. 19 p.

Preliminary Inventory of Records of the Special Committee of the Senate to Investigate the National Defense Program, 1941–48. Compiled by Harold E. Hufford and Toussaint L. Prince. PI 48. 1952. 227 p.

Preliminary Inventory of the Records of the United States Senate. Compiled by Harold E. Hufford and Watson G. Caudill. PI 23. 1950. 284 p.

RECORDS OF OR RELATING TO OTHER GOVERNMENTS

WAR DEPARTMENT COLLECTION OF CONFEDERATE RECORDS (RECORD GROUP 109)

Preliminary Inventory of War Department Collection of Confederate Records. Compiled by Elizabeth Bethel. PI 101. 1957. 310 p.

NATIONAL ARCHIVES COLLECTION OF FOREIGN RECORDS SEIZED, 1941–(RECORD GROUP 242)

Guides to German Records Microfilmed at Alexandria, Va. Distribution restricted to institutions, but guides 1–56 are available in Microfilm Publication T733.

Index of Microfilmed Records of the German Foreign Ministry and the Reich's Chancellery Covering the Weimar Period. 1958. 95 p.

Supplement to the Guide to Captured German Documents. 1959. 69 p. (Original prepared by Gerhard L. Weinberg and the War Documentation Project Staff. Maxwell Air Force Base, Ala.: Air University, 1952).

REFERENCE INFORMATION PAPERS

Audiovisual Records in the National Archives of the United States Relating to World War II. RIP 70. 1974. 41 p.

Audiovisual Records Relating to Naval History. RIP 73. 1975. 12 p.

Cost Determination Data for World War I Naval Vessels. RIP 62. 1973. 12 p.

Geographical Exploration and Mapping in the 19th Century: A Survey of the Records in the National Archives. RIP 66. 1973. 22 p.

Wage Data among 19th-Century Military and Naval Records. RIP 54. 1973. 5 p.

PUBLISHED SOURCES ON NAVAL HISTORY

GENERAL REFERENCE

Albion, Robert G. *Naval and Maritime History: An Annotated Bibliography.* 4th ed. Mystic, Conn.: Munson Institute of American Maritime History, 1972. 370 p.

Allard, Dean C., and Bern, Betty, comps. *U.S. Naval History Sources in the Washington Area and Suggested Research Topics.* Washington, D.C.: Government Printing Office, 1970. 82 p.

Cooney, David M. *A Chronology of the U.S. Navy: 1775–1965.* New York: Watts, 1965. 471 p.

Heinl, Robert D. *Dictionary of Military and Naval Quotations.* Annapolis: U.S. Naval Institute, 1966. 367 p.

Higham, Robin, ed. *A Guide to Sources of United States Military History.* Hamden, Conn.: Archon Books, 1975. 599 p.

Karsten, Peter. *The Naval Aristocracy: The Golden Age of Annapolis and the Emergence of Modern American Navalism.* New York: Free Press, 1972. 462 p.

Knox, Dudley W. *A History of the United States Navy.* Rev. ed. New York: Putnam's, 1948. 704 p.

Lovette, Leland P. *Naval Customs: Traditions and Usage.* 4th ed. Annapolis: U.S. Naval Institute, 1959. 358 p.

Mitchell, Donald W. *History of the Modern American Navy, from 1883 through Pearl Harbor.* New York: Knopf, 1946. 477 p.

Neeser, Robert W. *Statistical and Chronological History of the United States Navy, 1775–1907.* 2 vols. New York: Macmillan Co., 1909.

Potter, Elmer B. *The Naval Academy Illustrated History of the United States Navy.* New York: Crowell, 1971. 320 p.

———, and Nimitz, Chester W., eds. *Sea Power: A Naval History.* Englewood Cliffs, N.J.: Prentice-Hall, 1960. 932 p.

U.S. Department of the Navy. Naval History Division. *Checklist: Unpublished Naval Histories in the "Z" File, Record Group 45, U.S. National Archives, 1911–1927.* Washington, D.C.: Naval History Division, 1971. 18 p.

_____. Naval History Division. *Civil War Naval Chronology, 1861–1865.* Washington, D.C.: Government Printing Office, 1971. 477 p.

_____. Naval History Division. *Guide to United States Naval Administrative Histories of World War II.* Washington, D.C.: Naval History Division, 1976. 219 p.

_____. Naval History Division. *Partial Checklist: World War II Histories and Historical Reports in the U.S. Naval History Division.* Washington, D.C.: Naval History Division, 1973. 226 p.

_____. Naval History Division. *The War at Sea: France and the American Revolution, a Bibliography.* Washington, D.C.: Government Printing Office, 1976. 48 p.

_____. Naval History Division. *United States Naval Chronology, World War II.* Washington, D.C.: Government Printing Office, 1955. 214 p.

_____. Naval History Divison. *United States Naval History: A Bibliography.* Washington, D.C.: Government Printing Office, 1972. 92 p.

_____. Office of the Chief of Naval Operations. *United States Naval Aviation, 1910–1970.* 2d ed. Washington, D.C.: Government Printing Office, 1970. 440 p.

Wedertz, Bill. *Dictionary of Naval Abbreviations.* Annapolis: U.S. Naval Institute, 1970. 249 p.

Westcott, Allan F., ed. *American Sea Power since 1775.* Rev. ed. Philadelphia: Lippincott, 1952. 609 p.

BIOGRAPHIES

AMERICAN REVOLUTION AND NINETEENTH CENTURY

Clark, William Bell. *Captain Dauntless: The Story of Nicholas Biddle of the Continental Navy.* Baton Rouge: Louisiana State University Press, 1949. 317 p.

_____. *Gallant John Barry, 1745–1803: The Story of a Naval Hero of Two Wars.* New York: Macmillan, 1938. 530 p.

_____. *Lambert Wickes, Sea Raider and Diplomat: The Story of a Naval Captain of the Revolution.* New Haven: Yale University Press, 1932. 466 p.

Cooling, Benjamin F. *Benjamin Franklin Tracy: Father of the Modern American Fighting Navy.* Hamden, Conn.: Archon Books, 1973. 211 p.

Cummings, Damon E. *Admiral Wainwright and the United States Fleet.* Washington, D.C.: Government Printing Office, 1962. 266 p.

Dearborn, Henry A. *The Life of William Bainbridge, Esq., of the United States Navy.* Princeton: Princeton University Press, 1931. 218 p.

de Meissner, Sophie (Radford). *Old Naval Days: Sketches from the Life of Rear Admiral William Radford, U.S.N.* New York: Holt, 1920. 389 p.

Dewey, George. *Autobiography of George Dewey, Admiral of the Navy.* 1913. Reprint. St. Clair Shores, Mich.: Scholarly Press, 1971. 337 p.

DuPont, Henry A. *Rear Admiral Samuel Francis DuPont, United States Navy: A Biography.* New York: National Americana Society, 1926. 320 p.

Durkin, Joseph T. *Stephen R. Mallory: Confederate Navy Chief.* Chapel Hill: University of North Carolina Press, 1954. 446 p.

Dutton, Charles J. *Oliver Hazard Perry.* New York: Longmans, Green, 1935. 308 p.

Eliot, George Fielding. *Daring Sea Warrior, Franklin Buchanan.* New York: Messner, 1962. 191 p.

Ferguson, Eugene S. *Truxton of the Constellation: The Life of Commodore Thomas Truxton, U.S. Navy, 1775–1822.* Baltimore: Johns Hopkins University Press, 1956. 322 p.

Fiske, Bradley A. *From Midshipman to Rear Admiral.* New York: Century, 1919. 694 p.

Gleaves, Albert. *James Lawrence, Captain, United States Navy, Commander of the Chesapeake.* New York: Putnam's, 1904. 337 p.

———. *Life and Letters of Rear Admiral Stephen B. Luce, U.S. Navy, Founder of the Naval War College.* New York: Putnam's, 1925. 381 p.

Hall, Claude H. *Abel Parker Upshur, Conservative Virginian, 1790–1844.* Madison: State Historical Society of Wisconsin, 1964. 271 p.

Henderson, Daniel M. *The Hidden Coasts: A Biography of Admiral Charles Wilkes.* 1953. Reprint. Westport, Conn.: Greenwood, 1970. 306 p.

Hobbs, William H. *Peary.* New York: Macmillan, 1936. 502 p.

Hoppin, James M. *Life of Andrew Hull Foot, Rear Admiral United States Navy.* New York: Harper, 1874. 411 p.

Hull, Isaac. *Commodore Isaac Hull: Papers of Isaac Hull, Commodore, United States Navy.* Edited by Gardner W. Allen. Boston: Boston Atheneum, 1929. 341 p.

Johnson, Robert E. *Rear Admiral John Rodgers, 1812–1882.* Annapolis: U.S. Naval Institute, 1967. 426 p.

Lewis, Charles L. *Admiral de Grasse and American Independence.* Annapolis: U.S. Naval Institute, 1945. 404 p.

———. *The Romantic Decateur.* Philadelphia: University of Pennsylvania Press, 1937. 296 p.

Livingston, Dorothy M. *The Master of Light: A Biography of Albert A. Michelson.* New York: Scribner's, 1973, 376 p.

McKee, Christopher. *Edward Preble: A Naval Biography, 1761–1807.* Annapolis: Naval Institute Press, 1972. 394 p.

Morison, Samuel Eliot. *John Paul Jones: A Sailor's Biography.* Boston: Little, Brown, 1959. 453 p.

Niven, John. *Gideon Welles: Lincoln's Secretary of the Navy.* New York: Oxford University Press, 1973. 676 p.

Paullin, Charles O. *Commodore John Rodgers, Captain Commodore and Senior Officer of the American Navy, 1773–1838*. 1910. Reprint. Annapolis: U.S. Naval Institute, 1967. 434 p.

Perry, Matthew C. *The Japan Expedition, 1852–1854: The Personal Journal of Commodore Matthew C. Perry*. Edited by Roger Pineau. Washington, D.C.: Smithsonian Institution Press, 1968. 241 p.

Puleston, William D. *Mahan: The Life and Work of Captain Alfred Thayer Mahan, U.S.N*. New Haven: Yale University Press, 1939. 380 p.

Roske, Ralph J., and Van Doren, Charles. *Lincoln's Commando: The Biography of Commander W. B. Cushing, U.S.N*. New York: Harper, 1957. 310 p.

Selfridge, Thomas O. *Memoirs of Thomas O. Selfridge, Jr., Rear Admiral, U.S.N*. New York: Putnam's, 1924. 288 p.

Semmes, Raphael. *Service Afloat, or the Remarkable Career of the Confederate Cruisers Sumter and Alabama*. Baltimore: Baltimore Publishing Co., 1887. 833 p.

Smith, Philip C. *Captain Samuel Tucker (1747–1833), Continental Navy*. Salem, Mass.: Essex Institute, 1976. 115 p.

Waddell, James I. *C.S.S. Shenandoah: The Memoirs of Lieutenant Commanding James I. Waddell*. Edited by James D. Horan. New York: Crown, 1960. 200 p.

Wagner, Frederick. *Submarine Fighter of the American Revolution: The Story of David Bushnell*. New York: Dodd, Mead, 1963. 145 p.

Wells, Tom H. *Commodore Moore and the Texas Navy*. Austin: University of Texas Press, 1960. 218 p.

West, Richard S. *Gideon Welles, Lincoln's Navy Department*. Indianapolis: Bobbs-Merrill, 1943. 379 p.

————. *The Second Admiral: A Life of David Dixon Porter, 1813–1891*. New York: Coward-McCann, 1937. 376 p.

Williams, Frances L. *Matthew Fontaine Maury: Scientist of the Sea*. New Brunswick, N.J.: Rutgers University Press, 1963. 720 p.

TWENTIETH CENTURY

Buell, Thomas B. *The Quiet Warrior: A Biography of Admiral Raymond A. Spruance*. Boston: Little, Brown, 1974. 486 p.

Clark, Joseph J., and Reynolds, Clark G. *Carrier Admiral*. New York: McKay, 1967. 333 p.

Dyer, George C. *The Amphibians Came to Conquer: The Story of Admiral Richmond Kelly Turner*. 2 vols. Washington, D.C.: Government Printing Office, 1972. 1278 p.

Forrestal, Emmet P. *Admiral Raymond A. Spruance, USN: A Study in Command*. Washington, D.C.: Government Printing Office, 1966. 275 p.

King, Ernest J., and Whitehill, Walter M. *Fleet Admiral King: A Naval Record*. New York: Norton, 1952. 674 p.

Leahy, William D. *I Was There: The Personal Story of the Chief of Staff to Presidents Roosevelt and Truman* . . . New York: McGraw-Hill, 1950. 527 p.

Merrill, James M. *A Sailor's Admiral: A Biography of William F. Halsey.* New York: Thomas Y. Crowell, 1976. 271 p.

Morison, Elting E. *Admiral Sims and the Modern American Navy.* Boston: Houghton Mifflin, 1942. 547 p.

Potter, Elmer B. *Nimitz.* Annapolis: Naval Institute Press, 1976. 507 p.

Taylor, Theodore. *The Magnificent Mitscher.* New York: Norton, 1954. 364 p.

von Doenhoff, Richard A., ed. *The McCully Report: The Russo-Japanese War, 1904–05.* Annapolis: Naval Institute Press, 1977. 338 p.

Wheeler, Gerald E. *Admiral William Veazie Pratt, U.S. Navy: A Sailor's Life.* Washington, D.C.: Government Printing Office, 1974. 456 p.

NAVAL HISTORY BY PERIOD

AMERICAN REVOLUTION

Allard, Dean C. "The Potomac Navy of 1776." *Virginia Magazine of History and Biography,* October 1976, pp. 411–30.

Allen, Gardner W. *Massachusetts Privateers of the Revolution.* Boston: Massachusetts Historical Society, 1927. 356 p.

_____. *A Naval History of the American Revolution.* 2 vols. 1913. Reprint. Williamstown, Mass.: Corner House, 1970.

Barnes, John S., ed. *The Logs of the* Serapis–Alliance–Ariel, *under the Command of John Paul Jones, 1779–1780.* New York: Naval Historical Society, 1911. 138 p.

Bemis, Samuel F. *The Diplomacy of the American Revolution.* 1935. Reprint. Gloucester, Mass. Peter Smith, 1957. 293 p.

Clark, William Bell. *Ben Franklin's Privateers: A Naval Epic of the American Revolution.* 1956. Reprint. Westport Conn.: Greenwood, 1969. 198 p.

_____. *George Washington's Navy: Being an Account of His Excellency's Fleet in New England Waters.* Baton Rouge: Louisiana State University Press, 1960. 275 p.

_____. and Morgan, William James, eds. *Naval Documents of the American Revolution.* 7 vols. Washington, D.C.: Government Printing Office, 1965–.

Dupuy, Richard E. *The American Revolution: A Global War.* New York: McKay, 1976. 311 p.

Greenwood, Bart, comp. *The American Revolution, 1775–1783: An Atlas of 18th Century Maps and Charts, Theaters of Operations.* Washington, D.C.: Government Printing Office, 1972.

Knox, Dudley W. *The Naval Genius of George Washington.* Boston: Houghton Mifflin, 1932. 138 p.

Larrabee, Harold A. *Decision at the Chesapeake.* New York: Potter, 1964. 317 p.

Lundeberg, Philip K. *The Continental Gunboat* Philadelphia *and the Northern Campaign of 1776.* Washington: Smithsonian Institution, 1966. unp.

Metzger, Charles H. *The Prisoner in the American Revolution.* Chicago: Loyola University Press, 1971. 309 p.

Middlebrook, Louis F. *History of Maritime Connecticut during the American Revolution, 1775–1783.* 2 vols. Salem, Mass.: The Essex Institute, 1925.

Morgan, William J. "The Governor's Floating Town." *The Iron Worker* 35 (Autumn 1971): 2–10.

———. "The Pivot upon Which Everything Turned: French Naval Superiority That Ensured Victory at Yorktown." *The Iron Worker* 22 (Spring 1958): 1–9.

Paullin, Charles O. *The Navy of the American Revolution: Its Administration, Its Policy and Its Achievements.* 1906. Reprint. New York: Haskell, 1970. 549 p.

Peckham, Howard H. *The War for Independence: A Military History.* Chicago: University of Chicago Press, 1958. 226 p.

WAR OF 1812

Beirne, Francis F. *The War of 1812.* 1949. Reprint. Hamden, Conn.: Shoe String, 1965. 410 p.

Brown, Wilburt S. *The Amphibious Campaign for West Florida and Louisiana, 1814–1815: A Critical Review of Strategy and Tactics at New Orleans.* University, Ala.: University of Alabama Press, 1969. 233 p.

Byron, Gilbert. *The War of 1812 on the Chesapeake Bay.* Baltimore: Maryland Historical Society, 1964. 94 p.

Cranwell, John P. and Crane, William B. *Men of Marque: A History of Private Armed Vessels out of Baltimore during the War of 1812.* New York: Norton, 1940. 427 p.

Forester, Cecil S. *The Age of Fighting Sail: The Story of the Naval War of 1812.* Garden City, N.Y.: Doubleday, 1956. 284 p.

Mahan, Alfred T. *Sea Power in Its Relation to the War of 1812.* 2 vols. 1905. Reprint. New York: Haskell, 1970.

Porter, David. *Journal of a Cruise Made to the Pacific Ocean, by Captain David Porter, in the United States Frigate* Essex, *in the Years 1812, 1813, and 1814.* 2 vols. 1815. Reprint. Boston: Gregg, 1970.

Pullen, Hugh F. *The* Shannon *and the* Chesapeake. Toronto: McClelland & Stewart, 1970. 174 p.

Roosevelt, Theodore. *The Naval War of 1812; or, the History of the United States Navy during the Last War with Great Britain, to Which is Appended an Account of the Battle of New Orleans.* 6th ed. 1897. Reprint. (1883 ed.). New York: Haskell, 1968.

MEXICAN WAR

Bauer, Karl J. *Surfboats and Horse Marines: U.S. Naval Operations in the Mexican War, 1846–48.* Annapolis: U.S. Naval Institute, 1969. 291 p.

_____. *The Mexican War, 1846–1848.* New York: Macmillan Co., 1974. 399 p.

Knox, Dudley W. *Naval Sketches of the War in California.* New York: Random House, 1939. 74 p.

Scheina, Robert L. "The Forgotten Fleet: the Mexican Navy on the Eve of War, 1845," *American Neptune,* 30 (1970): 46–55.

Semmes, Raphael. *Service Afloat and Ashore during the Mexican War.* Cincinnati: W. H. Moore, 1851. 480 p.

CIVIL WAR, 1861–1865

Anderson, Bern. *By Sea and by River: The Naval History of the Civil War.* New York: Knopf, 1962. 303 p.

Baxter, James P. *The Introduction of the Ironclad Warship.* 1933. Reprint. Hamden, Conn.: Shoe String, 1968. 398 p. Chapters 12 and 14 relate to the Civil War.

Beers, Henry P. *Guide to the Archives of the Government of the Confederate States of America.* Washington, D.C.: Government Printing Office, 1968. 536 p. Records of the Confederate Navy Department are described on pp. 337-87.

Bernath, Stuart L. *Squall across the Atlantic: American Civil War Prize Cases and Diplomacy.* Berkeley: University of California Press, 1970. 229 p.

Canfield, Eugene B. *Civil War Naval Ordnance.* Washington, D.C.: Government Printing Office, 1969. 24 p.

Case, Lynn M., and Spencer, Warren F. *The United States and France: Civil War Diplomacy.* Philadelphia: University of Pennsylvania Press, 1970. 747 p.

Eller, Ernest M., and Knox, Dudley W. *The Civil War at Sea.* Washington, D.C.: Naval Historical Foundation, 1961. 22 p.

Fox, Gustavus V. *Confidential Correspondence of Gustavus V. Fox, Assistant Secretary of the Navy, 1861 1865,* 2 vols. edited by Robert M. Thompson and Richard Wainwright. New York: Naval History Society, 1918-19.

Jones, Virgil C. *The Civil War at Sea.* 3 vols. New York: Holt, 1960-62.

Keeler, William F. *Aboard the USS* Florida, *1863-65: The Letters of Paymaster William Frederick Keeler to His Wife Anna.* Edited by Robert W. Daly. Annapolis: U.S. Naval Institute, 1968. 252 p.

Merli, Frank J. *Great Britain and the Confederate Navy, 1861-1865.* Bloomington: Indiana University Press, 1970. 342 p.

Munden, Kenneth W., and Beers, Henry P. *Guide to Federal Archives Relating to the Civil War.* Washington, D.C.: National Archives and Records Service, General Services Administration, 1962. 721 p. Records of the Navy Department are described on pp. 439-498.

Summersell, Charles G. *The Cruise of C.S.S.* Sumter. Tuscaloosa, Ala.: Confederate Pub. Co., 1965. 187 p.

U.S. Department of the Navy. Naval History Division. *Civil War Naval Chronology, 1861-1865.* Washington, D.C.: Government Printing Office, 1971. 477 p. Originally published in six parts plus index, 1961-1966.

Welles, Gideon. *Diary*. Edited by Howard K. Beale. 3 vols. New York: Norton, 1960. Welles served as secretary of the navy under Presidents Lincoln and Johnson. Diary originally published in 1911 by Houghton Mifflin. New edition indicates all additions, alterations, and omissions made either by Welles, or by the editor.

THE STEEL NAVY

Braisted, William R. *The United States Navy in the Pacific, 1897-1909*. Austin: University of Texas Press, 1958. 282 p.

_____. *The United States Navy in the Pacific, 1909-1922*. Austin: University of Texas Press, 1971. 741 p.

Hoehling, Adolph A. *The Jeannette Expedition: An Ill-Fated Journey to the Arctic*. New York: Abelard-Schuman, 1967. 224 p.

Johnson, Robert E. *Thence Round Cape Horn: The Story of United States Naval Forces on Pacific Station, 1818-1923*. Annapolis: U.S. Naval Institute, 1963. 276 p.

Livermore, Seward W. "The American Navy as a Factor in World Politics, 1903-1913," *American Historical Review* 63 (1958):863-79.

_____. "Theodore Roosevelt, the American Navy, and the Venezuelan Crisis of 1902-1903," *American Historical Review* 51 (1946): 452-71.

Matthews, Franklin. *Back to Hampton Roads: Cruise of the U.S. Atlantic Fleet from San Francisco to Hampton Roads, July 7, 1908-February 22, 1909*. New York: B. W. Huebsch, 1909. 292 p.

_____. *With the Battle Fleet: Cruise of the Sixteen Battleships of the United States Atlantic Fleet from Hampton Roads to the Golden Gate, December 1907-May 1908*. New York: B. W. Huebsch, 1908. 321 p.

Peary, Robert E. *The North Pole, Its Discovery in 1909 under the Auspices of the Peary Artic Club*. 1910. Reprint. Westport, Conn.: Greenwood, 1968. 373 p.

Seager, Robert. "Ten Years before Mahan: The Unofficial Case for the New Navy, 1880-1890," *Mississippi Valley Historical Review* 40 (1953):491-512.

Sweetman, Jack. *The Landing at Veracruz: 1914; the First Complete Chronicle of a Strange Encounter in April, 1914, When the United States Navy Captured and Occupied the City of Veracruz, Mexico*. Annapolis: U.S. Naval Institute, 1968. 221 p.

Taussig, Joseph K. "Experiences during the Boxer Rebellion," *U.S. Naval Institute Proceedings* 53 (1927):403-20.

U.S. Congress. House. *Bombardment of the Taku Forts in China*. 57th Cong., 1st sess., House Doc. No. 645. Washington, D.C.: Government Printing Office, 1902.

SPANISH AMERICAN WAR

Chadwick, French E. *The Relations of the United States and Spain: The Spanish American War*. 2 vols. 1911. Reprint. New York: Russell, 1968.

Freidel, Frank B. *The Splendid Little War*. Boston: Little, Brown, 1958. 314 p.

Mahan, Alfred T. *Lessons of the War with Spain, and Other Articles*. 1899. Reprint. Plainview, N.Y.: Books for Libraries, 1970. 320 p.

Niblack, Albert P. "Operations of the Navy and Marine Corps in the Philippine Archipelago, 1898-1902," *U.S. Naval Institute Proceedings* 30 (1904):745-53, ibid. 31 (1905):463-64, 698.

Sargent, Nathan, comp. *Admiral Dewey and the Manila Campaign*. Washington, D.C.: Naval Historical Foundation, 1947. 128 p.

WORLD WAR I, 1917-1918

Albion, Robert G., and Pope, Jennie B. *Sea Lanes in Wartime: The American Experience, 1775-1945*. 2 ed. Hamden, Conn.: Archon, 1968. 386 p.

Alden, Carroll S. "American Submarine Operations in the War," *U.S. Naval Institute Proceedings* 46 (1920):811-50, 1013-48.

Beers, Henry P. *U.S. Naval Forces in Northern Russia (Archangel and Murmansk), 1918-1919*. Navy Department Administrative Reference Service Report No. 5. Washington, D.C.: Department of the Navy, 1943. 55 p.

Belknap, Reginald R. *The Yankee Mining Squadron; or, Laying the North Sea Mine Barrage*. Annapolis: U.S. Naval Institute, 1920. 110 p.

Clark, William Bell. *When the U-Boats Came to America*. Boston: Little, Brown, 1929. 359 p.

Clephane, Lewis P. *History of the Naval Overseas Transportation Service in World War I*. Washington, D.C.: Government Printing Office, 1969. 283 p.

Daniels, Josephus. *The Cabinet Diaries of Josephus Daniels, 1913-1921*. Edited by E. David Cronon. Lincoln: University of Nebraska Press, 1963. 648 p. Lacks diaries for 1914 and 1916.

———. *Our Navy at War*. New York: Doran, 1922. 390 p.

Frothingham, Thomas G. *The Naval History of the World War*. 3 vols. 1924-26. Reprint. Plainview, N.Y.: Books for Libraries, 1971.

Gleaves, Albert. *A History of the Transport Service: Adventures and Experiences of United States Transports and Cruisers in the World War*. New York: Doran, 1921. 284 p.

Grant, Robert M. *U-Boats Destroyed: The Effect of Anti-Submarine Warfare, 1914-1918*. London: Putnam, 1964. 172 p.

Kittredge, Tracy B. *Naval Lessons of the Great War: A Review of the Senate Naval Investigation of the Criticisms by Admiral Sims of the Policies and Methods of Joseph Daniels*. Garden City, N.Y.: Doubleday, 1921. 472 p.

Sims, William S. *The Victory at Sea*. Garden City, N.Y.: Doubleday, Page, 1920. 410 p.

U.S. Department of the Navy. Bureau of Ordnance. *Navy Ordnance Activities, World War, 1917-1918*. Washington, D.C.: Government Printing Office, 1920. 323 p.

———. Bureau of Yards and Docks. *Activities of the Bureau of Yards and Docks, Navy*

Department, World War, 1917-1918. Washington, D.C.: Government Printing Office, 1921. 522 p.

————. Office of Naval Records and Library. *German Submarine Activities on the Atlantic Coast of the United States and Canada.* Monograph No. 1. Washington, D.C.: Government Printing Office, 1920. 163 p.

————. *The Northern Barrage and Other Mining Activities.* Monograph No. 2. Ibid. 146 p.

————. *Digest Catalogue of Laws and Joint Resolutions, the Navy and the World War.* Monograph No. 3. Ibid. 64 p.

————. *"The Northern Barrage"* (*Taking up the Mines*). Monograph No. 4. Ibid. 79 p.

————. *History of the Bureau of Engineering.* Monograph No. 5. Ibid., 1922. 176 p.

————. *The United States Naval Railway Batteries in France.* Monograph No. 6. Ibid. 97 p.

————. *The American Naval Planning Section London.* Monograph No. 7. Ibid., 1923. 537 p.

————. *American Ship Casualties of the World War.* Monograph (unnumbered). Ibid. 24 p.

BETWEEN WORLD WARS, 1919-1941

Beers, Henry P. *U.S. Naval Detachment in Turkish Waters, 1919-1924.* Navy Department Administrative Reference Service Report No. 2. Washington, D.C.: Department of the Navy, 1943. 15 p.

Byrd, Richard E. *Discovery: The Story of the Second Byrd Antarctic Expedition.* 1935. Reprint. Detroit: Gale, 1971. 405 p.

————. *Little America: Aerial Exploration in the Antarctic, the Flight to the South Pole.* New York: Putnam's, 1930. 422 p.

Koginos, Manny T. *The Panay Incident: Prelude to War.* Lafayette, Ind.: Purdue University Studies, 1967. 154 p.

Lockwood, Charles A., and Adamson, Hans C. *Tragedy at Honda.* Philadelphia: Chilton, 1960. 243 p.

Quinlan, Robert J. "The United States Fleet: Diplomacy, Strategy and the Allocation of Ships (1940-1941)." In *American Civil-Military Decisions: A Book of Case Studies,* edited by Harold Stein, pp. 153-201. Birmingham: University of Alabama Press, 1963.

Roskill, Stephen W. *The Period of Anglo-American Antagonism, 1919-1929.* Naval Policy between the Wars, vol. 1. London: Collins, 1968-.

Sprout, Harold, and Sprout, Margaret. *Toward a New Order of Sea Power: American Naval Policy and the World Scene, 1918-1922.* 2d ed. 1943. Reprint. Westport, Conn.: Greenwood, 1969.

Tolley, Kemp. *Yangtze Patrol: The U.S. Navy in China.* Annapolis: U.S. Naval Institute, 1971. 320 p.

WORLD WAR II, 1941–1945

Abbazia, Patrick. *Mr. Roosevelt's Navy*: *The Private War of the U.S. Atlantic Fleet, 1939–1942*. Annapolis: Naval Institute Press, 1975. 520 p.

Adamson, Hans C., and Kosco, George F. *Halsey's Typhoons*: *A Firsthand Account of How Two Typhoons, More Powerful than the Japanese, Dealt Death and Destruction to Admiral Halsey's Third Fleet*. New York: Crown, 1967. 206 p.

Auphan, Gabriel A., and Cras, Herve. *The French Navy in World II*. Annapolis: U.S. Naval Institute, 1959. 413 p.

Ballantine, Duncan S. *U.S. Naval Logistics in the Second World War*. Princeton: Princeton University Press, 1947. 308 p.

Barbey, Daniel E. *MacArthurs Amphibious Navy*: *Seventh Amphibious Force Operations, 1943–1945*. Annapolis: U.S. Naval Institute, 1969. 375 p.

Beach, Edward L. *Submarine*. New York: Holt, 1952. 301 p.

Bekker, Cajus. *Hitler's Naval War*. New York: Doubleday, 1974. 400 p.

Belote, James H. *Typhoon of Steel*: *The Battle of Okinawa*. New York: Harper, 1970. 368 p.

―――― and Belote, William M. *Titans of the Seas*: *The Development and Operations of Japanese and American Carrier Task Forces during World War II*. New York: Harper, 1975. 336 p.

Best, Herbert. *The Webfoot Warriors*: *The Story of UDT, the U.S. Navy's Underwater Demolition Team*. New York: John Day, 1962. 187 p.

Blair, Clay. *Silent Victory*: *The U.S. Submarine War against Japan*. Philadelphia: Lippincott, 1975. 1072.

Blassingame, Wyatt. *The Navy's Fliers in World War II*. Philadelphia: Westminster Press, 1967. 258 p.

Borg, Dorothy, and Okamoto, Shumpei, eds. *Pearl Harbor as History*: *Japanese-American Relations, 1931–1941*. Studies of the East Asian Institute. New York: Columbia University Press, 1973. 801 p.

Bulkley, Robert J. *At Close Quarters*: *PT Boats in the United States Navy*. Washington, D.C.: Government Printing Office, 1962. 574 p.

Bunker, John G. *Liberty Ships*: *The Ugly Ducklings of World War II*. Annapolis: Naval Institute Press, 1972. 287 p.

Campbell, Ian, and MacIntyre, Donald G. *The Kola Run*: *A Record of Arctic Convoys, 1941–1945*. London: Muller, 1958. 254 p.

Carter, Worrall R. *Beans, Bullets and Black Oil*: *The Story of Fleet Logistics Afloat in the Pacific during World War II*. Washington, D.C.: Government Printing Office, 1953. 482 p.

―――― . *Ships, Salvage, and Sinews of War*: *The Story of Fleet Logistics Afloat in Atlantic and Mediterranean Waters during World War II*. Edited by Worrall R. Carter and Elmer E. Duvall. Washington, D.C.: Government Printing Office, 1954. 533 p.

Connery, Robert H. *The Navy and the Industrial Mobilization in World War II.* 1951. Reprint. New York: Da Capo, 1972.

Cook, Charles. *The Battle of Cape Esperance*: *Strategic Encounter at Guadalcanal.* New York: Crowell, 1968. 192 p.

Craig, William. *The Fall of Japan.* New York: Dial Press, 1967. 368 p.

Cunningham, Winfield S. *Wake Island Command.* Boston: Little, Brown, 1961. 300 p.

Fuchida, Mitsuo, and Okumiya, Masatako. *Midway, the Battle That Doomed Japan*: *The Japanese Navy's Story.* Annapolis: U.S. Naval Institute, 1955. 266 p.

Furer, Julius A. *Administration of the Navy Department in World War II.* Washington, D.C.: Government Printing Office, 1959. 1042 p.

Gallery, Daniel V. *Twenty Million Tons under the Sea.* Chicago: H. Regnery, 1956. 344 p.

Garfield, Brian W. *The Thousand-Mile War*: *World War II in Alaska and the Aleutians.* Garden City, N.Y.: Doubleday, 1969. 351 p.

Glines, Carroll V. *Doolittle's Tokyo Raiders.* Princeton, N.J.: Van Nostrand, 1964. 447 p.

Hashimoto, Mochitsura. *Sunk*: *The Story of the Japanese Submarine Fleet, 1942-1945.* Translated by E. H. M. Colegrave. London: Cassell, 1954. 218 p.

Helm, Thomas. *Ordeal by Sea*: *The Tragedy of the U.S.S.* Indianapolis. New York: Dodd, Mead, 1963. 243 p.

Hoehling, Adolph A. *The Lexington Goes Down.* Englewood Cliffs, N.J.: Prentice-Hall, 1971. 208 p.

Hough, Richard A. *The Battle of Midway.* New York: Macmillan, 1970. 90 p.

Hoyt, Edwin P. *How They Won the War in the Pacific*: *Nimitz and His Admirals.* New York: Weybright and Talley, 1970. 554 p.

————. *The Battle of Leyte Gulf*: *The Death Knell of the Japanese Fleet.* New York: Weybright & Talley, 1972. 314 p.

Inoguchi, Rikihei. *The Divine Wind*: *Japan's Kamikaze Force in World War II.* By Rikihei Inoguchi and Tadashi Nakajima with Roger Pineau. Annapolis: U.S. Naval Institute, 1958. 240 p.

Ito, Masanori. *The End of the Imperial Japanese Navy.* Translated by Andrew Y. Kuroda and Roger Pineau. New York: Norton, 1962. 240 p.

The Japanese Navy in World War II. Introduction and commentary by Raymond G. O'Connor. Annapolis: U.S. Naval Institute, 1969. 147 p. An anthology of articles by former officers of the Imperial Japanese Navy and Air Defense Force.

Kemp, Peter K. *Key to Victory*: *The Triumph of British Sea Power in World War II.* Boston: Little, Brown, 1957. 382 p.

King, Ernest J. *The United States Navy at War, 1941-45*: *Official Reports to the Secretary of the Navy.* Washington, D.C.: Government Printing Office, 1946. 305 p.

Lenton, Henry T. *American Battleships, Carriers, and Cruisers.* Navies of the Second World War Series. Garden City, N.Y.: Doubleday, 1968. 160 p.

————. *American Fleet and Escort Destroyers.* 2 vols. Navies of the Second World War Series. Garden City, N.Y.: Doubleday, 1971.

Lockwood, Charles A. *Battles of the Philippine Sea*. Edited by Charles A. Lockwood and Hans C. Adamson. New York: Crowell, 1967. 229 p.

_____. *Sink 'em All: Submarine Warfare in the Pacific*. New York: Dutton, 1951. 416 p.

Lord, Walter. *Day of Infamy*. New York: Holt, 1957. 243 p. A description of the Pearl Harbor attack.

_____. *Incredible Victory*. New York: Harper, 1967. 331 p. A description of the Battle of Midway.

Lott, Arnold S. *Brave Ship, Brave Men*. Indianapolis: Bobbs-Merrill, 1964. 272 p. The battle between U.S.S. *Aaron Ward* and Japanese Kamikaze suicide planes off Okinawa.

_____. *Most Dangerous Sea: A History of Mine Warfare and an Account of U.S. Navy Mine Warfare Operations in World War II and Korea*. Annapolis: U.S. Naval Institute, 1959. 322 p.

Miles, Milton E. *A Different Kind of War: The Little-Known Story of the Combined Guerrilla Forces Created in China by the U.S. Navy and the Chinese during World War II*. Garden City, N.Y.: Doubleday, 1967. 629 p.

Morison, Samuel E. *History of United States Naval Operations in World War II*. 15 vols. Boston: Little, Brown, 1947-62.

   Vol. 1. *The Battle of the Atlantic, September 1939-May 1943*.
   Vol. 2. *Operations in North African Waters, October 1942-June 1943*.
   Vol. 3. *The Rising Sun in the Pacific, 1931-April 1942*.
   Vol. 4. *Coral Sea, Midway and Submarine Actions, May 1942-August 1942*.
   Vol. 5. *The Struggle for Guadalcanal, August 1942-1943*.
   Vol. 6. *Breaking the Bismarcks Barrier, 22 July 1942-1 May 1944*.
   Vol. 7. *Aleutians, Gilberts and Marshalls, June 1942-April 1944*.
   Vol. 8. *New Guinea and the Marianas, March 1944-August 1944*.
   Vol. 9. *Sicily-Salerno-Anzio, January 1943-June 1944*.
   Vol. 10. *The Atlantic Battle Won, May 1943-May 1945*.
   Vol. 11. *The Invasion of France and Germany, 1944-1945*.
   Vol. 12. *Leyte, June 1944-January 1945*.
   Vol. 13. *The Liberation of the Philippines: Luzon, Mindanao, the Visayas, 1944-1945*.
   Vol. 14. *Victory in the Pacific, 1945*.
   Vol. 15. *Supplement and General Index*.

_____. *Strategy and Compromise*. Boston: Little, Brown, 1958. 120 p.

_____. *The Two-Ocean War: A Short History of the United States Navy in the Second World War*. Boston: Little, Brown, 1963. 611 p.

Morton, Louis. *Writings on World War II*. Washington, D.C.: Service Center for Teachers of History, 1967. 54 p.

Potter, Elmer B., and Nimitz, Chester W., eds. *The Great Sea War: The Story of Naval Action in World War II*. Englewood Cliffs, N.J.: Prentice-Hall, 1960. 468 p. Adapted from the naval history of World War II as told by the editors in their book entitled *Sea Power*.

Reynolds, Clark G. *Command of the Sea*. New York: William Morrow, 1974. 642 p.

_____. *The Fast Carriers*; *the Forging of an Air Navy*. New York: McGraw-Hill, 1968. 498 p.

_____. "Submarine Attacks on the Pacific Coast, 1942," *Pacific Historical Review* 33 (1964):183-93.

Rohwer, Jurgen, and Hummelchen, G. *Chronology of the War at Sea, 1939-1945*. Translated by Derek Masters. New York: Arco, 1974. 650 p.

Roscoe, Theodore. *United States Destroyer Operations in World War II*. Annapolis: U.S. Naval Institute, 1953. 581 p. An abridgement entitled *Tin Cans* was published in 1960 by Bantam Books.

_____. *United States Submarine Operations in World War II*. Annapolis: U.S. Naval Institute, 1949. 577 p. An abridgement entitled *Pigboats* was published in 1958 by Bantam Books.

Roskill, Stephen W. *The War at Sea, 1939-1945*. (3 vols. in 4.) London: H.M.S.O., 1954-61.

_____. *White Ensign*: *The British Navy at War, 1939-1945*. Annapolis: U.S. Naval Institute, 1960. 480 p.

Ruge, Friedrich. *Der Seekrieg*: *The German Navy's Story, 1939-1945*. Annapolis: U.S. Naval Institute, 1957. 440 p.

Salomon, Henry. *Victory at Sea*. Garden City, N.Y.: Doubleday, 1959. 256 p.

Schofield, Brian B. *The Russian Convoys*. Philadelphia: Dufour, 1964. 224 p.

Smith, Stanley E., ed. *The United States Navy in World War II*: *The One-Volume History, from Pearl Harbor to Tokyo Bay, by Men Who Fought in the Atlantic and the Pacific and by Distinguished Naval Experts, Authors and Newspapermen*. New York: Morrow, 1966. 1049 p.

Smith, William W. *Midway*: *Turning Point of the Pacific.* New York: Crowell, 1966. 174 p.

Toland, John. *But Not in Shame*: *The Six Months after Pearl Harbor*. New York: Random House, 1961. 427 p.

_____. *The Rising Sun*: *The Decline and Fall of the Japanese Empire, 1936-1945*. New York: Random House, 1970. 954 p.

Tuleja, Thaddeus V. *Climax at Midway*. New York: Norton, 1960. 248 p.

_____. *Twilight of the Sea Gods*. New York: Norton, 1958. 284 p. Operations of the German Navy.

U.S. Congress. Joint Committee on the Investigation of the Pearl Harbor Attack. *Pearl Harbor Attack. Hearings before the Joint Committee on the Investigation of the Pearl Harbor Attack*. 79th Cong., 1st and 2d sess. 39 vols. 1946. Reprint. New York: AMS Press, 1972.

U.S. Department of the Navy. Bureau of Medicine and Surgery. *The History of the Medical Department of the United States Navy in World War II*. 3 vols. Washington, D.C.: Government Printing Office, 1950-53. The series includes a narrative and pictorial volume; a compilation of the Killed, Wounded, and Decorated Personnel (of the Medical Department); and the statistics of Diseases and Injuries.

_____. Bureau of Ordnance. *U.S. Navy Bureau of Ordnance in World War II*. By

Buford Rowland and William Boyd. Washington, D.C.: Government Printing Office, 1953. 539 p.

_____. Bureau of Ships. *An Administrative History of the Bureau of Ships during World War II*. 4 vols. Washington, D.C.: Government Printing Office, 1952.

_____. Bureau of Yards and Docks. *Building the Navy's Bases in World War II: History of the Bureau of Yards and Docks and the Civil Engineering Corps, 1940–1946*. 2 vols. Washington, D.C.: Government Printing Office, 1947.

_____. Naval History Division. *United States Naval Chronology, World War II*. Washington, D.C.: Government Printing Office, 1955. 214 p.

_____. *United States Submarine Losses, World War II, Reissued with an Appendix of Axis Submarine Losses*. Washington, D.C.: Government Printing Office, 1964. 244 p.

_____. Office of Naval Operations. *U.S. Naval Aviation in the Pacific*. Washington, D.C.: Government Printing Office, 1947. 56 p.

_____. Strategic Bombing Survey. *Campaigns of the Pacific War*. 1946. Reprint. Westport, Conn.: Greenwood, 1969. 395 p. Information obtained from Japanese sources after World War II.

_____. *Interrogations of Japanese Officials*. 2 vols. Washington, D.C.: Government Printing Office, 1947.

_____. *Summary Report (Pacific War)*. Washington, D.C.: Government Printing Office, 1946. 32 p.

Wallin, Homer N. *Pearl Harbor: Why, How, Fleet Salvage and Final Appraisal*. Washington, D.C.: Government Printing Office, 1968. 377 p.

Waters, John M. *Bloody Winter*. Princeton, N.J.: Van Nostrand, 1967. 279 p. Account of the Battle of the Atlantic during the winter of 1942–43.

Waters, Sydney D. *The Royal New Zealand Navy*. Wellington: War History Branch, Department of Internal Affairs, 1956. 570 p.

Winton, John. *The Forgotten Fleet: The British Navy in the Pacific, 1944–1945*. New York: Crown-McCann, 1969. 433 p.

Wohlstetter, Roberta. *Pearl Harbor: Warning and Decision*. Stanford, Calif.: Stanford University Press, 1962. 426 p.

Woodward, David. *The Secret Raiders: The Story of the Operations of the German Armed Merchant Raiders in the Second World War*. New York: Norton, 1955. 288 p.

SPECIAL SUBJECTS

DIPLOMACY AND FOREIGN RELATIONS

Alden, Carroll S. *Lawrence Kearny, Sailor Diplomat*. Princeton: Princeton University Press, 1936. 231 p.

Andrews, Craig Neal. *Foreign Policy and the New American Military*. Beverly Hills: Sage Publications, 1974. 46 p.

Bailey, Thomas A. "Dewey and the Germans at Manila Bay," *American Historical Review* 45 (1939):59–81.

Billingsley, Edward B. *In Defense of Neutral Rights*: *The United States Navy and the Wars of Independence in Chile and Peru.* Chapel Hill: University of North Carolina Press, 1967. 266 p.

Blair, Leon B. *Western Window in the Arab World.* Austin: University of Texas Press, 1970. 328 p. Traces the development of U.S. military bases in Morocco.

Bloomfield, Lincoln Palmer. *In Search of American Foreign Policy*: *The Humane Use of Power.* New York: Oxford University Press, 1974. 182 p.

Borg, Dorothy. *The United States and the Far Eastern Crisis of 1933-1938*: *From the Manchurian Incident through the Initial Stage of the Undeclared Sino-Japanese War.* Cambridge: Harvard University Press, 1964. 674 p.

Braisted, William R. *The United States Navy in the Pacific, 1897-1909.* Austin: University of Texas Press, 1958. 282 p.

————. *The United States Navy in the Pacific, 1909-1922.* Austin: University of Texas Press, 1971. 741 p.

Buckley, Thomas H. *The United States and the Washington Conference, 1921-1922.* Knoxville: University of Tennessee Press, 1970. 222 p.

Case, Lynn M., and Spencer, Warren F. *The United States and France*: *Civil War Diplomacy.* Philadelphia: University of Pennsylvania Press, 1970. 747 p.

Challener, Richard D. *Admirals, Generals, and American Foreign Policy, 1898-1914.* Princeton, N.J.: Princeton University Press, 1973. 433 p.

Chayes, Abram. *The Cuban Missile Crisis*: *International Crises and the Role of Law.* New York: Oxford University Press, 1974. 157 p.

Davidonis, Anthony C. "The American Naval Mission in the Adriatic, 1918-1921." Navy Department Administrative Reference Service Report No. 4. Washington, D.C.: Department of the Navy, 1943. 99 p.

Dulles, Foster R. *Yankees and Samurai*: *America's Role in the Emergence of Modern Japan*: *1791-1900.* New York: Harper, 1965. 275 p.

Fenwick, Charles Ghequiere. *Foreign Policy and International Law.* Dobbs Ferry, N.Y.: Oceana Publications, 1968. 142 p.

George, Alexander L., and Smoke, Richard. *Deterrance in American Foreign Policy*: *Theory and Practice.* New York: Columbia University Press, 1974. 666 p.

Hagen, Kenneth J. *American Gunboat Diplomacy and the Old Navy, 1877-1889.* Contributions in Military History, No. 4. Westport, Conn.: Greenwood, 1973. 262 p.

Hall, Claude H. "Abel P. Upshur and the Navy as an Instrument of Foreign Policy," *Virginia Magazine of History and Biography* 69 (1961):290-99.

Healy, David. *Gunboat Diplomacy in the Wilson Era*: *The U.S. Navy in Haiti, 1915-1916.* Madison: University of Wisconsin Press, 1976. 268 p.

Leopold, Richard W. *The Growth of American Foreign Policy*: *A History.* New York: Knopf, 1962. 848 p.

Merli, Frank J. *Great Britain and the Confederate Navy, 1861-1865.* Bloomington: Indiana University Press, 1970. 342 p.

Morison, Samuel E. *"Old Bruin": Commodore Matthew C. Perry, 1794–1858, The American Naval Officer Who Helped Found Liberia.* . . . Boston: Little, Brown, 1967. 482 p.

Neumann, William L. *America Encounters Japan: From Perry to MacArthur.* 1963. Reprint. Baltimore: Johns Hopkins University Press, 1963. 353 p.

O'Connell, D. P. *The Influence of Law on Sea Power.* Annapolis: Naval Institute Press, 1975. 204 p.

O'Connor, Raymond G. *Force and Diplomacy: Essays, Military and Diplomatic.* Coral Gables: University of Miami Press, 1972. 167 p.

_____. *Perilous Equilibrium: The United States and the London Naval Conference of 1930.* 1962. Reprint. Westport, Conn.: Greenwood, 1969.

Paul, Roland A. *American Military Commitments Abroad.* New Brunswick: Rutgers University Press, 1972.

Paullin, Charles O. *Diplomatic Negotiations of American Naval Officers, 1778–1883.* 1912. Reprint. Gloucester, Mass.: Peter Smith, 1967. 380 p.

Preble, George H. *The Opening of Japan: A Diary of Discovery in the Far East, 1853–1856, from the Original Manuscript in the Massachusetts Historical Society.* Edited by Boleslaw Szczesniak. Norman: University of Oklahoma Press, 1962. 453 p.

Trask, David F. *Captains & Cabinets: Anglo-American Naval Relations, 1917–1918.* Columbia: University of Missouri Press, 1972. 396 p.

Tuleja, Thaddeus V. *Statesmen and Admirals: Quest for a Far Eastern Naval Policy.* New York: Norton, 1963. 256 p.

U.S. Department of Defense. *United States-Vietnam Relations, 1945–1967: Study.* 12 vols. Washington, D.C.: Government Printing Office, 1971. This twelve-volume committee print of the House Committee on Armed Services contains the first forty-three volumes of the original forty-seven-volume study. Popularly known as the "Pentagon Papers."

von Doenhoff, Richard A. "Biddle, Perry, and Japan," *U.S. Naval Institute Proceedings* 92 (1966):78–87.

Walworth, Arthur. *Black Ships off Japan: The Story of Commodore Perry's Expedition.* 1946. Reprint. Hamden, Conn.: Shoe String, 1966.

Wheeler, Gerald E. *Prelude to Pearl Harbor: The United States Navy and the Far East, 1921–1931.* Columbia: University of Missouri Press, 1963. 212 p.

SCIENCE AND TECHNOLOGY

Allen, Everett S. *Arctic Odyssey: The Life of Rear Admiral Donald B. MacMillan.* New York: Dodd, Mead, 1962. 340 p.

Anderson, William R., and Blair, Clay. Nautilus, *90 North.* Cleveland: World, 1959. 251 p. History-making voyage of the atomic submarine U.S.S. *Nautilus* under the North Pole ice.

Baldwin, Hanson W. *The New Navy.* New York: Dutton, 1964. 191 p.

Baxter, James P. *The Introduction of the Ironclad Warship.* 1933. Reprint. Hamden, Conn.: Shoe String, 1968.

Bennett, Frank M. *Steam Navy of the United States: A History of the Growth of the Steam Vessel of War in the U.S. Navy, and of the Naval Engineer Corps....* 1896. Reprint. Westport, Conn.: Greenwood, 1970. 953 p.

Bixby, William. *The Forgotten Voyage of Charles Wilkes.* New York: McKay, 1966. 184 p.

Byrd, Richard E. *Discovery: The Story of the Second Byrd Antarctic Expedition.* 1935. Reprint. Detroit, Mich.: Gale, 1971.

_____. *Little America, Aerial Exploration in the Antarctic: The Flight to the South Pole.* New York: Putnam's, 1930. 422 p.

Christman, Albert B. *Sailors, Scientists, and Rockets: Origins of the Navy Rocket Program and of the Naval Ordnance Test Station, Inyokern.* History of the Naval Weapons Center, China Lake, California, vol. 1. Washington, D.C.: Government Printing Office, 1971. 303 p.

Cole, Allan B. *Yankee Surveyors in the Shogun's Seas: Records of the United States Surveying Expedition to the North Pacific Ocean, 1853-1856.* 1947. Reprint. Westport, Conn.: Greenwood, 1969. 161 p.

DeLong, George W. *The Voyage of the* Jeannette: *The Ship and Ice Journals of George W. DeLong, Lieutenant-Commander U.S.N., and Commander of the Polar Expedition of 1879-1881.* 2 vols. Boston: Houghton Mifflin, 1883. 243 p.

Dufek, George J. *Operation Deepfreeze.* New York: Harcourt Brace, 1957. The 1955-56 naval Antarctic expedition.

Dupree, A. Hunter. *Science in the Federal Government: A History of Policies and Activities to 1940.* Cambridge: Harvard University Press, 1957. 460 p.

Furer, Julius A. "Naval Research and Development in World War II." *Journal of the American Society of Naval Engineers* 62 (1950):21-53.

Gebbard, Louis A. *Evolution of Naval Radio-Electronics and Contributions of the Naval Research Laboratory.* New York: Oxford University Press, 1974. 157 p.

Gimpel, Herbert J. *The United States Nuclear Navy.* New York: Watts, 1965. 199 p.

Henderson, Daniel M. *The Hidden Coasts: A Biography of Admiral Charles Wilkes.* 1953. Reprint. Westport, Conn.: Greenwood, 1971. 306 p.

Hewlett, Richard G., and Duncan, Francis. *Nuclear Navy, 1946-1962.* Chicago: University of Chicago Press, 1974. 475 p.

Hezlet, Arthur. *Electronics and Sea Power.* New York: Stein and Day, 1975. 318 p.

Howeth, Linwood S. *History of Communications-Electronics in the United States Navy.* Washington, D.C.: Government Printing Office, 1963. 657 p.

Hughes, Thomas P. *Elmer Sperry: Inventor and Engineer.* Baltimore: Johns Hopkins University Press, 1971. 348 p.

Lewis, Richard S. *A Continent for Science: The Antarctic Adventure.* New York: Viking Press, 1965. 300 p.

Long, Edward J. *Ocean Sciences.* Annapolis: U.S. Naval Institute, 1964. 304 p.

Lynch, William F. *Narrative of the United States' Expedition to the River Jordan and the Dead Sea.* 6th ed. Philadelphia: Lea & Blanchard, 1849. 509 p.

Maury, Matthew Fontaine. *Physical Geography of the Sea and Its Meteorology.* Edited by John Leighly. Cambridge: Harvard University Press, 1963. 432 p. Prepared from the eighth edition published in 1861.

Morison, Elting E. *Men, Machines, and Modern Times.* Cambridge, Mass.: M.I.T. Press, 1966. 235 p. The nature and impact of technological change is described. Four of the six essays concern the navy.

Page, Robert M. *The Origin of Radar.* Garden City, N.Y.: Anchor Books, 1962. 196 p.

Peary, Robert E. *The North Pole: Its Discovery in 1909 under the Auspices of the Peary Arctic Club.* 1910. Reprint. Westport, Conn.: Greenwood, 1968. 373 p.

Pouko, Vincent. *Ships, Seas, and Scientists.* Annapolis: Naval Institute Press, 1974. 283 p.

Schroeder, Peter B. *Contact at Sea: A History of Maritime Radio Communications.* Ridgewood, N.J.: Gregg, 1967. 139 p.

Scott, Lloyd N. *Naval Consulting Board of the United States.* Washington, D.C.: Government Printing Office, 1920. 288 p.

Sloan, Edward W. *Benjamin Franklin Isherwood, Naval Engineer: The Years as Engineer in Chief, 1861-1869.* Annapolis: U.S. Naval Institute, 1966. 299 p.

Stanton, William. *The Great United States Exploring Expedition of 1838-1842.* Berkeley: University of California Press, 1975. 433 p.

Tyler, David B. *The Wilkes Expedition: The First United States Exploring Expedition, 1838-1842.* Philadelphia: American Philosophical Society, 1968. 435 p.

U.S. Department of the Navy. Office of Naval Research. *A Decade of Basic and Applied Science in the Navy: A Symposium Sponsored by the Office of Naval Research as Part of Its Decennial Year, March 19 and 20, 1957.* Washington, D.C.: Government Printing Office, 1958. 630 p.

_____. *Research in the Service of National Purpose: Proceedings of the Office of Naval Research Vicennial Convocation.* Edited by F. Joachim Weyl. Washington, D.C.: Government Printing Office, 1966. 133 p.

U.S. President's Science Advisory Committee. Panel on Oceanography. *Effective Use of the Sea.* Washington, D.C.: Government Printing Office, 1966. 144 p.

Ward, Ralph G., ed. *American Activities in the Central Pacific, 1790-1870: A History, Geography, and Ethnography Pertaining to American Involvement and Americans in the Pacific Taken from Contemporary Newspapers.* 8 vols. Ridgewood, N.J.: Gregg, 1966-1971.

Weems, John E. *Peary: The Explorer and the Man, Based on His Personal Papers.* Boston: Houghton Mifflin, 1967. 362 p.

Index

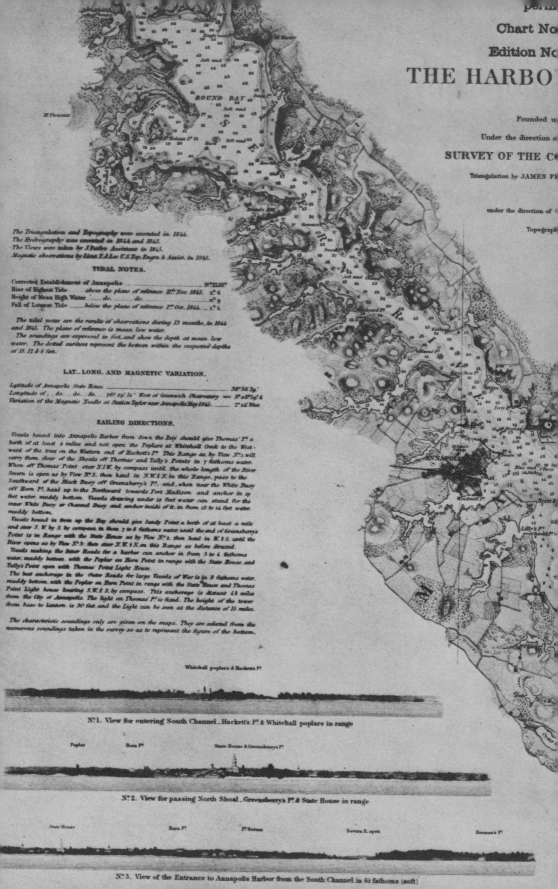

Chart No.

Edition No.

THE HARBO

Founded u

Under the direction o

SURVEY OF THE C

Triangulation by JAMES F

under the direction o

Topograph

The Triangulation and Topography were executed in 1844.
The Hydrography was executed in 1844 and 1845.
The Views were taken by J.Faulke Assistant in 1845.
Magnetic observations by Lieut. T.R.Lee U.S.Top.Engrs. & Assist. in 1845.

TIDAL NOTES.

Corrected Establishment of Annapolis _____ XII.h XLIII.m
Rise of Highest Tide _____ above the plane of reference II.th Nov. 1845. 2.ft 6
Height of Mean High Water _____ do. _____ do. _____ 0.ft 9
Fall of Lowest Tide _____ below the plane of reference 1.st Oct. 1844. 1.ft 4

The tidal notes are the results of observations during 13 months, in 1844
and 1845. The plane of reference is mean low water.
The soundings are expressed in feet, and show the depth at mean low
water. The dotted surfaces represent the bottom within the respective depths
of 18, 12 & 6 feet.

LAT., LONG. AND MAGNETIC VARIATION.

Latitude of Annapolis State House _____ 38° 58′ 39″
Longitude of _ do. _ do. _ do. _ 76° 29′ 51″ West of Greenwich Observatory = 5.h 05.m 59.s 4
Variation of the Magnetic Needle at Station Taylor near Annapolis May 1845. _ 2° 14′ West

SAILING DIRECTIONS.

Vessels bound into Annapolis Harbor from down the Bay should give Thomas' P.t a
berth of at least 2 miles and not open the Poplars at Whitehall Creek to the West-
ward of the trees on the Western end of Hackett's P.t This Range as, by View N.º 1, will
carry them clear of the Shoals off Thomas' and Tally's Points in 7 fathoms water.
When off Thomas' Point steer N.¼ W. by compass until, the whole length of the River
Severn is open as by View N.º 3, then haul in N.W.¼ N. in this Range, pass to the
Southward of the Black Buoy off Greensberry's P.t, and, when near the White Buoy
off Horn P.t, haul up to the Northward towards Fort Madison and anchor in 19
feet water, muddy bottom. Vessels drawing under 12 feet water can stand for the
inner White Buoy or Channel Buoy and, anchor inside of it, in from 13 to 14 feet water,
muddy bottom.

Vessels bound in from up the Bay should give Sandy Point a berth of at least a mile
and steer S. W. by S. by compass, in from 7 to 8 fathoms water, until the end of Greensberry's
Point is in Range with the State House as by View N.º 2, then haul in W.½ S. until the
River opens as by View N.º 3, then steer N.W.¼ N. on this Range as before directed.

Vessels making the Inner Roads for a harbor can anchor in from 3 to 4 fathoms
water, muddy bottom, with the Poplar on Horn Point in range with the State House, and
Tally's Point open with Thomas' Point Light House.

The best anchorage in the Outer Roads for large Vessels of War is in 8 fathoms water,
muddy bottom, with the Poplar on Horn Point in range with the State House and Thomas'
Point Light house bearing S.W.½ S. by compass. This anchorage is distant 4½ miles
from the City of Annapolis. The light on Thomas' P.t is fixed. The height of the tower
from base to lantern is 30 feet, and the Light can be seen at the distance of 15 miles.

The characteristic soundings only are given on the maps. They are selected from the
numerous soundings taken in the survey so as to represent the figure of the bottom.

Whitehall poplars & Hackets P.t

N.º 1. View for entering South Channel. Hackett's P.t & Whitehall poplars in range

Poplar — Horn P.t — State House & Greensberry's P.t

N.º 2. View for passing North Shoal. Greensberry's P.t & State House in range

State House — Horn P.t — P.t Severn — Severn R. open — Rieman's P.t

N.º 3. View of the Entrance to Annapolis Harbor from the South Channel in 6½ fathoms (soft)

ROUND BAY